# FRANTZ FANON

# Frantz Fanon

## Combat Breathing

Nigel C. Gibson

polity

First published in 2024 by Polity Press

Polity Press
65 Bridge Street
Cambridge CB2 1UR, UK

Polity Press
111 River Street
Hoboken, NJ 07030, USA

ISBN-13: 978-1-5095-4875-0
ISBN-13: 978-1-5095-4876-7(pb)

A catalogue record for this book is available from the British Library.

Library of Congress Control Number: 2023945890

Typeset in 10.5pt on 14pt Janson by
Cheshire Typesetting Ltd, Cuddington, Cheshire
Printed and bound in Great Britain by TJ Books Ltd, Padstow, Cornwall

For further information on Polity, visit our website:
politybooks.com

# Contents

# Preface: What would Fanon say?

The original impetus behind writing *Frantz Fanon: Combat Breathing* was the Black Lives Matter movement that exploded across the world after the 2020 police murder of George Floyd. Although the book was already at the publisher when the horrific Hamas attacks on Israeli citizens (as well as on military occupation facilities) took place, followed by Israel's immediate catastrophic response (a collective punishment resulting in a genocide of Palestinians in Gaza), I felt compelled to add a short preface to this book as another global movement is emerging in support of Palestinian national self-determination.

There is a remarkable staying power and urgency to Fanon's thought. Just short of one hundred years after his birth, he always seems to have something to say that connects with our contemporary moment. In the critique of orientalism expressed in one of his first articles, "The 'North African Syndrome,'" he lays out the thesis that when North Africans (i.e. Arabs) come "on the scene," they enter "into a pre-existing framework." This pre-existing orientalist framework extending beyond North Africa is seen every day in the commentaries about the Arabs' constitutional inferiority, violence, fanaticism, and lies. This ideology reemerged unmistakably after October 7, 2023 when Hamas fighters stormed into villages in southern Israel and killed civilians, young and old, many of whom were opposed to Netanyahu and the settlers.

The prevailing orientalist discourse emanated not only from the Israeli state, but also became the dominant narrative across the Western media: Hamas came to represent the generic Arab. Of course, the violence and daily brutality required to police Israel's Manichean world of colonizer and colonized was normalized, and remained so even after October 7, as the world began to watch a genocide unfold.

Israel's European "brightly lit" cities with their vibrant nightlife, on the one hand, and the high-tech border fences and military guards of the occupied territories, on the other, "a world without spaciousness" (Fanon 1968: 39), harkens back to the Manichean geography of the colonial world described by Fanon. It is a juridical world of compartments, divided by the police and the military. However, after October 7, the survival of Gaza – already an "open-air prison" – itself came into doubt as daily atrocities and massacres were unleashed against Palestinian civilians there who have nowhere to escape to. This obliteration is justified in the indisputable moral name of "never again."

This reference to the Holocaust takes us back to Fanon's first book, *Black Skin, White Masks*, in which, in connecting anti-Semitism with negrophobia, he is reminded of his philosophy teacher from the Antilles saying, "'When you hear someone insulting the Jews, pay attention; he is talking about you.' And I believed at the time he was universally right, meaning that I was responsible in my body and soul for the fate reserved for my brother." It was around that time that Fanon left Martinique to join the Free French Army, which was committed to the anti-Nazi fight. "Since then," he added, "I have understood that what he meant quite simply was that the anti-Semite is inevitably a negrophobe" (2008: 100). Back in Martinique in late 1945, Fanon heard a speech from Aimé Césaire's political campaign: "When I switch on my radio and hear that Black men are being lynched in America, I say that

they have lied to us: Hitler isn't dead. When I switch on my
radio and hear that Jews are being insulted, persecuted, and
massacred, I say that they have lied to us: Hitler isn't dead"
(2008: 70). Just a few years later, Césaire would argue that
Nazism is the product of a "boomerang effect" of European
colonialism, where the exclusive savagery, violence, and brutality – the racism – toward non-European people rebounds
with the largest holocaust in history, the systematic elimination of 6 million Jews. "At the end of formal humanism,"
Césaire adds, "there is Hitler" (2000: 37), making it clear that
Hitler was not dead but would continue to appear in new
forms.

After October 7, mention of the Holocaust in Israel became
weaponized as a justification for the removal (and, indeed, the
wished-for annihilation) of Palestinians. It is true that the idea
of self-determination for Jews after the Holocaust contained
contradictory tendencies, including liberal and socialist. More
importantly, there is also a direct line of Zionism in power
– from the fascist-terrorist Irgun, through Menachem Begin,
to Benjamin Netanyahu – that from its inception cared more
about consolidating land and power than adhering to the
principle of the self-determination of nations that declares no
nation can be free if it oppresses another.

In *Les Damnés de la terre*, Fanon describes the colonial world
as Manichean (going back to the Persian religion of Mani,
which viewed the creators of the world, God and the Devil,
as still fighting it out). From the colonizer's standpoint, the
colonized do not lack values but are simply evil. Thus, the
police and army play the role of containing the colonized and
keeping them in place (and, as Fanon critically points out,
they play the same role in the post-independence neocolonial
national regime).

To return to Fanon's conception of colonial Manicheanism,
its relevance now is borne out by the use of the term "apart-

heid" to describe conditions of life for Palestinians. Introduced after World War II in South Africa with genuinely fascist connections, apartheid was about "population control" (i.e. labor control) of South Africa's Africans, including pass laws and the forced removal of people. The creation of Homelands or "Bantustans" for 87 percent of the population on 13 percent of the land was an attempt by late settler colonialism to develop a system of indirect rule based on apartheid state-sanctioned and supported "tribal" rule outside "White South Africa." In apartheid Israel, the "Bantustans" of Gaza and the West Bank are not primarily about labor control – though the pass laws work in a similar way – but about keeping the Palestinian population fixed in their exiled place, as in Gaza, where this surplus population is essentially locked down. Fanon's writings, focused as they are on the lived experience of being denied freedom of movement, hemmed into "this narrow world, strewn with prohibitions" (1968: 37), have an immediate resonance. In *Les Damnés de la terre*, for example, he writes of a million Algerian hostages behind barbed wire and 300,000 refugees on the Moroccan and Tunisian frontiers forced there by the French. The unheard-of levels of brutality, terror, and vengeance unleashed on the populace created a continuous "apocalyptic atmosphere" that, Fanon concludes, is "the sole message [of] French democracy" (1965: 26). In extreme poverty and precarious living conditions, Fanon continues, the colonized live in a state of permanent insecurity; in flight from endless aerial bombardments, families are broken up and there is hardly anyone who does not suffer from mental disorders. This "shameless colonialism" is only matched by apartheid South Africa (1965: 26). Palestinians live under similar conditions and are also expected to express an emotional and affective control of the self that is situationally impossible. As Hamas's bloody murders of Israeli civilians on October 7 dominated the news, it was quickly forgotten that those breaching the fences and breaking into "forbidden quarters" (1968: 40) were experiencing a physical moment of liberation. As a psychiatrist and political theorist, Fanon engaged with these contradictory and dehumanized realities. While recognizing the role that the October 7 attacks have played in putting the Palestinian question back on a global stage, Fanon would also be critical of Hamas's ideology and authoritarianism. Concerned about the difficult question of how to rebuild a resistance that is democratic, his warning in 1959 could very much be directed at Hamas:

> Because we want a democratic and a renovated Algeria, because we believe one cannot rise and liberate oneself in one area and sink in another, we condemn, with pain in our hearts, those brothers who have flung themselves into revolutionary action with the almost physiological brutality that centuries of oppression give rise to and feed. (1965: 25)

In Fanon's schematic mapping of anticolonial activity, he argues that resistance is determined by the colonizer. He appreciated the power of this militant and Manichean anticolonial inversion, proclaiming that the colonized respond "to the living lie of the colonial situation by an equal falsehood" and adding that, in this colonist context, "there is no truthful behavior: and the good is quite simply that which is evil for 'them'" (1968: 50). While recognizing the logic of this inversion of colonial Manicheanism, Fanon also considered it incredibly problematic, warning that, along with the "brutality of thought and a mistrust of subtlety which are typical of revolutions . . . there exists another kind of brutality which . . . is typically antirevolutionary, hazardous and anarchist." If it is not "immediately combatted . . . this unmixed and total brutality . . . invariably leads to the defeat of the movement" (1968 147). Political education, Fanon argues, is necessary to introduce "shades of meaning" and, in doing so, challenges the tendency among leaders to underestimate the people's reasoning capabilities. This might sound almost idealistic, but it is essential to the cognitive break that Fanon argues can be brought about by a revolutionary moment. This is not the old, but a new politics, he argues, where "leaders and organizers living inside of history . . . take the lead with their brains and their muscles in the fight for freedom. These politics are national, revolutionary and social" (1968: 147).

Warning of the degeneration of nationalism into chauvinism and ethno-nationalism, Fanon argues in *Les Damnés de la terre* that national consciousness is not nationalism, quickly adding that national consciousness also has to open up during the struggle for freedom: "If it is not enriched and deepened by a very rapid transformation into a consciousness of social and political needs, in other words into humanism, it leads to a dead-end" (1968: 204). We continue to see these dead-ends reappear in brutal and nihilistic ways, reminding us that developing radical humanism mediated through political and social (human) action and thought requires both intention and clarity. Radical humanism calls not only for political organization, but also, crucially, for an image of the future society based on human foundations that must be worked out and discussed with the people (reflecting their social needs) involved in the struggle for liberation.

For Fanon, to perceive the reason in revolt – which will be discussed throughout this book – requires the development of new ways of thinking and new ways of understanding that seem implausible. The attitudes to the bombing of al-Ahli Arab Hospital in Gaza City in mid-October 2023 expressed the Manichean situation and thinking that Fanon describes. While Israel and the US immediately insisted that it could not have been an Israeli bomb, across the region, mass demonstrations and expressions of outrage (including against their own Arab leaders) rejected that assessment. As Fanon puts it, "the 'truth' of the oppressor" becomes "an absolute lie," and is countered by "another, an acted truth" (1967: 76). Despite whatever proof was produced, the masses had already made up their minds, connecting the violent destructive act directly to *their* experiences: the Palestinian experience of Israeli's military might, as well as the fear of a genocide. They knew that this would happen, and that thousands upon thousands of Palestinian children would be killed by Israeli airstrikes.

To reiterate, the colonizer/colonized relationship is a Manichean one. The arming of the ultra-rightwing Religious Zionists to steal Palestinian land and the silencing of opposition to the war inside Israel are logical expressions of Manichean thinking. While there is some opposition among Israelis to the settlers, there is, at the same time, a widespread sense of existential dread of Arabs. Among these groups, it would not be surprising to hear them repeat what Fanon heard the Algerian colonists say, "Let's each one of us take ten of them and bump them off and you'll see the problem solved in no time" (1965: 56).

But colonialism is not only a simple occupation of a territory. It is also, argues Fanon, the occupation of body and mind where, "in its initial phase, the action ... of the occupier ... determines the resistance around which a people's will to survive becomes organized" (1965: 47). After all the years since Fanon wrote these words, we keep returning to this initial phase, mediated by violence. As Gideon Levy put it in the liberal Israeli daily newspaper *Haaretz* immediately after the Hamas attacks: "They are already talking about wiping out entire neighborhoods in Gaza, about occupying the Strip and punishing Gaza 'as it has never been punished before.'" Implicitly critical of the idea of Israel being seen as a liberal democracy, he adds: "Israel hasn't stopped punishing Gaza since 1948, not for a moment ... Gaza, most of whose residents are refugees created by Israel. Gaza, which has never known a single day of freedom."[1]

Fanon's understanding of the pathology of colonialism is described in both *L'An V de la revolution algérienne* (*A Dying Colonialism*) and in *Les Damnés de la terre*. At the same time, he recognizes the emergence of the new "reality of the nation" (2018: 679) out of the process of decolonization. In *L'An V*, he argues that a radical change in consciousness is taking place as a new reality of the nation is being born, and critically warns of the pathological excesses of violence. But Fanon's relevance has to be understood in a context where no such new reality of the nation seems to be emergent. Manicheanism reigns, reflecting and underlining Fanon's discussion of violence as a ceaseless pathological dystopian reality of permanent social dysfunction manifested so vividly in Hamas's politics of pathological violence. It is a politics that is held up to the world ostensibly as distinct from the religion-driven violence of ultra-orthodox Jewish settlers in the West Bank, the state-sponsored persecution of occupied Palestine, and the Arab abandonment of the principle of Palestinian national self-determination. The massacre of Israeli civilians on October 7, 2023, a pathological act of anti-Jewish violence, exposed the multiple layers and facets of Palestinian oppression. And it is this dialectic that has elicited global responses of support for Palestinian national self-determination, as well as, not surprisingly, global anti-Semitic and Islamophobic rhetorical and actual violence. The images of Gaza as a graveyard of children have been seen around the world, motivating a global response, especially among youth, offering a challenge to both Israelis and Palestinians, as well as new possibilities.[2] As Fanon puts it in the conclusion to *Black Skin, White Masks*: "To move away from the inhuman voices of their respective ancestors so that a genuine communication can be born . . . to touch the other, feel the other, discover each other" (2008: 206).

As you read this book, you will see how Fanon's analysis and vision remain vital and speak powerfully to our situation. You will also read of Fanon's consistent concern about human liberation and the crucial need for disalienation. In his 1960 speech "Why We Use Violence," he responds to the colonist in Algeria who says that Algeria belongs to them, laying out his radical humanist challenges:

> We do not say . . . "You are a stranger, go away." We do not say . . . "We will take over the leadership of the country and make you pay for your crimes and those of your ancestors." We do not tell him that "to the past hatred of the Black we will oppose the present and future hatred of the White" . . . We say . . . "We are Algerians, banish all racism from our land, all forms of oppression and let us work for the flourishing and enrichment of humanity." We agree, Algeria belongs to all of us, let us build it on democratic bases and together build an Algeria that is commensurate with our ambition and our love. (2018: 657)

This is the "important theoretical problem" Fanon discusses at the end of *Les Damnés de la terre*, which includes an existential self-critique, explaining that it is "necessary at all times and in all places to make explicit, to de-mystify, and to hunt down the insult to humankind that exists in oneself" (1968: 304; 2004: 229; translation altered). The theoretical problem concerns how to create a new society that supports and nurtures a liberating consciousness. It is a problem that Fanon addresses throughout his psychiatric and political work. Understanding that "people are imperceptibly transformed by revolutionary processes in perpetual renewal," he adds that "there must be no waiting until the nation has produced new people." Consciousness, Fanon insists, "must be helped" by giving people back their dignity and what he calls "opening the mind to human things" (1968: 304, 205). Indeed, we should not forget that the beginning of the end of apartheid in South Africa – the Soweto uprising of 1976 – was opened up by a philosophy of liberation called Black Consciousness, for which Fanon was an essential theorist (see Gibson 2011). Revolutionary theory (and this is what makes *Les Damnés de la terre* a "handbook of revolution") must contribute to total and complete human liberation.

November 20, 2023

# Acknowledgments

This book was meant to be completed earlier. George Owers contacted me just before the Covid-19 lockdown in March 2020 about Polity's new Black Lives series. We talked about a book on Fanon and I submitted a proposal later in the year. At the time, I was working on *Fanon Today: Reason and Revolt of the Wretched of the Earth*, an edited collection that would be published in November 2021 on the sixtieth anniversary of *Les Damnés de la terre* (Daraja Press). During that time, I was struggling with a medical condition that was not improving. To keep me sane I worked, when I could, on *Frantz Fanon: Combat Breathing*. Medical leave followed by a teaching sabbatical gave me the time to concentrate and live with the book. A big thanks to Amy Ansell, my dean at Emerson College, for helping to make this possible.

*Frantz Fanon: Combat Breathing* could not have been completed without the aid of many people. First, I want to thank Lou Turner, who commented on every chapter. It was, while I was living in London in 1980 that John Alan and Lou Turner's *Frantz Fanon, Soweto, and American Black Thought* first introduced me to Fanon and to Steve Biko's Fanonian praxis. After the formal end of apartheid in 1994, Fanon became newly alive, though his books were not being taught at South African universities. In 1999 I had my first opportunity to visit South Africa and speak there about Fanon; in the early 2000s, I presented the annual Frantz Fanon lecture in Durban. Students there told me that, as they read Fanon's *Les Damnés de la terre*, they would write down South African names as they applied "the Pitfalls of National Consciousness" to their own situation. But it was the emergence of the shack-dweller movement, Abahlali baseMjondolo, in 2005 that expressed the reason and revolt of the wretched of the earth in post-apartheid South Africa. For me, the relevance today of Fanon is visible in these conversations in South Africa, in the Arab Spring revolutions, and in the #Black Lives Matter movements. This Fanonian praxis was expressed by the activists and scholars who contributed to *Fanon Today: Reason and Revolt of the Wretched of the Earth* including Flávio Almada, Elizabeth Berger, Alejandro De Oto, Deivison Faustino, Rosemere Ferreira, Levi Gahman, Razan Ghazzawi, Hamza Hamouchene, Samah Jabr, Kurtis Kelly, Wangui Kimari, Toussaint Losier, Ayyaz Mallick, Feargal Mac Ionnrachtaigh, David Pavón Cuéllar, Johannah Reyes, Annette Rimmer, Ato Sekyi-Otu, Léa Tosold, Lou Turner, and S'bu Zikode, as well as, most crucially, the publisher, Firoze Manji. In addition, Jim Fabris, Michelle Gubbay, Yasser Munif, Michael Neocosmos, Richard Pithouse, and Jennifer Rycenga were also important interlocutors during this important moment. The sudden death of Miraj Desai, a contributor to *Fanon Today*, is truly mourned. A true Fanonian, his work with Fanon was connected with his commitment to anti-racist community psychiatry and healing.

Students from my Fall 2020 Fanon seminar who, with me, at that very Covid-19 and George Floyd moment, read, discussed, and were fully engaged in Fanon backwards, from *Les Damnés de la terre* to *Black Skin, White Masks*, include Eric Dolente, Maya Faerstein-Weiss, Griffin Fisher, Claire Foley, Leah Kindler, Sam Kiss, Hunter Logan, Tess Rauscher, Michael Rocco, Salah Shams, Madison Shaw, Liam Thomas, Weiting Tian, Lin Vega, and Vedaaya Wadhani. Leah

Kindler's poetry from the class is included in *Fanon Today*; and the artwork of Griffin Fisher, who heartbreakingly died before *Frantz Fanon: Combat Breathing* was completed, is present in the book.

Just before the Covid-19 lockdown, I had a chance to meet with members of the South African shack-dweller organization, and to engage in a four-hour discussion on Fanon's work and its meaning, sitting around a table with National Council Members S'bu Zikode, Mqapheli Bonono, Nomusa Sizani, Zanele Mtshali, Bathabile Makhoba, Joyce Majola, Thuso Mohapi, Mfanufikile Sindane; KwaZulu-Natal Provincial Secretary, Nhlanhla Mtshali; Youth Comrades, Busisiwe Diko, Lindokuhle Mnguni, Nhlakaniphi Mdiyastha; and Financial Officer, Asiphe Mpumela. Since then Abahlali baseMjondolo has established a Frantz Fanon school in the eKhenana Commune in Durban.

When the first draft of *Frantz Fanon: Combat Breathing* was complete in the spring of 2022, John Trimbur offered invaluable support, reading, commenting, and provided critical editorial advise. At Polity, the book was shepherded by Julia Davies, who went through the whole manuscript, suggesting edits and calmly explaining each element of the publishing process, aided by Sarah Dancy, Helena Heaton, and Maddie Tyler. The work also benefited from a research appointment at Brown University's Department of Africana studies from 2022 to 2024, thanks to chair and Professor Noliwe Rooks. In the Spring of 2023, Matthieu Renault invited me to the Fanon en Pratiques Colloque in Paris, my first Fanon trip in three years. There I saw the marvelous Frantz Fanon graphic book, and had the opportunity to meet its author, Frédéric Ciriez. In Paris, I had the chance to reconnect with my friends from the "Fanon: Decolonizing Madness" project: Alice Cherki, Roberto Beneduce, and Lisa Damon.

I am grateful to have been involved in Caribbean Philosophy

Association events, and value my long acquaintance and work with Jane Gordon and Lewis R. Gordon. And last, my debt to Raymond Geuss, Edward Said, and the late George C. Bond for their intellectual generosity remains boundless. While Aidan Gibson generously offered humor, relief, and advice, Kate Josephson was a constant interlocutor, companion, critic, and comrade.

# Introduction

We inhabit extraordinary times: times of crisis and possibility in which we are acutely aware of the intensity of what revolutionary thinker Frantz Fanon called "the glare of history's floodlights." Around the world, the invisible has become visible as rebellions from Black Lives Matter following the death of George Floyd on May 25, 2020 spread with astonishing speed, creating new solidarities around the globe (see Gibson 2021).[1] And in 2022, after the death of Mahsa Amini on September 16, 2022, the movement, under the banner of "Woman. Life. Freedom," escalated quickly across Iran into North Africa, the Middle East, and Turkey. It is impossible to predict – but then, in retrospect, it seems utterly predictable. As the police murders of George Floyd and Mahsa Amini become nodal points, calling for action as well as rethinking and self-clarification, many are reminded of an observation attributed to Lenin – that "there are weeks where decades happen." What will happen next? How can we play a role in determining the future, making sure that these rebellions are not taken over and watered down, and realizing the truly human-centered transformations that people crave?

Fanon's statement in the conclusion to his first book, *Black Skin, White Masks*, that the Vietnamese revolt not because they have discovered a culture but "quite simply . . . because it became impossible for them to breathe" (2008: 201) quickly became reproduced and reanimated on placards, public art, and social media posts after the murder of Eric Garner in 2014 and again following the murder of George Floyd. The lament of their dying words "I can't breathe" – the same phrase uttered by 40 people in the US killed by police in 2020[2] – became transformed into the reason for revolt.

Asking the question, what to do after the revolution has failed, the incarcerated revolutionary philosopher James Yaki Sayles created a remarkable guide to discussing Fanon (2010: 353). By describing the Manichean world, Sayles argued, Fanon is talking about mental liberation "reflecting on the state of consciousness of colonized people as they struggle to become NEW PEOPLE" (2010: 180). And from within the hellholes of the Pelican Bay State Prison, the hunger strikes (2011–13) began as a humanist refusal to the "killing of our minds."[3]

Fanon is acutely aware of consciousness and the lived experience of the body in space, structured and ordered by racism and colonialism. Throughout his work, he uses the terms "suffocated," "smothered," and "imprisoned" to describe racialized and colonial reality. In *Les Damnés de la terre* (*The Wretched of the Earth*), he describes the spatial reality of the colonial world where the colonized are forced to live in a "narrow world strewn with prohibitions" (1968: 37; 2004: 3). And in *L'An V de la révolution algérienne*,[4] he describes colonization as the crushing of life and the denial of space, food, water, and air. In a colonial situation, life is not perceived "as flowering," he writes, "but as a permanent struggle against an omnipresent

Photograph by Tony Webster. "We revolt simply because for many reasons we can no longer breathe" – Frantz Fanon. Outside Minneapolis Police Department 4th precinct following the police officer-involved shooting of Jamar Clark on November 15, 2015.

death" because "there is not occupation of territory, on the one hand, and independence of persons on the other. It is the country as a whole, its history, its daily pulsation that are contested." Under these conditions, breathing itself is a threat, "it is an observed, occupied breathing . . . a combat breathing." Combat breathing is not only the struggle to survive under the continued threat of political, economic, and psychological violence. Fanon does not forget to inform us of the clandestine forms of existence that become the oxygen "shap[ing] a new humanity" (1965: 12, 65, 181).

Fanon's philosophy of liberation is intimately connected to the fight for another life. In such a struggle, he observes, every breath is a challenge, and "a clandestine form of existence." Because life cannot be conceived "otherwise than as a kind of combat," titling this work combat breathing also echoes Fanon's vision for another history and another society, "porous to all the breaths of the world" (Aimé Césaire, quoted in Fanon 2008: 104, 107).

This book is an introduction to the life and ideas of Frantz Fanon, the radical psychiatrist and revolutionary humanist. There is really nothing to separate his politics and his therapeutic approaches to mental health. By focusing on this dialectic, *Combat Breathing* brings into focus a living Fanon who continues to emerge at historical junctures of revolutions, social movements, and rebellions.

Fanon died young, at the age of 36 in 1961. In the short period between 1952 and 1961, he wrote and published three books, *Black Skin, White Masks*, *L'An V de la révolution algérienne*, and *The Wretched of the Earth* (*Les Damnés de la terre*),[5] all of which have become classics discussed in radical social movements.

As well as a political activist and thinker, Fanon was a psychiatrist who spent much of his short professional life working in hospitals in France, colonial Algeria, and postcolonial Tunisia. In all these contexts, treating the suffering of mental disorders was connected to the necessity of disalienating and decolonizing the institutions themselves, encouraging active engagements with the patients, and democratizing the hospitals (Fanon used the term "boarder" rather than "patient" to highlight his view that the institution works to "transform the mad into a patient"). His active participation in the Algerian revolution changed the primary focus of his work: he resigned in late 1956 to work as a full-time revolutionary. In his letter of resignation he wrote that after three years of working to disalienate the hospital, "there comes a time when silence becomes dishonesty" (1967: 52, 54).

My focus on Fanon's life and thought will offer up some important insights into his theory of liberation. Thinking about this moment with Fanon, we need to be aware of continuities and discontinuities – or, as he puts it, opacities

– between our age and his. Fanon is often speaking to us, but generally in ways we cannot hear. We have to work to hear him and to understand the new situations and their meanings.

Since his death, each generation has read Fanon and applied his ideas to their time. In Africa, Fanon's warning of the pitfalls of national consciousness was played out across the continent to such an extent that Ngugi wa Th'iongo (1993: 84), argued that the literature of Africa at the time was a "series of imaginative footnotes" to Fanon's "Pitfalls" chapter in *Les Damnés de la terre*. In Africa and Latin America, with the world's largest reserves of cobalt, coltan, copper, lithium, and uranium, and other minerals, neocolonialism remains incredibly adaptive and violent to any resistance.[6]

In South Africa, students read Fanon after the end of formal apartheid, adding local examples to his analysis. Fanon's idea of "development" from the ground up, based in the community need and discussion articulated in *Les Damnés de la terre*, resonate today with rural people in the Eastern Cape of South Africa fighting government-supported expropriation of land. And Abahlali baseMjondolo, the shack-dweller and activist movement in Durban (eThekwini), South Africa, have recently created a political education school named after Fanon as they developed the eKhenana commune on occupied land.[7] They continue to be under constant and often deadly attack from the police and the state as well as from local ruling African National Congress (ANC) organizations. Even as Fanon's words take on fresh meanings among new generations of activists, we should heed his caution that he does not come with timeless truths. This takes us directly to his warning that each generation must find, fulfill, or betray its mission, as he puts it.

Fanon's first "home" after his death in 1961 was not in fact Algeria or France, but the United States where, by the late 1960s, he had become infamous (Turner and Kelley 2021).

*Les Damnés de la terre* was first published in the US in 1963, on the 100th anniversary of the Emancipation Proclamation, coinciding with the murder of Medgar Evers, who was involved in desegregation at the University of Mississippi and voting rights struggles, and the televised police violence against civil rights demonstrators in Birmingham, Alabama. It occurred at the moment when the nonviolent strategy, including the overall philosophy of the civil rights movement, was being challenged. Fanon was acutely aware of the struggles in the US; when he noted in *Les Damnés de la terre* that "Black radicals in the US have formed armed militia groups" (2004: 39), he was perhaps referring to Rob Williams and the 1959 announcement that he and other Black North Carolinians had taken up armed self-defense. The reprint of *Les Damnés de la terre* in the US in 1965 coincided with Martin Luther King Jr.'s opposition to the Vietnam war and the turn to "Black Power" within the civil rights movement. In the wake of the 1965 Watts rebellion, Fanon's description of violence as the daily experience of colonialism and his idea that counterviolence was the only language colonialism understood immediately resonated with his readers. By 1968, Fanon had become central to the movement's debates: as *Les Damnés de la terre* was republished in a cheap mass paperback edition, his name became well known in the Black movements and among White leftists (in 1968, the book was second on the list, behind *The Autobiography of Malcolm X*, as suggested reading for new members of the Black Panthers).[8]

Reacting to this, influencers from the popular press and in intellectual circles equated Fanon's thought with violence.[9] As the philosopher Hannah Arendt said at the time, very few people read past the first chapter, "On Violence," with many focusing on Sartre's preface, which "was more violent than the book it introduced" (Bernasconi: 2010: 40). The idea of Fanon as an "apologist of violence" has unfortunately remained

Griffin Fisher, *Frantz Fanon*. Boston 2019

dominant. Even today, the idea that every one of Fanon's comments "on violence is framed or qualified by an argument about healing" is reduced to an argument for healing through violence rather than, for example, a starting point for "understanding how his thought unfolds over time" (Gilroy et al. 2019: 180, 181). Assuming "a moral equivalence" between colonial and anticolonial violence (see Turner 2011) was not Fanon's argument, and elides both the geo-historical specificity of colonial violence and the goals of organized anticolonial counterviolence. As Fanon's biographer and colleague Alice Cherki puts it, Fanon was "a thinker about violence, not its apologist" (2006: 2).

Today, the return to Fanon is framed by a more nuanced view, helped by the English translation of his psychiatric and medical writings (see Fanon 2018; Gibson and Beneduce 2017), but we should not forget that this always formed part of his activist engagements (see Turner and Neville 2020). It has become a characteristic of Black Lives Matter as a psychosocial political movement for expressions of the subjective element of Black trauma that had not occurred previously. Perhaps it was because the George Floyd uprising happened in the midst of COVID-19 – when the high numbers of deaths of Black and Brown "essential" workers shone a light on Black life not mattering – that space was made for these subjective expressions. The movement continued to highlight police abuse and murder, including those whose names were being added to a growing list, such as Breonna Taylor who was shot by police deploying a no-knock warrant. The no-knock warrant became law 50 years earlier in response to another moment of the Black uprising in 1970. Deeply connected to "search and destroy" in Vietnam, it grew exponentially, echoing its militarism, equipment, tactics, and mindset, just as the police in Ferguson employed military-grade equipment in response to the rebellion after the murder of Michael Brown in 2014. In a Fanonian sense, Black trauma became politicized and expressed in the heartfelt testimonies from the immediate families who spoke in much clearer terms than the leaders as they testified in the trial of Floyd's murderers. Writing about suffering in the Blida-Joinville Psychiatric Hospital's *Notre Journal*, Fanon understood George Floyd's call out, explaining: "In hours of great suffering, the adult again has need of a consoling mother ... A mother is someone who has protected us from suffering, from troubles" (2018: 345).

It is Fanon's revolutionary humanism and humanity, his sensibility to the lived experience of racial objectification, oppression, and suffering that cannot be hidden, that make him so present for a new generation of thinkers and activists. He knew nothing about intersectionality or nonbinary gender identities; one can find in his writings terms and norms that very much reflect the period in which he wrote. But "to accuse Fanon of not thinking beyond his historical and cultural context," as argued by Bhopal and Preston (2011: 215), "is to accuse Fanon of being stuck in a singular consciousness, focused on 'race.'" It is his quest for human liberation – not as an abstract principle, but grounded in the daily lives of those who have been objectified, alienated, and dehumanized – and his willingness to "rethink everything" that mark him out as a thinker for our age. As his last words sum up, "we must make a new start, develop a new way of thinking, and endeavor to create a new human" (1968: 239).

Fanon is primarily a theorist of liberation, and his engagement with philosophy, politics, and mental health is always grounded by his concerns about dehumanization and alienation. He was a psychiatrist, philosopher, and political theorist but not at all interested in academic disciplines. Fanon's psychoanalytical approach in Black Skin, White Masks engages above all with the world around him (politically, culturally, medically), and he continually reminds us that such critical engagements require radical action. In thinking about taking such action, he is reminded of the psychiatrist and philosopher Karl Jaspers, who argues that each person is "co-responsible for every wrong and every injustice in the world, especially for crimes committed in their presence or with their knowledge. If I fail to do whatever I can to prevent them, I too am guilty" (quoted in Fanon 2008: 69n.9). Many in the Black community in Minneapolis expressed this in response to the murder of George Floyd, feeling guilty that they had not been able to do more to stop the police from killing him. Darnella Frazier, the young woman who stood a few feet away recording his death on her cellphone, said she felt powerless. For her, it was a life-changing and traumatic experience. Suffering from anxiety and panic attacks for months afterwards, she couldn't sleep. All she would see was a man "Brown like me, lifeless on the ground." Her mom would have to rock her to sleep: "George Floyd . . . I want you to know you will always be in my heart.

I'll always remember this day because of you" (McDonnell Nieto del Rio 2021).

Revealing a lifelong commitment to human freedom and the struggle against tyranny, Fanon would use a Jasperian argument in response to his brother Joby, who asked him why he was joining the Free French in 1944. In the year that followed, he would find out that France's humanism was an "obsolete ideal." This represented a transformational moment, but he still remained committed to fighting for freedom: indeed, he widened this commitment to focus on the struggle against racism and colonialism. And he would develop a "new humanism" in the 1950s connected to constructing a new ideal in the struggles for freedom in the Third World, which was most explicitly expressed in the conclusion to *Les Damnés de la terre*.

To remember Fanon, the man, the person, and the thinker, is to remember Claude Lanzmann's reflection after visiting him as he lay dying. Fanon, he said, "was a gentle man whose delicacy and warmth were contagious" (Lanzmann 2012: 347).

## A question of biography

Wary of what Lewis Gordon calls the "problem of biography in Africana thought," where "White intellectuals provide theory; Black intellectuals provide experience" (2000: 29), one is faced with a number of problems writing about Fanon in a book series called "Black Lives." Fanon felt the lived reality of the racial gaze reproduced on a daily basis, which for him meant that wherever he went he had to struggle to change that reality.

Another problem with writing about Fanon is that we don't know much about his private and domestic life. We know of his life in Martinique through his brother Joby and his friends. But as his neighbor Maiotte Daiphite remarked, Frantz Fanon was an average (not brilliant) student, and was "quite normal": "I was far from imagining he would become *the* thinker. I mean *the* thinker. I wonder what was brewing in his mind then" (Djemai 2001).

As a full-time member of Algeria's National Liberation Front (FLN) after 1957, and one of its leading spokespeople, Fanon was cautious by necessity. He was a public figure involved in a war against the French. He did not share personal stories even with those who knew him. There are very few photographs of him, and none (as far as I know) of him and his wife Josie; apart from one with his son Olivier in Tunis, there are no family photos. And as Daniel Nethery put it in the foreword to Joby Fanon's *Frantz Fanon, My Brother* (2014), "Josie remains an elusive character in all of the Fanon biographies."

The Fanons attended a Christmas Eve party at Marie-Jeanne Manuellan's house in 1959. Manuellan had been working with Fanon for more than a year, transcribing sessions with his patients and then typing *L'An V de la révolution algérienne*, but their relationship was strictly professional. Fanon had essentially invited himself, and Manuellan could hardly say no. But she could not imagine "dancing in front of Fanon" (Manuellan 2017: 41). Josie went too, along with Fanon's bodyguard Youssef Farès (who was also a nurse at the Charles Nicolle psychiatric day hospital in Tunis). A few years younger than Fanon, Youssef was a dark-skinned Algerian who took care of Fanon's car, carefully opened his packages, and also sometimes took care of Olivier. Farès was also Fanon's official name at the hospital; in addition, Fanon used the name Nadia Farès, writing in the third person to his publisher François Maspero. Having the same name and the same fake passports under the Farès name, Youssef could easily pick up Fanon's packages at the post-office. Aware of Tunisian racism, Fanon would ironically remark: "Between two Blacks, the Tunisians will not know the difference" (see Cherki 2006: 131). Many at the hospital, at the clinics, and at the borders, writes Manuellan, thought Youssef was Fanon's brother (Manuellan 2017: 81).

Fanon turned out to be the life and soul of the Manuellans' party. This was a "different Fanon" from the one at work. He cracked jokes, was happy and relaxed. He sang biguines,[10] and he might have even have played a bit of guitar. Pictures were taken of the party, but Fanon destroyed the film. This reflected his intelligence, not paranoia. For his own safety and that of all the guests, the photos could not exist. It simply was too dangerous. These were the practices that Frantz and Josie Fanon carried out, almost automatically, on a daily basis. It was a war situation with informants and spies everywhere. Alice Cherki suggests that although Fanon may have said to Manuellan, "I am a very important person in the FLN and cannot fraternize with French people," he was only truly at ease with those who "belonged to Tunis's cosmopolitan circles – Tunisian Jews, French volunteer workers, French people who had decided to remain in independent Tunisia, Europeans who worked with the FLN. These were the people with whom he went to the beach and to the movies, with whom he listened to music and conversed" (Cherki 2006: 125).

The party at the Manuellans was so enjoyable that the Fanons were invited to gather again on New Year's Eve to sing and dance and, of course, talk about the Algerian war, independence, and the future of the Third World (see Manuellan 2017: 143). Over the next few months, Fanon would spend quite a bit of time with the Manuellans and also with the Taïebs. All were ex-communists who supported the Algerian revolution. Roger Taïeb was a Tunisian lawyer who had defended imprisoned communists during the Tunisian struggle for independence. Fanon would write a powerful letter to him from his deathbed, which is discussed later. Yoyo

Taïeb was a musician and Gilbert Manuellan a jazz aficionado, and Fanon would sometimes talk with them about jazz. Some Sundays, notes Cherki, "Fanon would relax by playing cards," which he would also do with his Algerian comrades Omar Oussedik and Si Saddek (see Cherki 2006: 126).

Fanon's critical interest in popular culture (comics, novels, films), indicated in *Black Skin, White Masks*, continued. At Blida-Joinville, he created a film discussion club and included film screenings as part of socio-psychotherapy programs. We know from Manuellan that he watched *Hiroshima Mon Amour* in Tunis. Because he was short-sighted (a fact rarely spoken about in the biographies, even though there is a famous photo of him with his nose in a text) and refused to wear glasses, he insisted on others joining him in the front row (see Manuellan 2017: 153–4). He liked the film and wanted to hear the others' opinions.

After Fanon's death, Josie avoided talking about their personal life. Into this void, stories and innuendos surfaced. For a few months before Fanon left for Accra in February 1960, he and Josie spent time with the Manuellans; Marie-Jeanne's *Sous la Dictée de Fanon* provides some useful insights. Like Fanon, Gilbert Manuellan, Marie-Jeanne's husband, had signed up for the fight against Nazism as a young man, and both had been wounded in the winter of 1944. Both had been denied their humanity by the French: Fanon because he was Black, Manuellan because he was a Métèque (a pejorative word for a "shifty-looking" immigrant of Mediterranean origin). They were both concerned with creating a post-independence society and had many discussions concerning questions of land and agriculture.

This is not to say that Marie-Jeanne and Josie were not also involved in political discussions, but they were the ones taking care of the children. Manuellan reminds us that relations between men and women in 1960 were quite different from how they are today: "Of course, Josie and I put our grain of salt in the political discussions of men. But it was just a 'grain of salt'. Yet our men in no way relegated us to the kitchen." But when Fanon said that "a child must smell the smell of jams made by his mother," it was the women who started making the strawberry jam and asked the children to watch. But Manuellan insists there were no divisions about what was spoken: "All four of us also talked about psychiatry, children's education, ways of being of others, and of ourselves ... We commented on the news on the radio that we listened diligently and on the articles in the 'progressive' [French] newspapers of the time" (2017: 147–8).

Fanon would talk about the possibility of new social relations, which he called "revolutionary love" (1965: 114–15), whereby each was the owner of their own freedom while respecting the freedom of others – but he would add you'd have to make the revolution first (see Manuellan 2017: 155). The revolution was in motion, as he argued in the first chapter of *L'An V de la révolution algérienne*, and the Algerian revolution had women at the "heart of the combat" (1965: 66). It is clear that when he said that revolution comes first, he was not disconnected from the new questions and new social relations that the revolution itself was creating. The truth is that Fanon, in theory and practice (whether that be as a psychiatrist, a political analyst, or a philosopher), was a revolutionary who called for disalienation in all its forms. What he had said in *Black Skin, White Masks* about transforming the world and changing the social structure (2008: 1, 80) had become a live possibility with the Algerian revolution.

An ardent supporter of the Algerian revolution, Josie was fearful about what would happen to her and Olivier after Frantz died, but she was always committed to "returning to Algeria" (Manuellan, 2017: 170). After Algerian independence, she became a naturalized Algerian, writing for *Afrique action* and other publications. She interviewed Che Guevara for *Révolution africaine* in 1964. She remained committed to keeping Fanon's work in print and was skeptical of the new generation of American biographers in the early 1970s (such as Peter Geismar and Irene Gendzier) who wanted to know personal details about the Fanons. But, just as Fanon never said much about himself, so his wife rarely spoke about their life after his death. This was in the period when Fanon was being stereotyped as an angry man of violence in the US popular media. While Joby Fanon made himself available to biographers, he was taken aback by Gendzier's claim that Frantz's relationship with his mother was difficult because Frantz "was the darkest of the family." In response, Joby decided to write his own biography of his brother. While Joby's biography certainly gives us a good sense of their childhood, and includes family letters, the physical distance between them (especially after Frantz left Algeria) meant that they would only see each other occasionally.

Alice Cherki was a colleague of Fanon's first at Blida-Joinville and then at Charles Nicolle Hospital in Tunis. Her *Fanon: A Portrait* (2006) provides some important details, especially concerning his years in Algeria and Tunis. In response to a question about Fanon's family life, Cherki said he was a "dedicated husband and father. At the same time, he was a very busy man. But he was very dedicated to his family." "Fanon loved life," she added later, "He had a great sense of humor ... He liked to go out to dinner, go dancing, things like that" (2016). Marcel Manville later recounted that while they were in the French army in North Africa, a Gaullist official turned up at the army camp where they were stationed. The camp commanders organized a parade of 300 troops to be inspected by the official, who asked them if they had any concerns or questions. Three raised their hands and met the official privately: they were the Antillean friends, Fanon, Manville, and

Pierre Mosole. Worried, the commanding officers intercepted them, wanting to find out what they would say. Since they had raised their hand for fun, they found it quite enjoyable, recalled Manville later, as he had advised them not to say a thing. "The [W]hite officers got more and more excited while the [B]lack servicemen refused to talk ... Manville was using all his strength not to giggle; he always enjoyed laughing. Especially when he looked at Fanon, the most ferocious-looking soldier imaginable" (Geismar 1971: 33).

To talk about Fanon's life is to talk about Fanon's intellectual work. This is especially the case of his first book *Black Skin, White Masks*, in which he used the first person singular and plural. It was published when he was 26 and is the most intentionally "biographical" of his works, but it would be a mistake to associate the author with the pathologies he describes. Rather, the alienation of the person with a Black skin, forced to put on the White mask in an almost unconscious striving toward the ideal of Whiteness, is social; disalienation requires not only making the unconscious conscious, "but also [acting] along the lines of a change in social structure." In other words, bringing into conscious reflection through psychoanalytic work the patient's unconscious feelings, desires, fantasies, anger, and so on, is not enough because the "hallucinatory lactification" is not an individual neurosis but a social one, a product of a racist society. Very much connected to contemporary discussions in psychoanalysis, Fanon would tell his patients: "It's the environment; it's society that is responsible for your mystification" (2008: 80). But that knowledge alone would not bring about liberation.

Just as Fanon begins *Black Skin, White Masks* stating that it is a product of a very specific moment and insists that he does not posit timeless truths, the same can be said of his second book, *L'An V de la révolution algérienne* , literally the fifth year of the revolution. In his last book, *Les Damnés de la terre*, he argues: "Each generation must discover its mission, fulfill it or betray it, out of relative opacity" (2004: 145). He thus demands that the reader discover their mission and act in good faith in the struggle for human freedom. For Fanon, this is very much tied to his historic moment and its meaning: the birth of a new "Third World." As he put it in the FLN newspaper *El Moudjahid* in 1959, while the colonialists can't imagine a time without them, "'a historic look at history'" requires the end of the colonialism, "for it has become historically necessary for the national time . . . to exist" (1967: 159). This new history would need to rethink everything from the ground up (2004: 237–9, 57).

## A note on psychiatry

Fanon's first full-time appointment was as a *chef de service* at Blida-Joinville Psychiatric Hospital in Algeria from 1953 to 1956. After leaving to work full-time for the Algerian revolution in Tunis, he continued to work as a psychiatrist at the same time as being part of the editorial group and writing for *El Moudjahid*. His work as a psychiatrist ended in February 1960 when he became the FLN's ambassador to Africa, based in Accra, Ghana. During 1960, "the year of Africa,"[11] he acted as the representative of the Provisional Government of the Algerian Republic (GPRA), engaging with radical leaders and militants about African freedom.

During the 1950s, Fanon's psychiatric opinions and methods (as well as his interest in psychoanalytic theories) had been developing and changing. After writing *Black Skin, White Masks*, he spent the year before passing his final oral exam for his degree (1953) at Saint-Alban Psychiatric Hospital under the supervision of François Tosquelles, the "founder" of a radical psychoanalytic approach that would be called "institutional psychotherapy" (or socio-[psycho]therapy). Critical of hospital hierarchies and the treatment of patients, Tosquelles addressed ideas of transforming the hospital from an alienating and pathologizing structure by including patients in discussions and decisions about the hospital's daily running. Like many institutional psychotherapists at the time (including those at Saint-Alban like Tosquelles and Jean Oury and Félix Guattari at La Borde,[12] as well as others who would be associated with critical and antipsychiatry in the late 1960s),[13] Fanon was pragmatic about the use of electroconvulsive therapy (ECT), insulin shock therapy, and other drug treatments. He was critical of the indiscriminate use of ECT and the new medications that made patients passive and controllable from the institution's point of view. But he and others were not wholly against shock therapy; in a paper co-written with Tosquelles in 1953, they argued that ECT could "be legitimated only in terms of efficacy" (see 2018: 291). To understand Fanon as a psychiatrist, one has to remember that he studied and worked in a period quite different from the present where the medicalization (and, indeed, the chemicalization) of mental health and the focus on "brain chemistry" is virtually hegemonic.[14] Fanon would be opposed to such an approach, since it avoids what he calls a situational sociodiagnosis. Chemical diagnosis elides any criticisms of society and its institutions.

There is a long history to today's chemicalization of mental health, which started with Largactil (Thorazine), developed in France in 1950 as an antipsychotic used to treat schizophrenia. Fanon was completely opposed to the use of Largactil to treat agitated patients with a "total ignorance of the pathological mechanisms involved" (2018: 447). The elision of situational and social diagnostics meant that any form of protest was always pathologized (see Metzl 2010).

The history of mental health is intimately connected with the history of racism and imperialism. The sheer longevity, reproduction, and materiality of racism include an awareness of changes wrought by social struggles and by the "evolution of exploitation" even if racism "no longer dares appear without disguise" (Fanon 1967: 37). But the latent messages are remarkably consistent. Black boys are seen as threatening; Black girls are defiant; reaction to objectification is seen as "aggressive."

For colonial ethnopsychiatrists, schizophrenia was said to be the most frequent form of psychosis among Africans. The same would be said about Black Americans in the 1960s, where "schizophrenia was a condition that also afflicted 'Negro men,' and that Black forms of the illness were more hostile and aggressive than were White ones" (Metzl 2010: xvi; see also Metzl, 2012). Fanon engaged earlier discussions around the question of neuropsychiatry in his medical dissertation and throughout his career emphasized the importance of subjectivity in any social and situational diagnosis. This approach would provide him with a quite different and radical standpoint from which to think about mental health. Two critical articles of Fanon's are worth mentioning in this regard. The first is his criticism of the racist medical practice toward people from North Africa, "The 'North African Syndrome,'" published in 1952, and the second (which implicitly decenters the hegemonic view of the mad and madness), is "Maghrebi Muslims and their Attitude toward Madness," published in 1956. In the colonial world, Fanon argued, "the colonized's affectivity is kept on edge like an open sore flinching from a caustic agent." The psyche retracts, he argued, and "finds an outlet through muscular spasm" that the experts classify as "hysterical and violent" (2004: 19). Black power in the US in the 1960s was conceived as "delusional anti-whiteness" and diagnosed as "protest psychosis" (Metzl 2010: xv). And within mainstream psychiatry a shift was occurring in the early 1970s toward the idea that depression was biochemical in nature (a characterization that we are still living with today). By 1980, the listing of criteria in the *DSM* (*Diagnostic and Statistical Manual*) *III* made the assumption that the "core symptoms of mental disorders stemmed from aberrant brain functioning" (Healy 1997: 234), marking the birth of "a new biomedical self" (Healy 2004: 7).[15] The instrumentalization of diagnosis went hand-in-hand with an emphasis on function (namely, functioning uncritically within a racist society). The quantification of symptoms almost completely erases the subjective and the social, connected with the development of SSRIs (selective serotonin reuptake inhibitors) as the pharmacological answer to depression to "sculpt personalities" rather than treat illness (see Healy, 2004: 169).[16] And still the medical model trades on "race norming," the numerical adjustment of values for organ function of Black patients based upon a White norm, built on a premise that Black people and White people are physiologically and cognitively different (see Trimbur 2021). Connected to this is the estimate that on average one Black person is killed everyday by the police. "We accumulate data," writes Fanon, "but with every line we write . . . we get the feeling of something unfinished" (2008: 147).

Across eight chapters, this book discusses Fanon's life, his commitments, his action, and his intellectual work with reference to each of his three major books. Chapters 1–3 focus on Fanon's life in Martinique and France, ending with a discussion of his first book, *Black Skin, White Masks*. Chapters 4–6 look at Fanon's appointment to the Blida-Joinville Psychiatric Hospital and his growing involvement in the Algerian liberation struggle. Moving to Tunis to work full time for the FLN, he wrote *L'An V de la révolution algérienne*. He became the representative of the GPRA in Accra in 1960, and his final work, *Les Damnés de la terre*, was published just before his death in 1961. Highlighting a thread connecting all his work, a new humanism is linked with the Third World revolution, which in its original meaning was "the third age of humanity."

## A note on Fanon and the language of race, gender, and translations

Throughout this book, I use the modern convention of capitalizing B for "Black" and W for "White," including in quotations.

Since French is gendered, "Le Noir" is used to translate "the Black man." In other words, "L'homme Noir" would be redundant. However, Fanon also uses the word "homme" to talk about generic "Man" as human (similarly, Simone de Beauvoir ended *The Second Sex*, writing that it is "for man to establish the reign of liberty . . . men and women unequivocally affirm their brotherhood" (1989: 732)). This is typical of the period before the women's liberation movement of the 1970s, when these commonplaces were called into question. I have avoided this gendering unless Fanon is explicitly referring to women and men. It may be argued that I am doing Fanon favors, but wherever possible I see no reason to reproduce dated gendered language that was not being challenged as such in 1952. The English translations of Fanon's major works in the 1960s use the language of race and skin color that is also dated. The translations of the 2000s are better on that score.

In *Black Skin, White Masks*, Fanon uses the term "Black" in the title of a number of chapters. His use of the term "Le Noir" in 1952 is not the same as the way in which "the Black" or "the Black man" is understood today.

In the 1890s, some Black people in the US described themselves as Afro-Americans and although that didn't catch on then as it did later, an important moment came in the period after World War I with arguments and actions for capitalizing the N in "Negro." At the time, "Black" was considered derogatory and capital N "Negro" was preferred by Marcus Garvey, as in the "Universal Negro Improvement Association" founded in 1914, "Negro World" founded in 1918, and in the 1920 "Declaration of Rights of the Negro Peoples of the World." W.E.B. Du Bois and others at the time used it in titles of their publications. Capital N "Negro" had some correspondence with the French "Le Noir."

The move from Negro to Black in the US in the late 1960s and 1970s, connected with the move from Civil Rights to Black Power, was an important shift, which also carried over into the UK (Black British) and South Africa (Black Consciousness) in the same period. In France there was also a period when the English term "Black," understood politically and culturally, was preferred over "Le Noir," reflecting Black consciousness as a world phenomenon.

One question concerns what role Fanon gives to the lower case "nègre" and the upper case "Nègre." The English translations are reflective of their periods, so that "Nègre" in *Black Skin, White Masks* has been translated as "Negro" (1967), "Black" (2004), and "nègre" as the "N-word." Depending on who is speaking, the term "nègre" can be used as an insult or a compliment. As David Macey points out, adding the "Creole equivalent (nèg) can be used to mean simply 'man' or even 'friend'" (Macey 2012: 47).

I do not use the English N-word. Instead, although the lower case "nègre" is contested and rejected as offensive and pejorative, I will, following Fanon, use it with all its ambiguities. Most certainly, Aimé Césaire and Fanon used this word and underscored it as a derogatory term. It was Césaire who, using the term, turned it inside out and created the neologism "negritude"; Fanon is partly building on Césaire's appropriation of the pejorative term as a rallying call, while also emphasizing its ambiguity and its psychical and emotional power, not only as a reminder of slavery and colonialism but also the lived experience of racism.

The sixth chapter of *Black Skin, White Masks*, "Le Nègre et la psychopathologie," has been translated as either "The Negro and Psychopathology" (the 1967 Markmann translation) or "The Black Man and Psychopathology" (the 2008 Philcox translation). Since Fanon is talking about the psychopathologization of the Black man as an object of fear, the Black man becomes "le nègre," a phobic object. That the subject of the chapter is the Black man is clear when Fanon writes: "Those who grant our conclusions on the psychosexuality of the White woman may ask what we have to say about the woman of color. I know nothing about her." He goes on to explain that in fact he does know something about the woman of color insofar as he is talking of women of color who have internalized the racial gaze and the psycho-pathologizations of the Black man, the subject of *Black Skin, White Masks*: "What we can suggest, nevertheless, is that for many Antillean women, whom we shall call the almost White, the aggressor is represented by the typical Senegalese or in any case by a so-called inferior" (2008: 157).

There are two translations of *Les Damnés de la terre*. The first, by Constance Farrington, is still widely available, but uses the terms "settler" and "native" rather than "colonizer" and "colonized." The later (2004) translation by Richard Philcox fixes this problem, but introduces other issues. I have privileged the Philcox translation, but also refer to the Farrington translation when needed.

# 1

## Martinique, France, and Metaphysical Experiences

The title of this chapter refers to Fanon's argument in his essay "Antilleans and Africans" (1967) that a number of metaphysical experiences occurred in Martinique between 1939 and 1945 that changed Martinican self-consciousness and contributed to the development of a political consciousness that would remove the Vichy government in 1943. Thus, he argues, after 1945 Antilleans "changed their values" (1967: 24). Fanon also experienced a change in values. He left to join the Free French in 1943 before the end of the Vichy regime. In an important letter to his family in 1945 he writes that the ideal for which he had risked his life was obsolete. He returned to Martinique a changed man.

### Childhood

Frantz Fanon was born on July 25, 1925 in Fort-de-France, Martinique. His name was Frantz Omar Fanon.[1] Frantz was the fifth of eight children. His father, Casimir, was a civil servant and described as a "free thinker" (Hansen 1974: 26). His mother, Eléonore, ran a small haberdashery. Patrick Ehlen writes that Eléonore was a "mulatto" whose "family had traveled to Martinique from Alsace" and what was "essential to her social standing" was not her Alsatian background but "the fairness of her skin." The politics of skin color was an essential marker of social standing. Three centuries of "mercantilism and imperial expansion," writes Ehlen, "had cast together complex and varied backgrounds of Europeans, Africans, East Asians, Chinese, and other nationalities, hosting one of the most culturally diverse populations of its time" (2001: 18–19).

Despite being a Black middle-class family in uncertain economic times, the family was fairly stable. Eléonore gave a fair bit of autonomy to the younger children, and Frantz had what could be considered a carefree childhood, spending a lot of his time with his brother Joby who was two years older. They were very close, "more friends than brothers," Joby remarked. After schoolwork was completed, they spent the rest of the day playing with friends: "We often followed him, even me, though I was older, because his ideas were good fun," Joby recounted. "When we were messing around he was the one who had the idea . . . he was very imaginative [and] had a good sense of organization and charisma." They played a lot of sport and also participated in what their parents called "vagabonding" (Fanon, 2014: 17), which included stealing fruit from the market more for fun than out of hunger.

There is also a remarkable story about an eight-year-old Frantz told by his older brother Félix. Clébert, a friend of Félix, had come around to see him. Told that Félix was running an errand, he was invited inside and went upstairs, where he saw Frantz. Clébert spoke with him briefly and then showed him his father's revolver, which he had brought along to impress Félix.

[Clébert] took off the safety, began to clean it, and, in the process pulled the trigger, unaware that the revolver was loaded. Frantz was nearly killed in this accident. As it turned out, the bullet tore Clébert's index finger slightly. Frantz kept his head. When Madame Fanon, hearing the shot, asked from downstairs what the two boys were doing, Frantz calmly told her that it was a toy backfiring. Meanwhile, he was tearing a sheet and wrapping Clébert's bleeding finger. Shortly after, Frantz told his mother that he was taking a walk with Clébert, but he actually accompanied him to the hospital. Asked whether this indicates the sangfroid of a child, Felix responded in the negative and added: "It was in his nature to be like that. Playing football, it was the same thing. He never got too excited; he was always very efficient." (Bulhan 1985: 20)

## Césaire and negritude

As late as 1940 no Antillean found it possible to think of himself as *un nègre*. It was only with the appearance of Aimé Césaire that the acceptance of negritude and the statement of its claims began to be perceptible.

Fanon, "West Indians and Africans",
*Black Skin, White Masks*

We adopted the word *nègres* as a term of defiance.

Césaire, *Discourse on Colonialism*

In "West Indians and Africans," published in *Esprit* in 1955, Fanon describes a shift in attitudes among a new generation of Antilleans, including himself, marked by a series of events, including Césaire's return to Martinique, the fall of France, the arrival of the French fleet blockaded there throughout the war, and the speeches from London by Charles de Gaulle. Before we turn to Fanon's teenage years during the war, let us consider a crucial influence on Fanon's thinking: Aimé Césaire and his book-length poem *Notebook of a Return to My Native Land*. Césaire returned to Martinique in 1939 around the time the poem was first published in a Parisian periodical, *Volontés*. In 1941 he, together with his wife Suzanne Roussi and René Ménil, founded the magazine *Tropiques*. It was a literary event on the island and beyond, which young intellectuals, like Joby and Frantz, would have known about. The surrealist André Breton, who had escaped from France, came across *Tropiques* while looking for ribbon in a draper's shop. The shop was owned by Reni Ménil's sister, who put him in touch with the editors. Breton would soon leave for New York and would help get Césaire's poem published in a bilingual edition prefaced by his own essay, "A Great Black Poet" (first published in *Tropiques*).

Twelve years Fanon's senior, Césaire was born in Basse-Pointe, a small town on Martinique's north coast. Like the Fanons, his was a lower-middle-class Black family, his father a tax inspector and his mother a dressmaker. From Basse-Pointe they moved to the capital, Fort-de-France, where Césaire became a prizewinning student at the Lycée Victor Schoelcher. Easily adapting to the elitist French lycée system, which was alien to the great majority of Creole-speaking rural Martinicans, he won a scholarship to the Lycée Louis-le-Grand in Paris. From there he enrolled at the École normale supérieure, where he studied literature and philosophy. Like other Antillean students, Césaire's goal was to "make it" in France. Instead, he became a central figure in the creation of negritude as a result of, and in reaction to, France's civilizing mission and its creation of the colonized *évolué*. In Paris, Césaire met Léopold Senghor from Senegal (then part of French Western Africa) and declared himself an African.

Césaire, Senghor, and Léon-Gontran Damas (from French Guiana) together created *L'Étudiant noir* in 1935. They had all been brought up to think of themselves as French, privileged to be in the Motherland, but unable to escape the racial gaze. Their Blackness became the point of connection. In its third (and last) issue, *L'Étudiant noir* published Césaire's "Racial Consciousness and Social Revolution," expressing what Césaire would coin as "negritude." The conception had been brewing for a number of years, especially seen in the US during the Harlem Renaissance; in France, the trail was blazed by the sisters Jane and Paulette Nardal, the first Martinican women to attend the Sorbonne, who wrote regularly for the Paris-based monthly *La Dépêche africaine* and met with African American writers such as Alain Locke (author of *New Negro*, published in 1925) and Claude McKay (a communist poet).

Césaire, Damas, and Senghor had three things in common: their color, their language, and their experience of French colonialism and education. In Paris, Césaire wrote: "I became conscious of the basic category of *nègre*. My poetry was born from that confrontation" (quoted in Gibson 2003: 62); he declared unequivocally: "I accept . . . I accept . . . completely, with no reservation . . . my race which no ablution of hyssop mixed with lilies could purify" (Césaire 1995: 121) and saw in this the disintegration and death of the "old negritude" (1995: 129).

No poem of negritude was more revolutionary than Césaire's *Notebook of a Return to My Native Land*. It was a scandal, Fanon noted, because here was Césaire – who was educated, and therefore respected – saying it was good to be Black. Through constant repetition that Blackness was invested with value, Césaire helped introduce Black consciousness to a new generation of young Antilleans.

Written in Yugoslavia on his "return" from France to Martinique, Césaire's poem discloses a memory of an earlier despondent return to the "inert" and "breathless" town of Fort-de-France. In contrast to this picture, there is a return to Africa, and (more importantly) a turn to a self-created Black self-consciousness. To communicate his African heritage and self-consciousness, Césaire created a new language. This creativity of Black consciousness is the message of his assertions in the poem that "negritude is not a rock," not a primeval self-consciousness, but a modern and global one. For Césaire, the "return" is a creative journey that both parallels and opposes the return to the poverty of alienated Martinique.

Surrealism furnished him a method of negativity and Césaire viewed this as a weapon that "exploded the French language." Moreover, it represented for him a "liberating factor" and a "process of disalienation," which helped him summon up unconscious forces to "plumb the depths" and "reclaim Africa." During the war years, surrealism became synonymous in Martinique with the revolutionary opposition to the war. "Poetry," Césaire argued, "equaled insurrection": "Revolt against Western rationalism! Revolt against colonialism! Revolt against 'browsing peacefulness' of the Martinican. A fundamental revolt against 'a world torn by its own contradictions,' the modern world" (quoted in Kestleloot 1974: 61).

Words are the weapons that bring renewal. Argued in French, against the French, the language of the oppressor is used to convey the madness of slavery and the mad slaves. *Notebook of a Return to My Native Land* begins as a story of a split subject: one is defensively introspective, looking inward from a distance, fearing the shock of reality; the other is retrospective, looking back for the means to narrate the new truth of reality. The poem begins with a description of the capital, Fort-de-France: flat, soulless, and zombie-like, bubbling subterraneously with potential violence. It is not, though, the violence of potential liberation, but the violence of survival. Along with hunger and grief, there is reaction and hatred, but such sentiments are atomistic, "strangely babbling and mute." The island is itself a prison, a metaphor for the alienated self and the moment of self-evaluation. It is cut off from the "fresh oases of brotherhood . . . the archipelago arched with the anxious desire to deny itself" (1995: 89). This self-reflection is both an identity and a separation; it becomes, in other words, negritude as an elemental pan-Africanism:

> [M]y non-enclosure island, its clear boldness standing at the back of this Polynesia, before it, Guadeloupe split in two along its backbone and sharing our misery, Haiti where negritude stood up for the first time and said it believed in its humanity . . . and Africa gigantically caterpillaring as far as the Hispanic foot of Europe . . . And I tell myself Bordeaux and Nantes and Liverpool and New York and San Francisco. (Césaire 1995: 91)

The drama of the African diaspora introduces resistance.

The ambiguity of this claim is evidenced in Césaire's emphasis on the individual's alienation that passes into despair. Haiti represents the most heroic Antilles, "most African of the Antilles" (1995: 90) and it also prepares the way for the tragic suffering of an individual. Toussaint Louverture, the leader and hero of the Haitian revolution, is a single and solitary man, "imprisoned in Whiteness" (1995: 91), a Black man in a White jail, guarded by a White jailer and facing a "White death." Césaire portrays Antilleans as a suffering humanity. Cut off from their roots, experiencing collective domination but with no sense of collective resistance or memory. Crushed by poverty, they enjoy no solidarity; they do not mix but dodge and take flight. How can Toussaint, the first hero of negritude, be remembered when there is little memory of resistance? Eschewing the collective, the poet fixes his faith on his individual will.

But the dialectic of negritude expresses an opposition to the dominant White value system, expressed surrealistically against "White reason" celebrating irrationality in the context of the Black slave's resistance:

That 2 and 2 make 5
that the forest mews
that the trees pull the maroons out of the fire. (1995: 93)

The White slave master's calculating rationalism is subverted (2 + 2 = 5) and "the slaves taste liberty (the forest mewing the call of runaways to one another) as they seek refuge among the trees" (Gibson 2003: 66).

The moment of supposed irrationality is a turning point. For it is a "madness that remembers" the brutality of slavery; it is a madness that remembers the whips, the rapes, and the lynchings. Césaire's madness signifies a refusal to accept reality; "it also means putting faith, against all odds, in a seemingly unrealizable future" (Gibson 2003: 66). This madness bears a close affinity to the poet's inspiration, "a madness that creates memory out of imagination" (Gibson 003: 66). The irrational is pitted against a Reason with its whips and authority, and it is the supposed irrationality of the slaves that confronts the slave masters' Reason. Césaire reveals the slaves' madness to be an imaginative expression of anger: "Because we hate you, you and your Reason, we claim kinship with dementia praecox, with flaming madness, with tenacious cannibalism" (1995: 93).

"It is with thoughts of Africa that the poet gains freedom: 'Thinking of the Congo, I become a Congo'" (Gibson 2003: 66). With this Africanism, there is a shift in the geography of reason. Reason, formerly equated with the crack of the White master's whip, which scarred Black flesh with the instrumental rationality of the slaver's account books and shipping logs,

is now countered with "Black Reason" flourishing a soar-
ing banner of freedom. It is an empowering act of mind to
transform oneself into the Congo. The reference supplies a
genealogical origin and hence an identity, suggesting that in
one's imagination lies the force of a nation. At the same time,
Césaire's negritude is not of African monarchs and African
civilizations; it is of the African diaspora and the slave's
reason. It is a memory of lies and cowardice. It is a memory of
the master and the slave. In the dialectic of Black consciousness, negritude begins as a negative movement, an admission
of nonachievement by Europe's judgment: "For those who
never invented anything, for those who have never explored
anything, for those who have never subdued anything" (1995:
115). More importantly, Césaire's litany of nonachievements
is intoned "against the glorification of technology by the
Europeans, the bloody conquests and destruction of peoples
by colonization" (Kunene 1969: 22).

"Porous to all the breaths of the world," Césaire accepts
definition not by the representation of empires on maps, nor
by biology, but only by "the compass of suffering" (1995: 115,
125). Through this self-knowledge, negritude is presented as
creative, moving, developing, and in motion. It is opposed to
a static object: "My negritude is not a stone"; it is opposed
to the kind of monuments that are found in Europe: "My
negritude is neither a tower nor a cathedral" (1995: 115). It
is an acceptance of Blackness as the basis of a discovery of a
new pride, an attitude that respects "my repulsive ugliness"
(1995: 103). With this new sense of identity comes the power
to imagine rebellion. What Césaire expounds is the painful
birth of the new Black out of the death of the "old negritude"(1995: 129). The "great Black hole," in which Césaire
"wanted to drown," now becomes the fount of a new consciousness, a new movement, a "revolution" (1995: 135). His
long "journey" ends with acceptance. He is "no longer mis-

erably confined to a facial angle, to a type of hair, to a nose
sufficiently flattened, to a pigmentation sufficiently mela-
nose." Negritude is "no longer a cephalic index or plasma";
it is measured by the "compass of suffering." Césaire urges
humanity "to conquer . . . every rigid prohibition" and create
a new humanism: "No race holds a monopoly of beauty, of
intelligence, of strength and there is room for all at the ren-
dezvous of conquest" (1995: 127).

   "Before Césaire, Antillean literature was the literature
of the Europeans," argues Fanon. The Antillean not only
identified with the White man but "was a [W]hite man"
(1967: 21).

## Antillean metaphysics and Fanon's war years

"In the Antilles in 1939 no spontaneous claim of Negritude
rang forth," Fanon argues. Antilleans believed they were
French and volunteered in the colonial army and "served in
the European unit" (1967: 20). And, as he will argue in the
*Black Skin, White Masks*, they thought of themselves as assimilated and superior to the African. It was then that three events
occurred successively (1967: 21).

   The first event was the arrival of Césaire: "For the first
time a lycée teacher – a man, therefore, who was apparently
worthy of respect – was seen to announce quite simply to
West Indian society 'that it is fine and good to be un nègre'"
(Fanon 1967: 21). And just as that scandal was dying down,
a second event occurred, the fall of France, which was, in a
sense, like "the murder of the father." This national defeat
might have been endured, but on top of that the French fleet
"remained blockaded in the Antilles during the four years of
the German occupation" (1967: 22). With the pressure on
food and housing, the 10,000 French blockaded sailors created

a socioeconomic crisis and uncovered their "authentic racism" under Vichy rule. At the same time "came Free France," with de Gaulle speaking of the treason of Vichy France. All this became part of a new consciousness that convinced the Antilleans that "their France had not lost the war but traitors had sold it out" (Fanon 1967: 23). They now refused to take their hats off to the Marseillaise. Who "can forget those Thursday evenings when on the Esplanade de la Savane," Fanon asks, when "patrols of armed sailors demanded silence and attention while the national anthem was being played? What had happened?" (1967: 23) These events, one after another, created for the Antillean their first metaphysical experience. In other words, after living in an unreality, they came face to face with the nature of their reality. Césaire made it possible for a "new generation" of Martinicans to emerge and people joined him "chanting the once-hated song . . . that it is fine and good to be un nègre" (Fanon 1967: 23). The Antillean had to "recast their world" and by declaring that "the color Black was invested with value reject their previous valuation (1967: 24).

Frantz Fanon was 14 years old in 1939 and his brother Joby was 16 at the outbreak of the war in September of that year. The schools were closed in Fort-de-France, and the boys were sent by their mother to live with their uncle, who was a French teacher in Le François, a small town in a rural region on the Atlantic coast. With little for them to get up to outside school, their uncle guided their reading through his library. They read and re-read Balzac, Zola, and other "classics" (see Fanon 2014: 16). In Le François they met peasants who were deeply suspicious of urban people, as well as sugar workers whose realities began to open up different perspectives for the relatively privileged young Fanons. Frantz remembered these workers in a stirring rebuke of "exploitation, poverty, and hunger" in the conclusion to *Black Skin, White Masks*: "For the

Antillean working in the sugarcane plantations in Le Robert, to fight is the only solution, because quite simply he cannot conceive his life otherwise than as a kind of combat" (2008: 199).

Joby and Frantz returned to Fort-de-France the following school year and began to listen to de Gaulle speaking about freedom and the Republic, broadcast from the neighboring Islands of Domenica and Saint Lucia. In *Black Skin, White Masks*, Frantz remembered charting Montgomery's defeat of the Italian army at Benghazi on a map. He was with a friend, whose Italian father had married a Martinican woman. "Ascertaining the considerable territorial gains, I cried out enthusiastically: 'You're really getting hammered!' My friend, who was not oblivious of his father's origins, was extremely embarrassed. For that matter, so was I. Both of us had been victims of cultural imposition" (2008: 171).

In Fort-de-France, Joby attended the Lycée Victor Schoelcher; Aimé Césaire was one of his teachers and Joby shared with Frantz his bound notebook from the class (2014: 19).[2] Bored at his junior high school, Terres Sainville, Frantz would spend a lot of his time reading in the Bibliothèque Schoelcher. Because he always seemed to have his head in philosophy books, he became known as "Bergson," after the philosopher Henri Bergson.

Fanon recounts how, during the war, "teachers came from Guadeloupe to Fort-de-France to correct the baccalaureate exams." In the color-class hierarchy of the Antilles, the Guadeloupeans were considered darker. "Driven by curiosity," just as he was by the Senegalese soldiers, Fanon and his friends went to see the Black philosophy teacher who "was said to be excessively [B]lack." In the Antilles as well as in France, Fanon argues in *Black Skin, White Masks*, "we encounter the same stories. In Paris, they say he is Black but very intelligent. In Martinique, they say the same" (2008: 141n.25). The underlying point was that Antillean "was not un nègre" but "a quasi-metropolitan," and the "contempt for the African" was justified by [W]hites (1967: 20).

In 1943, with Joby's help, Frantz passed his written exams for the first part of the baccalauréat – no doubt his study at the library had been excellent preparation – but he didn't complete the baccalauréat, specializing in philosophy (at the Lycée Victor Schoelcher), until after he returned from the war in 1946.

In Fort-de-France's main park, La Savane, where the now-beheaded statue of Empress Josephine is located, the Fanon brothers would hang out and sometimes play pick-up football games. Later, Fanon was more damning of this after-school meeting place:

> As soon as school's out, they all gather on the Savane. Imagine a square 600 feet long and 120 feet wide, lined by worm-eaten tamarind trees down each side; at the top the huge war memorial, acknowledging the mother country's gratitude to her children; and at the bottom the Central Hotel – a square twisted with uneven paving stones and gravel that crunches underfoot, and walking up and down in it 300 or 400 young people, greeting one another, making contact, no, never making contact, then walking on. (2008: 8)

The last lines, describing the crowd making no contact, are reminiscent of the first pages of Césaire's *Return to My Native Land*, and Fanon tells us that Césaire has perhaps been too generous in his descriptions. The alienation Fanon is describing is repeated in the penultimate chapter of *Black Skin, White Masks*, where he argues that the Antilles is a *comparaison* society. He gives an example of the Martinican returning from France meeting his friends on the Savanna. "To protest against the inferiority" felt historically, Fanon argues, the returnee reacts with superiority, while their friends are waiting for "the slightest mistake." A mistake that "is seized upon, scrutinized, and in less than forty-eight hours it will be all over Fort-de-France." There is no forgiveness for the returning Martinican who "flaunts their superiority." They are judged harshly and any linguistic mistake is pounced upon. News of their failure quickly spreads and they become a joke. That the dominant term is "White" expresses the way in which school program heads in the French colonies had for years been "desperately try[ing] to make a [W]hite out of the [B]lack (2008: 8, 191).

But in the context of Vichy France something else was happening. Blockaded in the French colony, the 10,000 European sailors and the 2,000 European functionaries in Martinique behaved "as 'authentic' racists." The Martinicans increasingly became "shut in on themselves" (1967: 22). Geismar explains:

What money failed to do brute power accomplished. Cafés were immediately segregated ... In the stores sailors expected to be served before Martinicans. At first, segregation came about for economic reasons: With the influx of military money prices went up and the islanders could no longer afford to be customers. By 1941 ... the color lines were firmly established. The servicemen weren't going to fraternize with [B]lack males. The women were another matter: The [W]hite visitors requisitioned them; they considered every young girl on the island a prostitute. Rape often replaced the remuneration for those unwilling to conform to the sailors' expectations. The police, used to operating in a colonial environment where [B]lacks were always in the wrong, dismissed rape victims as overpriced prostitutes. In military courts, the navy's word always carried

more weight than the Martinican's complaints. It was a
totalitarian racism. (1971: 23)

Fanon experienced the Vichy regime's racism and
Hitlerism (for example, children having to *sieg heil* the High
Commissioner of the Vichy regime for the French overseas
territories, Admiral Georges Robert), as well as economic
hardships and shortages created by the blockade, and the
influx of French sailors making life even more difficult than
in the depression years. But then came de Gaulle's voice
speaking of treason. This voice "contributed to convinc-
ing the Antilleans that *their* France had not lost the war but
that traitors had sold it out" (1967: 23). Without telling
his parents, the 17-year-old Frantz decided that he would
join the Free French in Dominica (a British colony about
35 kilometers away). What Fanon called the first metaphysical experience (1967: 23) had a political expression.
In Martinique, liberation demonstrations toppled Admiral
Robert. Fanon had already left, but he did not get beyond
Domenica and soon returned to a "liberated" Martinique
before starting a new journey to help liberate France. Joby
remembers a conversation before Frantz left for the second
time. Joby quoted a speech from his philosophy teacher who
had argued in class that "what is currently taking place in Eur
ope is fundamentally not your problem. Yours is another.
Pay attention and do not mistake your objective. Messieurs,
heed my words and believe me, when [W]hites kill themselves, it's a benediction for [B]lacks" (2014: 23). Joby was
convinced by his teacher and tried the argument on Frantz.
But Frantz refused to be persuaded. "'Joby,' he replied, 'I'm
not a romantic. My feet are firmly on the ground. Whenever
liberty is in question, I feel concerned. We're all concerned,
whatever our color – white, black, yellow, coconut, dark
brown, cocoa. Your teacher is a bastard and I swear to you,

today, that whenever liberty is threatened, I'll be there'" (2014: 23).

Fanon's war experiences would represent an important turning point for him. The Free French had defied Vichy and risked their lives to join General de Gaulle in Europe's war against the Fascists. Why? Quite simply, because they believed they were French and that de Gaulle was the embodiment of good France. Just before a mission at the end of the war, Fanon wrote to his mother. He had become absolutely disillusioned, speaking of Free France as an "obsolete ideal," but he did not give up on *being present* where liberty is threatened. Not to be present was to act in bad faith, as he puts it in *Black Skin, White Masks*: "I cannot dissociate myself from the fate reserved for my brother. Every one of my acts commits me as a man. Every instance of my reticence, every instance of my cowardice, manifests the man" (2008: 69).

## Fanon and the Free French

> We realized that we who had fought for racial equality and human brotherhood, lived in loneliness and contempt.
>
> Manville, *Les Antilles sans fard*

Frantz was the youngest person aboard the troopship. Before leaving Martinique, his mother asked Marcel Manville, a lycée friend and classmate of Joby's, to take care of Frantz. Manville and Frantz, who had left together for Domenica, were often in the same regiment; when they weren't, they kept in touch, sharing experiences of the racially hierarchical military where the Antilleans wore the same uniforms as the Europeans and were considered superior to Arabs and to Africans. The position of Antilleans was "ambiguous in the extreme" (Macey 2012: 92) as Fanon explained: "The North Africans despised

[B]lack men," and he "found it impossible to have any contact with the native Arab population" (2008: 82).

From Morocco he was sent to Algeria in July 1944. From there, the invasion of France from the south would be launched. Fanon remembered how the settler colony resembles "a huge farmyard, where the only law is that of the knife":

> I can recall one horrible scene. It was in Oran in 1944. From the military camp where we were waiting to embark, the soldiers threw bits of bread to some Algerian children who fought for them in a frenzy of rage and hatred. A veterinarian could no doubt explain these events in terms of the famous "pecking order" noted in farmyards where the corn is bitterly fought over. The strongest birds gobble up all the grain while the less aggressive grow visibly thinner. (2004: 231–2)

Reflecting on the animosity of the Arab for the Black, Fanon tied it into a definitive racial-colonial logic:

> We left Africa for France without understanding the reason for this animosity. Certain facts, however, were food for thought. The Frenchman does not like the Jew, who does not like the Arab, who does not like the [B]lack. The Arab is told: "If you are poor it's because the Jew has cheated you and robbed you of everything." The Jew is told: "You're not of the same caliber as the Arab because in fact you are [W]hite and you have Bergson and Einstein." The [B]lack is told: "You are the finest soldiers in the French empire; the Arabs think they're superior to you, but they are wrong."

Fanon then immediately adds: "Moreover, it's not true; they don't say anything to the [B]lack man; they have nothing to say to him; the Senegalese infantryman is an infantryman, the good soldier who only obeys his captain, the good soldier who obeys orders" (2008: 82–3). Here, the Black man does and does not refer to the Antillean, but it does refer to the Senegalese (who is the absolute other). A good soldier who must respect and obey – especially obey. Fanon explained:

> Every time there was a rebellion, the military authorities sent only the colored soldiers to the front line. It is the "peoples of color" who annihilated the attempts at liberation by other "peoples of color," proof that there were no grounds for universalizing the process: if those good-for-nothings, the Arabs, got it into their heads to rebel, it was not in the name of reputable principles. (2008: 82–3)

This discussion comes in the chapter of *Black Skin, White Masks* that is devoted to Fanon's critique of Octave Mannoni's *The Psychology of Colonization*, in which the author discusses children's dreams during the brutal colonial repression of revolt in 1947. This exemplified one of Césaire's major points in *Discourse on Colonialism*: that the European victory against fascism allowed for its colonial form to resume in Vietnam and Madagascar (2000: 35–6). As we shall explore further, the Senegalese soldiers played an essential role in annihilating the attempts at liberation by the Malagasy. However, at the same time, after the European victory, the newly de-mobbed colonial troops would play an important role in the proto-anticolonial revolts and (perhaps more importantly) as recruits to liberation movements, using their training in armed struggles in Kenya and Algeria. Massive strikes also took place immediately after the end of the war, from "Durban to Tunis, and from Dakar to Dar es Salaam . . . unparalleled in scope, intensity, and political significance." In addition to the miners' strike in South Africa in 1946 (that Fanon refers to in *Black Skin, White Masks*), there were strikes across the entire French

West African railway in 1947–8 (see Oberst 1988).

In France before liberation, Fanon took part in the battle of Alsace in the freezing winter of 1944. His commanders considered him an "average soldier" without military commitment who "often makes his own opinion known," but he also "proved himself in combat to be courageous and coolheaded," volunteering "for several perilous missions," which he accomplished "with courage and tenacity, earning him the admiration of his comrades." Fanon was injured during the battle of Alsace and was sent to Nantua military hospital near Lyon. Toward the end of his convalescence, he started playing football with a local team and made friends in the Lyon area (see Geismar 1971: 39). In February 1945, he was awarded the Croix de Guerre by Colonel Raoul Salan, the same man who became a commanding general during the Indochina war – and a founder of the far-right French paramilitary organization in Algeria, Organization armée secrète (OAS). Salan was also one of the organizers of the failed coup d'état to stop the French withdrawal from Algeria in April 1961.[3]

## Disillusionment

By January 1945, Fanon had become "disgusted" with his decision to join the fight to liberate France from the Nazis. He wrote to Joby that he had "made a mistake and I'm paying the price." The war had aged him, he wrote, so that he now felt older than his brother. Still only 20 years old when he returned to Martinique from France, he was no longer the "happy, open and talkative" boy who had been "a bit of a joker" (Fanon 2014: 38).

On April 12, 1945, a year after he had left Martinique, Fanon wrote to his family, indicating his disillusionment before a military operation in which he thought it was likely he would die.

Dear family,
Today is April 12. A year since I left Fort-de-France. Why?
To defend an obsolete ideal. This time I feel I won't return
... I doubt everything, even myself. If I don't return, if you
are informed of my death at the hands of the enemy, con-
sole yourselves but never say, "he died for a just cause." Say,
"God called him to his side." Because we must no longer
look to this *false ideology*, behind which secularists and idi-
otic politicians hide, as our beacon. I was wrong! Nothing
here justifies that sudden decision I took to make myself the
defender of the farmer's interests, when the farmer himself
couldn't care less. (Quoted in Fanon 2014: 34; my emphasis)

Frantz continued that he, Manville, and Mosole had taken
notes guaranteeing that even if two of them are killed, "the
third will reveal to you the dreadful truth." He tells his
father that "you at times have been very inferior in your
duty as a father." If "we eight children become something in
this world," he added, "the glory belongs to *maman* alone."
According to Joby, the letter created a stir in the family and
"caused us to refine our relationships with each other." Their
mother refused to criticize their father, who took the letter
"philosophically and with humor." Fanon ended the letter
saying, "I leave tomorrow, a volunteer for a perilous mission. I
know that I will not return" (Fanon 2014: 34–5).
   Fanon returned to Martinique in October 1945 and stayed
for just under a year before leaving again for France.

## Back to Martinique

Back in Martinique, Fanon began working almost immediately on Aimé Césaire's parliamentary campaign, the first
of the Fourth Republic, on the Communist Party ticket.

Césaire's oratory skills had given him stature and his speeches were local events. Fanon quotes from memory a speech that was later rephrased by the anti-apartheid activist Steve Biko: "When I switch on my radio and hear that Black men are being lynched in America, I say that they have lied to us: Hitler isn't dead" (2008: 70; see also Biko 1979: 75). So great was Césaire's campaign oratory "that in the middle of his talk a woman fainted. The next day a colleague describing the event commented: 'His French was so dynamite the woman fell to the floor and started ketching malkadi.'"[4] "The power of language," remarked Fanon (2008: 22).

Fanon had no wish to stay in Martinique. He, like other lycée graduates, wanted to follow Césaire and go to university in France. To do so meant finishing the baccaleauréat by passing the oral exams. He spent the time studying and also joined Joby and Félix's football team, "Assault," whose games were reported in the local paper, highlighting the brothers. One report expresses the joy of their play: "Félix Fanon . . . dribbles with as much authority as his younger brother Frantz, drove to the left, leaving behind one, two, three opponents" (Fanon 2014: 40–1). But another report concludes "I agree with the reporter from last Sunday: Frantz Fanon is not a team player" (Fanon 2014: 40). This idea of Frantz Fanon was not held by his brother Félix, who, in an interview with Hussein Bulhan some years later, paid his brother a high footballing compliment, calling him "very efficient" (Bulhan 1985: 20).

Frantz left Martinique for France in the Fall of 1946. Although he spent a couple of months back on the island in 1952, this was the last time he would stay there for any length of time. It was also the last time he would see his father.

Before we move to the next chapter, let us turn back to the idea that Fanon was not a team player. Such an idea of him, whether on the football team, as a psychiatrist, or as member of the FLN, is worth further consideration. Just as Fanon was not an individualist, his universalism did not mean uncritically following orders. At Blida-Joinville Psychiatric Hospital, for example, we will see him challenging the status quo, leading the introduction of new sociotherapies as well as organizing a co-authored article with a range of section heads (including conservatives) that spoke to the shared condition of the over-crowded wards in the hospital and the success of sociotherapy programs. At Razi Hospital (in Tunis), he tried to work with a reactionary nationalist director there, until the director denied Fanon funds for a new program. He then turned to the Tunisian minister of health. Moreover, he became a rep-resentative of the FLN and then the GPRA; in this capacity, he promoted the armed struggle in Algeria and promoted the provisional government itself.

In *Les Damnés de la terre*, Fanon is specifically critical of the national bourgeoisie, the nationalist party leadership, and discusses the dialectic of organization in a liberated society. Perhaps taking from Lenin's idea in *What Is To Be Done?* (that the intellectual be disciplined by the worker members in the branches), Fanon argues that the party must be decentralized in the extreme and established in the rural areas where the majority of the people are. Building new decolonized societies has to be done in concert with everyone becoming decision-makers. Could one conclude from this that Fanon was not a team player? For him, the "team" would have to be taken as loyalty to human liberation. Fanon's changing attitude to the French struggle against fascism from inside the war reveals his lifelong commitment: being at the core of the struggle against tyranny and for a just freedom. This becomes what he calls a "new humanism" deepened by the anticolonial struggle he becomes engaged with.

# 2

## Fanon in France

After finishing his baccalauréat and working on Césaire's communist campaign, Fanon left Martinique for France in late 1946. As a veteran, he had been granted a small stipend. Traveling to France to go to university was very much part of the educated Martinican's French drama.

The Martinican metaphysical experience was also playing out in France, where the Resistance, which began in 1943, represented an important political divide that was still in play in 1946. The experiences of occupation, resistance, and the project of liberation were reflected across life, politically, culturally, and intellectually. In "discovering history," as Maurice Merleau-Ponty put it, the writings of Jean-Paul Sartre (who was at the height of his literary fame) and others expressed a commitment not only to resistance but also to building a liberated society. The idea of this commitment was reflected in the establishment of the journal *Les Temps Modernes* (named after the Charlie Chaplin film) founded in October 1945 with Merleau-Ponty as lead editor. Revolution had become an "existential requirement" and the idea of taking action was necessary to sustain "the authenticity of the individual" (Judt 2011: 40). Existentialism had become an idea whose time had come. The necessity of urgent radical – indeed, revolutionary – change was also expressed by existentialists like the Catholic left intellectual Emmanuel Mounier,[1] the founder of the magazine *Esprit* (which would publish Fanon's first articles), who argued that "an honest analysis of the French situation shows us it is revolutionary" (quoted in Judt 2011: 39).

Since its participation in the National Council of the Resistance, the Communist Party of France (PCF) had become an important national political force. From 1944 to 1947, it was a leading party in the Provisional Government of the French Republic. Sartre, however, was a prominent critic of the party and in 1947, alongside Merleau-Ponty, Mounier, and Georges Altman and David Rousset, editors of the resistance newspaper *Franc-Tireur* (free shooter) and *Combat*, he was involved in the establishment of a new leftwing political grouping referred to as the Rassemblement démocratique révolutionnaire (Revolutionary Democratic Assembly, RDR). The name suggested that it was more revolutionary than the socialists and more democratic than the communists. In 1948, the African American author Richard Wright addressed the RDR mass meeting in Paris alongside Albert Camus and André Breton. His speech, "Such Is Our Challenge" (1948) begins with these words:

> My body was born in America, my heart in Russia, and today I am quite ashamed of my two homelands. The American State of Mississippi gave me my body; the Russian October Revolution gave me my heart. But today these two giant nations – symbols of the nationalistic scourge of our times – rival each other in their efforts to establish projects for the debasement of the human spirit . . . Man ought to have

the freedom to remain a man ... Freedom is not negative, it ought to be not only the possibility "of" something, but to go freely "towards" something. It ought to let man create new values for life, otherwise it was not created for man.

In late 1946 Fanon traveled first to Le Havre with his sister Gabrielle (who was going to study pharmacy in Rouen), then to Paris, where he apparently planned to apply for dental school, but he soon left to attend medical school in Lyon. While this might have been provoked by his wish to study with Merleau-Ponty, who held a chair in psychology there, his desire to apply himself to psychiatry can be connected to an attempt at self-diagnosis and self-understanding of his layered trauma of war and racism. For example, while critical of the 1949 Hollywood film *Home of the Brave* and its treatment of war trauma, psychotherapy, and race, we might consider Fanon's engagement with it as a biopsy of his own war experiences, namely the trauma of Black colonial war veterans. His interest in dentistry could only have been momentary, whereas his decision to study psychiatry was virtually preordained.

Fanon had gone to Paris to meet up with his military comrades Manville and Mosole (who had remained in France following the war). His decision to move to Lyon was perhaps also connected to contacts he had made when he was convalescing from his war wounds. According to Manville, however, he left Paris because there were too many nègres there – "the less I see them, the better I feel" (quoted in Fanon 2014: 44).[2] What is meant by this is ambiguous and it is certainly not dismissive of Black consciousness; rather, it was the choice Antillean students had to make, as Fanon put it in *Black Skin, White Masks*:

When a group of Antillean students meet in Paris they have two options: Either support the [W]hite world ... Or reject Europe, "Yo," and come together thanks to Creole by settling comfortably in what we'll call the Martinican Umwelt. By this we mean – and this goes especially for our Antillean brothers – that when one of our comrades in Paris or another university town attempts to address a problem in all seriousness he is accused of putting on and the best way of disarming him is to brandish the Antilles and shift into Creole. (2008: 20)

It was a double bind. For Fanon neither option was authentic.[3]

At the University of Lyon, Fanon enrolled in three degree programs: a bachelor in arts, a bachelor in sociology, and a doctorate in medicine (which included introductory courses in biology, chemistry, and physics). Although he later reported to de Beauvoir that he found Merleau-Ponty "cold" (see Beauvoir 1992: 314), Fanon's work is certainly influenced by Merleau-Ponty. He cites *Phenomenology of Perception* (1945) in *Black Skin, White Masks* and in his psychiatric papers he also references Merleau-Ponty's critique of behaviorism in *The Structure of Behavior* (1942). In fact it was through Merleau-Ponty that Fanon became familiar with some of the current debates in phenomenology and psychiatry. From Merleau-Ponty he engaged ideas of lived experience and the centrality of the body in space: an object and subject in the world. "Our body does not occupy space like things do: it inhabits space or haunts it," opined Merleau-Ponty (1964: 5). In addition to taking courses with Merleau-Ponty and the philosopher Jean Lacroix, he took others with André Leroi-Gourhan, a paleo-anthropologist and anthropologist. Leroi-Gourhan's idea of the human group as a living organism influenced Fanon's discussion of neurology and mental illness in his medical thesis, as well as in his later "anthropological" fieldwork.[4]

## Fanon in Lyon

Lyon was a vibrant city with a rich history of struggle. The silk-weavers' uprisings (the Canut revolts of 1831, 1834, and 1848) marked the first organized working-class conflicts of the industrial revolution. They were massive and violent events. After the war, socialist ideas became dominant across the country; in Lyon, workers were militant, as they had been a century before, as preparations began for a 100-year commemoration of the 1848 revolution. But racism toward North African workers was rarely discussed.

As well as navigating life in the new city, Fanon confronted a personal tragedy. In January 1947 his father died. His brother argued that this considerably reduced Frantz's vitality, resulting in him failing an exam as he "seemed physically and morally overwhelmed" (Fanon 2014: 49). Joby and Gabrielle raised his morale, which, he wrote in a letter to his mother, "was in danger of collapsing" and he felt incapable of finding the energy necessary to sit the exam the following month.

Fanon's first year of study, including what he called "catching up," consumed a lot of time and energy and was made much more difficult following the death of his father and the distance from his family. At the same time, Fanon became involved in anticolonial activity and was "clubbed and trampled underfoot by the police" on a demonstration for the release of Paul Vergès, the leader of the Communist Party of Réunion, who was imprisoned in Lyon in 1947 awaiting trial. Fanon supported Vergès but showed little interest in the PCF. As strikes spread across France later that year, with 4 million workers (miners, autoworkers, metal workers, and teachers) on strike, the PCF played a conservative role (see Alexander 1991: 378) and student discussions about the counterrevolutionary role of the PCF, often connected with discussions about the Spanish revolution a decade earlier, were sharp and sometimes violent. According to Geismar, Fanon was involved in these debates to such an extent that "in 1947 and 1948 his political engagements threatened his academic career: He was always involved in debates, going to left-wing meetings, touring occupied factories." Fortunately for Fanon, "a special 1947 law exempting all army veterans from academic examinations" meant the exams could be put off (Geismar 1971: 46–7).

In another biography of Fanon, Pierre Bouvier (1971) notes that Fanon was also particularly interested in Trotskyist meetings during this time, though there is little indication that he was committed either to their politics or to the French left in general.[5] On this he remained consistent. In the concluding chapter of *L'An V*, "Algeria's European Minority," Fanon argues that "it can be said of Algeria's European democrats what has been endlessly repeated of the French parties of the Left: for a long time history is made without them . . . The Left has done nothing for a long time in France. Yet by its action, its denunciations, and its analyses, it has prevented a certain number of things." And then he reminds us that the Algerian Communist Party was confined in a reformist politics within the French Union as it denounced the Algerian FLN as "terroristes provocateurs" (1965: 150). In his conclusion to *Les Damnés de la terre*, Fanon remained pessimistic about European workers: while some "Europeans were found to urge the European workers to shatter this narcissism and to break with this unreality . . . in general, the workers of Europe have not replied to these calls; for the workers believe, too, that they are part of the prodigious adventure of the European spirit" (1968: 313).

While there are no works by Trotsky from Fanon's library, which was deposited by his son Olivier in Algiers (listed in Fanon 2018), Cherki says that Fanon "discovered Trotsky" on the rue Blondel in Paris, then asked Marcel Manville to bring him the proceedings of the Fourth International. Though Manville's membership of the Communist Party "separated the two friends," argues Gendzier (1973), Manville did bring Fanon the material. In fact, they would remain close friends for the rest of Fanon's life. Offering his legal services to the FLN, Manville was a frequent visitor to Algiers and stayed at Fanon's house.

Fanon's reading continued to be extensive and he kept up with the important debates in the new postwar journals, *Les Temps Modernes* and *Présence Africaine*. When Joby and Gabrielle visited their brother in 1948, they were astonished by the mess: "There were books piled up everywhere, even on the floor. A small mountain of clothes stood in the corner. The washbasin overflowed with cups and a coffee machine" (Fanon: 2014, 54).

This period in the late 1940s was one of intense creativity for Fanon: not only was he writing and thinking about what would become *Black Skin, White Masks*, but he also composed three plays and created a student newspaper *Tam Tam*. But his financial situation as a student remained desperate and for a time he was sleeping in a former brothel made available by the ministry of education for student housing, staying up late into the night reading and discussing questions of existentialism, psychiatry, and politics.

While he was finishing up undergraduate courses and before deciding to specialize in psychiatry in the faculty of medicine, Fanon got to know Nicole Guillet through his then-girlfriend Michèle Weyer. In 1948, Guillet had just started as a student at the school of medicine. Her father had been a bursar at Saint-Alban Psychiatric Hospital and, while at university, she lived in Paul Balvet's home; until a few years earlier, he had worked with Guillet as the doctor in charge at Saint-Alban Psychiatric Hospital. Fanon was a frequent guest at Balvet's house; he had regular discussions about psychiatry with Balvet (see Macey 2012: 139) and it is likely that it was these that sparked Fanon's interest in Jacques Lacan's (1932) dissertation, as well as in the work of François Tosquelles and Saint-Alban. While medical conservatism held sway (as Fanon would discover at medical school in Lyon), psychiatry in France was beginning to open up from the ground up and this was conveyed in his discussions with Balvet. Balvet's stories about Tosquelles's contempt of authority and commitment to the practice of a socially engaged and radical psychiatry must have been compelling to Fanon and he decided to embark on a course in psychiatry at Vinatier Hospital in Lyon, where Balvet worked, before deciding to study under Jean Dechaume at the University of Lyon medical school (Dechaume also had a position at Vinatier).

## Meeting Josie and the birth of Mireille

Fanon had a child with Michèle – Mireille, who was born in 1948. The relationship between Michèle and Fanon was not a committed one, and Fanon never saw the child. Joby and Gabrielle did go to see the baby, but Frantz didn't want to accompany them. Joby remembered: "Gabrielle and I talked about the child, her pretty face, her kindness, her intelligence and also her mischievousness ... In the end, he burst out: 'Well yes, that's why I don't want to see her. If she were with maman it'd be a different story'" (2014: 54–5). Today, Mireille Fanon Mendès-France is president of the Frantz Fanon Foundation.[6]

Fanon first met his future wife Josie (Marie-Josèphe Dublé) in 1948, "on the steps outside the theatre shortly after his arrival in Lyon," when she was a lycée student (Cherki 2006: 19). It was a memory that he would refer to in his last letter to his wife (Cherki: 2006: 166). Josie was 18 and Frantz was

23. "Josie and her big gypsy eyes ... And above all her voice, that happy contralto," remembers the novelist Assia Djebar, Josie's friend of more than 30 years (2000: 174–5).[7] Daughter of Lyonnais leftist trade unionists, according to Macey, Josie was of "mixed-Corsican descent." She played a major role in the creation of *Black Skin, White Masks* since Frantz composed the work orally and spoke it Josie, who typed it out. She was, as Lewis Gordon puts it, "his partner in struggle and ideas ... She was, then, in many respects the actual reader/listener/ audience, the flesh-and-blood presence, to whom the texts were addressed and who, to some extent, haunts his writings as one among their many subtexts" (2015: 14). They married in 1952.

## The plays

In late 1948 through 1949, Frantz spent quite a bit of time thinking about playwriting as a creative avenue for working out questions of action and commitment. He wrote three plays, "Parallel Hands," "The Drowning Eye," and "The Conspiracy," the first two of which survived and have now been translated into English.

There is a general agreement among his biographers that this was a difficult period for Fanon. Geismar says that, by 1948, he had "reached the depths of depression" and play-writing was a way to "relieve tensions" through "poetic retrospection" (1971: 49). Fanon's later publisher, François Maspero, called "The Drowning Eye" "a work of personal exorcism" (quoted in Fanon 2018: 29). This play, whose French title is "L'Oeil se noie," expresses an ambiguity: is the eye an active subject, drowning itself, or is it a passive object being drowned? If the eye is drowning, what and who drowns it? And in its drowning, what does it see and how is its perception (and, indeed, self-perception) obscured? The questions of subject and object of perception, the distortion of and lack of perception correspond well with Maurice Merleau-Ponty's *Phenomenology of Perception* (1945), which Fanon had recently read. In *Black Skin, White Masks*, he returns to the eye in a long footnote explaining a fundamental methodological and conceptual point:

> It might be argued that if the [W]hite man elaborates an *imago* of his fellow man, the same should be the case for the Antillean, since it is based on a visual perception. But we would be forgetting *that in the Antilles perception always occurs at the level of the imagination*. One's fellow is perceived in [W]hite terms. People will say of someone, for instance, that they are "very [B]lack"; it is not surprising to hear the mother of a family remark: "X . . . is the darkest of my children" (2008: 141n.25; my emphasis)

The question concerns the structure of perception. The colorism occurring at the level of the imagination perceived in White terms expresses Antillean subject positions. A philosophy teacher from Guadeloupe came to mark exams during the war, Fanon continued; "as they say in Martinique, not without a certain irony, he was 'blue.' One family was highly regarded: 'They're very [B]lack, *but* decent people'" (2008: 141n.25). Fanon suggests the transcendence of the narcissism of the White gaze can be achieved because

> [the eye is] not only a mirror, but a correcting mirror. *The eye must enable us to correct cultural mistakes.* I do not say the eyes; I say the eye – and we know what the eye reflects: not the calcarine fissure, but the even glow that wells up out of van Gogh's reds, that glides from a Tchaikovsky concerto, that clings desperately to Schiller's "Ode to Joy," and lets

itself be carried away by Césaire's vermiculate howl. (2008: 175; my emphasis)

In July 1949, Joby Fanon had just got a position as a customs inspector in Dunkirk; when Frantz visited him, he "appeared feverish and agitated." He had just finished writing "The Drowning Eye" and was working on another play "at the cemetery in Dunkirk, the only place where he was able to concentrate properly" (Fanon 2014: 59). He had a problem finishing "Parallel Hands" and asked Joby to find someone to type it out. "He was blocked," remembered Joby. "He did not know how to continue the play." "The wife of a colleague offered her services, and Frantz spent three full days dictating the third and fourth acts" (Fanon 2014: 61). Fanon would use this method of composition in future to compose his books, pacing up and down: "His thinking seemed to spring from the movement of his body, like something physical" (Aubenas 2017). His works were dictated without notes and mainly without corrections.

The protagonist of "The Drowning Eye" is named François; when his brother Joby quotes from the play, he does so as if François is Frantz, which makes sense, since it plays on the name as a cognate. The German (or Alsatian, since his grandfather was Alsatian) name Frantz means Frenchman or Freeman, and Frantz sounds like France. But the François of "The Drowning Eye" is not the Frantz of *Black Skin, White Masks*. Rather, issues of identity, of being and action, of consciousness and transcendence are not grounded in questions of race and racialization but rather focus on the desire to be self-determining and free of such objectifications. So as much as there is some autobiographical self-interrogation and self-analysis in the play, and as much as there are also echoes of some of the ideas in *Black Skin, White Masks* (see Arnall 2020; Young 2018), the focus of the play is neither race nor racism.

When color is mentioned, it is in terms of its reception and reflection mediated by stage directions. The color of the characters mirror and absorb the colors around them. Color shifts, it is distorted by lighting, stressing the audience's perspective and perception, which also shift.

But this perception and self-perception do offer an expression of what would be explored and analyzed in *Black Skin, White Masks*, namely a fissured consciousness of somebody who sees themselves as confronting mutually exclusive alternatives. When one of the primary characters in "The Drowning Eye," Lucien, says "a man will always have to choose between life and death" (2018: 95), he adds, "The greatness of man lies perhaps in his acceptance of life." In *Black Skin, White Masks*, the choice between life and death is really a false choice because Black life is a debilitating alienation and objectification experienced day in and day out in a racist anti-Black society, a kind of living death, a life within the zone of nonbeing. This zone is partially expressed in the first few pages of Césaire's *Cahier*, where he describes the broken-down state of Fort-de-France and its population as a town without movement. Fanon probably had something similar in mind when describing the fictional Greek island of Lébos in "Parallel Hands" as a stifling and inert town. It is from this stifling society that the protagonist must act *on behalf* of the others. When Fanon writes in the conclusion to *Black Skin, White Masks* that bourgeois society "is a closed society where it's not good to be alive, where the air is rotten and ideas and people are putrefying … stifling any development, progress, or discovery" (2008: 199), there is perhaps an echo with François in "The Drowning Eye": "I believe that a man who takes a stand against this living death is in a way a revolutionary" (2008: 199).

"Parallel Hands" is a tragedy. Its final scene depicts a "defeated Épithakos who accepts the inevitable return of order and the equally inevitable failure of his act" (Arnall 2020:

57). The question of human failure haunts Fanon's writing, addressed, for example, in his turn to psychoanalysis in *Black Skin, White Masks* and in the failure of the nationalist intellectuals and leaders in the pitfalls of national consciousness in *Les Damnés de la terre*. But the closing act of the play, like the closing of his major works, is nevertheless optimistic, indicating the possibility of a genuine new beginning.

Before putting the play aside, Fanon sent it to Jean-Louis Barrault, whose production of Paul Claudel's "Partage de midi" had played at Les Célestins theater in Lyon in February 1949, and was likely seen by Josie and Frantz. However, Barrault did not reply, and Fanon's plays were left to the gnawing criticism of the mice as he began to specialize in psychiatry and to work on *Black Skin, White Masks*. Importantly, at the end of his life he asked Joby to destroy the plays "because they did not correspond to his intellectual evolution and were far removed from his political choices at that time" (quoted in Young 2018: 11n.2). In short, the plays can be viewed as a clearing of the mind during a period of self-questioning and perhaps also set in a period of crisis, agitation, and change, including the birth of a daughter, Frantz's new relationship with Josie, and his decision to concentrate on his study in psychiatry.

At the same time, some of the concerns and concepts developed in the plays (namely, questions of existence and action, of freedom and meaning) would be developed and concretized in the remarkably productive period around the writing of his first book. *Black Skin, White Masks*, in its composition and critical content, is a culturally innovative and engaged work. It was published soon after Fanon's arrival at Saint-Alban Psychiatric Hospital. On January 6, 1953, he wrote to Richard Wright, by the way of Alioune Diop of *Présence Africaine* (Wright was a founding editor), telling him that he was working on a study of Wright's work. Revealing the scope

of Wright's influence, Fanon tells him that he "intended to
show the systematic misunderstandings between [W]hites
and [B]lacks" in *Black Skin, White Masks*, which had just been
published, and that he was "working on a study bearing on
the human scope of your works" (Ray and Farnsworth 1973:
150).

While both the plays and *Black Skin, White Masks* are didac-
tic, the subject of "Parallel Hands" is about an individual
alienated revolutionary hero who sacrifices himself so that
"the people of Lébos may be released from their insentient
subservience" (Young 2018: 68). The dialectic of *Black Skin,
White Masks*, as we shall see, is social, and the conclusion tells
a different story from that of the plays. There, after writing
that bourgeois society is an airless society, where it is not good
to be alive, Fanon turns to the ongoing anticolonial revolt in
Vietnam, which just a few years later would result in a massive
and historic French defeat at Dien Bien Phu.


## Words


During their adolescence, according to his brother Joby,
Frantz was "obsessed by the idea of death." Lying in bed,
they often spoke about the "true purpose of man and our
purpose on this earth" (Fanon 2014: 59). In "The Drowning
Eye," Lucien remarks: "It is said that man is great because
he accepts to die. But dying is nothing." Looking back, Joby
emphasizes Frantz's reference to "white death," quoting from
"The Drowning Eye" the "hemorrhaging stars that condemn
me" to "mute whiteness," articulated "with the knowledge that
Frantz died of leukemia" (2014: 61). He could have added that
Fanon died at a hospital in America, like Césaire's Toussaint,
"surrounded by whiteness" imprisoned at the Fort de Joux, in
Doubs, in Eastern France (where Fanon was injured fighting

against the German army in 1944, and awarded the military cross by Colonel Salan).

Although the plays were left on the shelf, they certainly could be considered part of the working out of what would become *Black Skin, White Masks*, which Fanon said "represents seven years of experiments and observations" and "should have been written three years ago. But at the time the truths made our blood boil" (2008: 41, xiii). The three years dates it to his playwriting period. But then, self-critically, he adds: "Today the fever has dropped and truths can be said without having them hurled into people's faces. They are not intended to endorse zealousness. We are wary of being zealous" (2008: xiii). The statements are not contradictory.

In response to a question from his editor, Francis Jeanson, to explain a sentence in *Black Skin, White Masks*, Fanon responded: "This sentence is inexplicable. I seek, when I write such things, to touch my reader with affect . . . that is to say irrationally, almost sensually." Like Césaire he wanted "to sink beneath the stupefying lava of words that have the color of quivering flesh," and added: "Words have a charge for me. I feel myself incapable of escaping the bite of a word, the vertigo of a question mark" (see Fanon 2011: 51–2). Fanon's desire to touch the reader physically, "almost sensually," and go beyond meaning, writing inside the sensory dimension of language to promote new ways of thinking, remained throughout his writing and is explicitly present in the plays. It is summed up in "Parallel Hands" when he writes: "Raise the world with language authorized by the ACT" (2018: 162).

"For Frantz," Joby argues, "language had a complete sense – a prelude to action. Words, he believed, were a mark of humanity, a means by which man distinguished himself from the animal. But he believed words must be a movement of penetration and emergence. It must be a movement supported by movement" (2014: 58), and is wonderfully expressed in the following excerpts:

> Words have fangs and must do harm. Soft, supple words must vanish from this hell. Man speaks too much. He must be taught to reflect. For that, he must be made to fear. To be very afraid . . .
>
> Before I pronounce a word, I want to see a mask of suffering, a mask of searching, of disappointment. Because words must be agile, cunning. They must appear, take a good look around and disappear without leaving a trace. (2014: 58)

In "Parallel Hands," words reach "volcanic extremes" and "assume the role of act." It is a language, Fanon writes, "haunted by exultant perception!" (2014: 59):

> I'll speak to your reasoning
> Your ardor fleeing the dawn
> And I, igniter of worlds
> Words! Words! Words!
> I'll seek stars to use as wings for reason
> I'll become myself
> Surging from the power of the act
> In absolute contestation. (2014: 59–60)

This volcanic power of language resonates with Césaire's *Notebook of a Return to the Native Land* and the reaction to the European master's use of words and reason as a volcanic eruption, calling himself a Pelean, after the Mount Pelée volcano that destroyed the city of Saint-Pierre in 1902. For Césaire, words invoke action, revolt and the "end of the world" (1995: 99).

Fanon had come face to face with life and death in the battle in Alsace, but here it is also highlighted by Césaire's words, asking not only "Who and what are we?" but also, "Who and what can we become?" Joby cites the following concept from the summary of "Parallel Hands," which is not present in the version included in *Alienation and Freedom*:

> Each of the consciousnesses on stage has made the LEAP
> From Nothingness to Justified Being
> From Unjustified Being to Nothingness
> Whence the COMPLETED finish of the Expression.
>   (2014: 58)

Leaps can be backwards and forward. The leap in consciousness can be from Nothingness to Justified Being and from Unjustified Being to Nothingness. One is a revolutionary leap and the other becomes the subject of *Black Skin, White Masks*, the unjustified Being living in a state of alienation. In "Parallel Hands," the progressive leap to Justified Being or revolutionary, actional Being constitutes the individual act: "freedom is the act through which I come to Myself."[8] In *Black Skin, White Masks*, that progressive leap constitutes the social act to change the world.

In the context of the Algerian revolution, in his 1956 letter to a Frenchman (that is, the liberal and good bourgeois Frenchman concerned about human rights but not about the Arabs), Fanon returns to the question of voice authorized by the act as he speaks "of man and his refusal, of the day-to-day rottenness of man, of his dreadful failure": "I want my voice to be harsh, I don't want it to be beautiful, I don't want it to be pure . . . I want it to be torn through and through, I don't want it to be enticing" (1967: 47). We should keep these words in mind as we read Fanon.

*Black Skin, White Masks* reflects the volume of reading that Fanon was doing in Lyon in the period between 1947 and 1951. Psychoanalytic and medical, cultural and literary, philosophical and political. Alongside these readings were novels and creative works, and he followed the representation of Blacks in popular culture. He was able to synthesize these representations brilliantly, putting into writing what would take years to become part of critical cultural theory, relating the representations of Blacks in children's comic books and films.

## Medical school

Written while he was a medical student, *Black Skin, White Masks* does tell us a little about Fanon's training. Critical of the researcher who simply describes the real as an external object, content with description like the anatomist, Fanon gives us an example of this practice of objectification, focusing "on others and never themselves" (2008: 145) from his early days as a medical student: "After several nauseating sessions of dissection, we asked an old-hand how we could avoid the malaise. He replied quite simply: 'My dear fellow, pretend you're dissecting a cat and everything will be OK'" (2008: 145–6). He was part also of a word association study that took place over a three-to-four-year period: "We questioned about 500 individuals from France, Germany, England, and Italy, who were all [W]hite." Then, having gained a certain trust, they would insert the word nègre during free association test. "Almost 60 percent gave the following answers: "'nègre=biological, sex, strong, athletic, powerful, boxer, Joe Louis, Jesse Owens, Senegalese infantrymen, savage, animal, devil, sin.' The mention of Senegalese infantrymen produced 'fearsome, bloody, sturdy, and strong'" (2008: 143–4).

In his essay, "The 'North African Syndrome,'" published in February 1952, and reprinted in *Toward the African Revolution*, Fanon focuses on a thesis by a new doctor from the University of Lyon, Leon Mugniery. He reproduces a few lines from

Mugniery's 1951 doctoral thesis (the same year that Fanon
received his doctorate), quoting examples of the "powerful sexual appetite that is characteristic of those hot-blooded
southerners . . . These are mostly young men (25 to 35) with
great sexual needs, whom the bonds of a mixed marriage
can only temporarily stabilize, and for whom homosexuality is a disastrous inclination" (1967: 11). Fanon also quotes
Mugniery's concern that granting French citizenship to a
"civilization still primitive . . . seems to have been precipitous"
(1967: 12). This "North African syndrome" was produced
and reproduced by university medical schools and was part
of the structure of Fanon's "education." Tosquelles described
the faculty of medicine in Lyon as a caricature of "analytic
Cartesianism," mechanical in its approach, with the treatment "summed up in a line": "What am I saying? Not a line.
One word will do. No possible error in the prescription. No
nuances, and no generous doses of lamentable errors. Here it
is in capitals: TREATMENT: COMMITAL. Nothing more,
nothing less" (quoted in Macey 2012: 143).

The narrowness of the faculty, not at all related to psychoanalytic approaches, meant that Fanon must have read all the
psychoanalytic material he engages with outside his formal
medical classes. He first wrote *Black Skin, White Masks* as a
draft of a medical dissertation. But this was then rejected. At
around the same time, he was working on two stand-alone
articles published in *Esprit*. The first, "The Lived Experience
of the Black" (published in May 1951) would be included in
*Black Skin, White Masks*; the second was "The 'North African
Syndrome.'"

Fanon submitted the first draft of his dissertation –
which was later included in *Black Skin, White Masks* – called
"Contribution à l'étude des mécanismes psychologiques
susceptibles de générer une compréhension saine entre les dif-
férents membres de la communauté" ("A contribution to the

study of psychological mechanisms likely to generate a healthy understanding between the different members of the French community"), in November 1950. We don't know how much of *Black Skin, White Masks* had been included in the dissertation. Perhaps it excluded what we now know as "The Lived Experience of the Black," a chapter in the book that, as Fanon makes clear in his introduction, is different from the others; as he points out: "There is nothing in common between the [B]lack man in this chapter and the [B]lack man who wants to sleep with the [W]hite woman. The latter wants to be [W]hite. Or has a thirst for revenge, in any case" (2018: xvii).

Many of the books and articles referred to in *Black Skin, White Masks* (*Présence Africaine, Les Temps Modernes, Esprit, Revue Française psychanalyse, Psyché*) are from the period 1948–50. The dating is important, indicating how much of the book was put together by November 1950 and also how it concretely emphasizes Fanon's point in the introduction (that is, the book's temporality) as it engages the literature of the time. Thus, even as the contemporary reader finds his use of Freud and the work of Freudians such as Marie Bonaparte on female sexuality problematic, for example, it was at the time new, just published material, as was Octave Mannoni's *Prospero and Caliban: The Psychology of Colonization* (1950), Germain Guex's *Abandonment Neurosis* (1950), and Sir Alan Burns's *Colour Prejudice* (1948).[9] Mannoni and Burns were both liberal colonial administrators, which meant that while they believed in self-governance, they were utterly opposed to any anticolonial revolt, insisting on a program of slow, incremental process controlled by the "enlightened" colonial regime building on its "civilizing missions," with chosen educated colonized elites performing roles in transitional parliamentary systems mirroring those in the metropole. It was perhaps not at all strange to hear that Kwasi Kwarteng, the UK's former Chancellor of the Exchequer, holds a similar view (see Kwarteng 2011) or that

Queen Elizabeth II followed this policy, which was praised at her death. It was against such patronizing views that Kwame Nkrumah spoke some decades earlier, in the early 1950s, of a new African freedom struggle: "Ready or not, here we come."

The decision to reject Fanon's medical dissertation was made in April 1951. It seems that his supervisor, Professor Jean Dechaume, was willing to let Fanon proceed only if certain political conditions were met (namely, if the study was put in a purely medical scientific framework), which could lead to conclusions that would reinforce the French Union. Fanon never knew this, and it is doubtful that he would have agreed. At any rate, in the end the dissertation was rejected.

Fanon responded to the decision by quickly writing an entirely new thesis connected to an ongoing case he was involved in at Vinatier Hospital. The new dissertation was titled "Mental Disturbances, Changes in Character, Psychic Disturbances and Intellectual Deficiency in Hereditary Spinocerebellar Degeneracy: A Case of Friedreich's Disease with Delusions of Possession." The foreword to the dissertation includes a quote attributed by Fanon to Nietzsche, addressed to his brother, Joby: "I speak only of *lived* things and do not present cerebral processes."[10]

The aim of the dissertation was to question the relationship between neurology and psychiatry, which was especially relevant given Dechaume's own interest in neurology and the department's lack of interest in (if not knowledge of) psychoanalytical methods or inquiry. Dechaume's main interest was psychosurgery and his approach has been considered "very 'biological' with anxiety cases treated with shock therapy and intravenous injections of succyl" (Razanajao and Postel 2007: 147). The thesis develops a critique of the dominant models of psychiatry and the relationship of psychiatry to neurology through a study of the rare cases of psychic disorders in Friedreich's disease. Whether mental disorders can arise independently of neurological lesions questions the assumption that every symptom was produced by a lesion, which Fanon would also address in "The 'North African Syndrome.'" At what point, he asks, "can a neurological disease be suspected of triggering a psychic alternation?" (2018: 224). The question of the psychological cause (rather than the biological organogenesis) of mental illness was at the core of Fanon's argument. In *Black Skin, White Masks*, he argues that Freud's demand "that the individual factor be taken into account in psychoanalysis" meant "replac[ing] the phylogenetic theory by an ontogenetic approach" (2008: xv). Since Black alienation "is not an individual question," Fanon adds a third term, *sociogeny*, to "phylogeny" and "ontogeny," arguing that the individual has to be understood sociogenetically. The importance Freud placed on the family might be correct for a White child in Europe (we might add, for a bourgeois White male child in Europe), but for a Black child in a colonial or racist society, the family plays a secondary role. Racism and race consciousness do not simply influence the individual's development, but become essential to contextualize discussions of unconscious "drives" and inhibitions. Fanon's innovation in *Black Skin, White Masks* is to argue that a psychoanalytic approach is necessary to understand Black alienation, while emphasizing the centrality of a sociodiagnostic approach connected to a fundamentally changing society. Understood as race, class, gender, sexuality, and ableism, the emphasis Fanon puts on body experience and sociogeny "has much in common with feminist reworkings of the psychoanalytic canon," argues Sally Swartz, "as well as relational rescriptings that enrich psychoanalysis with a deep appreciation of the effect of the political, economic and social on suffering and psyche" (2022: 75).

In Fanon's medical thesis, the sociogenesis of mental disorders is introduced through a discussion of Jacques Lacan:

The social category of human reality, to which I personally attach so much importance, is one to which Lacan has been attentive. He reprises the discoveries of the ethno-sociology of projection, as illustrated by Mauss and Lévy-Bruhl, and describes the phenomenon of representation. Some images, he says (stars in film, newspapers, sports) represent the necessities of dramatic space and of moral communion specific to the human personality. (2018: 266)

Alongside a review of cases presented in recent medical literature, Fanon includes the case of C. Odile, a patient hospitalized at Vinatier in 1951 (which, under Paul Balvet's directorship, had become a center of institutional psychotherapy). This "case of delusion of possession with hysterical structure" became central to Fanon's dissertation; he questioned whether the relationship between neurology and psychiatry – specifically, in a brain-based illness, the hereditary condition called Friedreich's ataxia – could be simply reduced to neurology.

The thesis includes a 25-page theoretical engagement with Lacan, Kurt Goldstein, Gestalt theory, and Henri Ey. Balvet's article in *Esprit*, "La Valeur humaine de la folie," ("The Human Value of Madness"), published in September 1947, is referred to, in connection with Lacan, indicating that Fanon's engagement with current debates was at "the forefront of intellectual life at the time" (Khalfa 2018: 179). Ey's conception of an "organo-dynamic psychiatry" was a useful starting point for Fanon, but in thinking about neuropsychiatry as a dialectical rather than a dualistic relationship between the brain and the body, Fanon was critical of Ey's approach because of the reification of symptoms it produces. Ey had developed the theory of organodynamism in an attempt to formulate a synthesis between psychiatric symptom and neurophysiological data. His position that the neurological is localizable, instrumental, and elementary, while psychiatry is "non-localizable, historical, global, and synthetic," meant that "character shifts and personality disorders are brought on by the disease itself." Fanon, in contrast, acknowledged the place of the situational – the social, historical, and biographical contexts of the "organic" disease – as well as the psychic and the body's integration of it. Lacan provided an important contrast to Ey's emphasis on the organodynamic.

The discussion of Lacan in Fanon's dissertation goes well beyond the important footnote on the mirror stage in *Black Skin, White Masks*. Arguing that "few men are as contentious as Lacan," Fanon sums up Lacan's position, perhaps mistakenly, as "a defense of the rights of madness to exist in man" (2018: 263). Asserting that "misrecognition is at the foundation of Lacan's thought," he argues that "Lacan goes beyond the concept of the image, making the projectional phenomena described by Lévy-Bruhl as a corollary of primitive thought, the cornerstone of his system. He links the unhappy consciousness to a conception of magic" (2018: 269). Whereas Fanon does not develop this argument further, other than saying that "internally Lacan seems to inhabit the meeting place of Hegel and Lévy-Bruhl" (2018: 269), he does suggest that Lacan's discussion "centers on the very limits of freedom, in other words, humanity's responsibility" (2018: 270). "Thus, says Lacan, 'there is an essential dissonance in human reality. And even if the organic conditions for intoxication are prevalent, one's freedom would still have to grant consent. The fact that madness only appears in man after the 'age of reason' corroborates the Pascalian intuition that "a child is not a man."'" Fanon asks what kind of conclusion should be drawn from these various considerations, adding: "And, is a conclusion even necessary? Would it not be best to leave open a discussion that centers on the very limits of freedom, or in other words, the responsibility of humanity?" (2018: 269–70). He notes that he has been undertaking a work in which he tackles "the problem of history from the psychoanalytic and ontological angles. In it, I will show that History is only the systematic valorization of collective complexes" (2018: 257).

Fanon's second thesis, "Mental Disturbances, Changes in Character, Psychic Disturbances and Intellectual Deficiency in Hereditary Spinocerebellar Degeneracy: A Case of Friedreich's Disease with Delusions of Possession," included a dedication to one of his professors, Denis de Rougemont, whom, as Joby Fanon reports (2014: 63), he considered to be a deep philosophical thinker. The dedication reads: "Given that philosophy is the risk that the mind takes to achieve dignity, we hold him in the highest respect." The thesis was accepted and defended by Fanon on November 29, 1951.

## "The 'North African Syndrome'"

"The 'North African Syndrome'" was written at the same time as *Black Skin, White Masks*, and was published in February 1952; subsequently, it was included as the first chapter of his posthumous collection, *Toward the African Revolution*. The essay is a political-ethical critique of contemporary medical practices, which includes parodies of common attitudes among medical professionals in Lyon (but applicable throughout the Francophone world) who considered North Africans to be lazy and criminal. "The 'North African Syndrome'" does not directly attack the dominant ethnopsychiatric theories that had been promoted by Professor Antoine Porot and the Algiers school of neuropsychology,[11] but there is a direct connection between Fanon's criticism of the racist and orientalist attitudes toward North Africans in France, and the theories of the Arab mind promulgated by the Algiers school, notably the idea of racial/cultural hierarchy in terms of anatomic-physiology – i.e. the absence, in their terms, of cortical integration. Fanon begins the essay with a belief that the human dilemma can be reduced to an existential question connected to the Hippocratic oath: "Have I not, because of what I have done or failed to do, contributed to the impoverishment of human reality? . . . Have I, in all circumstances, called forth the human inside me?" (1967: 3). For Fanon, it is not enough to understand that the North African's "impulsivity" is a product of the colonial situation. Rather, he implores his readers to change the way they act, and take a stand against the alienated social reality that has created it. Disalienation and demystification, as he puts it in *Les Damnés de la terre*, mean "to demystify (de-alienate), and to harry the insult that exists in oneself" (1968: 304). "The 'North African Syndrome,'" Fanon argues, is based on an a priori diagnosis founded on an idea: "The North African [is] . . . a foundation built by the European. In other words, the North African enters spontaneously, by his very presence, into a pre-existing framework" (1967: 4). The racist and dehumanizing pathology created and recreated by the medical establishment is reproduced in medical schools and rehearsed in every interaction between doctor and patient. The North African is objectified, spoken to as though lacking in intelligence and treated as a liar or shirker or, as Porot opined, an impulsive criminal. While French doctors continued to look for the diagnostic source of the symptom in a lesion, they refused to think of the patient's life. Moreover, by thingifying the North African, they refused to consider North Africans in France as anything other than people "without family, without love, without human relations, without the possibility of communion," and who thus live "in a bodily struggle with death, a death on this side of death, a death in life" (1967: 10). The patient (the sufferer) is reified and "dissolve[d] on the basis of an idea"; instead of seeing a human being, the doctor reconstructs the North African as something empty of substance. Once dehumanized, the patient's inability to express a specific symptom increases the doctor's disdain. Linguistic alienation simply reinforces the patient's sense of insecurity, along with the doctor's condescension and tendency to infantilize the patient. "The 'North African Syndrome'" is an ethical statement that challenges the medical profession to act with genuine reciprocity and dignity toward the poor and suffering immigrants. Not acting in this way is a form of neo-Hippocratism, Fanon argues, and reveals the bankruptcy of the Hippocratic oath. Fanon concludes that the North African would be happier at home; he would soon discover that North Africans in Algeria were also alienated, and he would continue to repeat the plea that he had made in his essay: treat the North African with dignity.

## Trip to Martinique

Fanon had spoken about going to Martinique to work on his thesis, but it was only after he had defended his dissertation (and when *Black Skin, White Masks* was already at the publishers) that he returned to Martinique with his brother Joby and took a temporary position at Colson Hospital, Fort-de-France. He found the experience disappointing.

The great shifts in consciousness that had taken place after the war had ground to a halt. The radicalism around Césaire's election in 1945 as deputy to the French National Assembly for Martinique had dissipated. He put enormous energy into getting departmentalization approved, the result of which was that, in 1946, Martinique officially became one of the four overseas departments of France (the other three being French Guiana, Guadeloupe, and Réunion[12]), but it produced very little immediate benefit for Martinicans or challenged French domination. Poverty remained entrenched and, for

Fanon, "most patients who came to see him suffered from causes which were nutritional deficiency, poor sanitation, and public health practices" (Bulhan 1985: 208). Fanon might have thought about reforms, but it seemed more of a hope than a reality.

While in Martinique, Fanon performed autopsies. One report reflects the social reality: "After exhuming the body of a woman who had died three months earlier he discovered that the corrupt doctor on the case had falsified her death certificate, hiding the fact that her husband had beaten her to death" (Mbom 2004: 212).

Politically, the "immense figure named Césaire" towered over everything and, at least subconsciously, Fanon "needed to tread his own path, and needed to do it in his own field" (Ehlen 2001: 105). He left after a few months, boarding a ship for France, never to return. He summarized his experiences as one where he had "met more trousers than men" (Cherki 2006: 19).[13]

## Institutional therapy and radical psychiatry

Paul Balvet had not only been in charge at Saint-Alban Psychiatric Hospital (1936–43); he had also been its only doctor. After the hospital lost 36 of its staff to the draft at the outbreak of World War II, he found 27-year-old François Tosquelles at the Septfonds internment camp in south-west France, running a clinic "in the mud" (Platt-Mills 2021). He was able to convince the authorities to release Tosquelles (see Macey 2012: 139, 145–6). Since Tosquelles's credentials were not recognized, Balvet hired him as a nurse and the first thing they did was to organize the hospital staff and patients to find food. Survival and the idea of social-psychotherapy became intimately connected.

After the fall of France in 1940, psychiatric hospitals across France became places of starvation and extermination as the Vichy regime followed the Nazi policy of systematic sterilization and murder of the mentally ill. During the war, 40 percent of the hospital population in France (about 45,000 people) died. The situation at Saint-Alban Psychiatric Hospital was unique: its death rate was less than 10 percent and nobody died from malnutrition. What became known as *psychothérapie institutionnelle* (known in English as institutional psychotherapy and also sociotherapy, using Tosquelles's term, *sociothérapie*)[14] emerged out of this necessity. The shortages were total. When Balvet found a delirious patient making sandals out of raffia, they began an occupational therapy program. But rather than "make-work," the goal was to allow patients to respond to community needs. Patients were involved in the hospital's farm, in cooking, cleaning, and working on the hospital's newspaper, which included articles about patients' lives and criticisms and examinations of "the purpose of psychiatry" (Platts-Mills 2021). Having the advantage of being relatively small and distant from any urban center, Saint-Alban also became a refuge for the Resistance. All this was not separate from the horizontal structure advocated by Tosquelles, where discussion and meetings included everyone, and their open participation became a central principle of Institutional psychotherapy. As Tosquelles put it, "nothing should ever be obvious, and everything is subject to discussion" (Platts-Mills 2021).

Balvet reported that he learnt "half of what I know about psychiatry" from Tosquelles, whose interest in Lacan was part of that education. In 1942, Balvet and Tosquelles put into practice and radically developed Hermann Simon's idea of an "active therapy."[15] The idea that the community as a whole (including the institution) was sick meant that everyone (including patients) had to be involved in decision-making about every aspect of the institution, including the most seemingly mundane. In addition, as well as breaking down the walls inside between the institution, active therapy meant breaking down the walls and opening doors between the institution and the world outside it.

Born in Catalonia in 1912, François Tosquelles passed his baccalaureate at the age of 15 and enrolled in Barcelona University's medical school, where he studied psychiatry with the phenomenologist and psychoanalyst Emilio Mira y López, who introduced him to Lacan. With Mira y López, Tosquelles took "part in an innovative experiment at the Catalonia General Hospital" reorganizing the health services (Dosse 2011: 42).[16] While in analysis, he met Sándor Eiminder and in the early 1930s he organized study groups on Marx and Freud and a reading group on Lacan, maintaining that without Marx "a psychiatrist is nothing" and without Marx and Lacan "we cannot understand anything" (quoted in Robcis 2021: 17). For Tosquelles, individual and social liberation, and psychiatry and politics were intimately connected.

Tosquelles was a founding member of the Spanish Workers, Party of Marxist Unification (POUM), an important anti-Stalinist revolutionary organization that was also critical of the popular front alliances and Communist Party politics. In Catalonia, the opposition to the military coup that led to the civil war took the form of collectivization and self-management among workers, and also rural workers taking over land (see Leval 1975). These self-organization practices particularly influenced Tosquelles as "mechanisms to prevent authoritarianism and reification" (Robcis 2016: 214). Toward the end of the Spanish Civil War, he became the head of the Republican Army's psychiatric services. These experiences, the struggle for independence and self-management in Catalonia, the Stalinist betrayal of the revolution, and the Fascists' "victory" in Spain "convinced Tosquelles that occupation was not only a social and political reality but also a psychic structure: Thus, the search for a true freedom needed to go through a form of psychic 'disoccupation.' To think through these issues, the psychiatric hospital appeared to offer a perfect platform" (Meyers 2014).

Sentenced to death by Franco's regime, Tosquelles escaped Spain for France in 1939, walking across the Pyrenees to France. He was carrying two books: Lacan's doctoral thesis on paranoid psychosis and Hermann Simon's *Psychotherapy in the Asylum.*

After being interned in camps for "undesirables," Tosquelles created a refuge for the suffering with direct links with resistance fighters. For him, institutional psychotherapy was a product of these experiences as the struggle for liberation against Francoism and Nazism became inseparable from the struggle for liberation inside the mental asylum. He insisted that the institution had to be transformed into a caring community. Rather than a professional administration of mental health that normalizes institutionalization and pathologizes patients, the institution had to become a space where the inmates (staff and "guests") could work out therapies in a supportive, nurturing environment.[17]

In 1943, Balvet left Saint-Alban and joined the psychiatric hospital of Vinatier near Lyon (where he started to introduce some of the same ideas). He was replaced by Lucien Bonnafé, a psychiatrist and communist militant, although he would also soon leave to become part of the resistance medical service. By this time Saint-Alban had become an underground resistance center, treating wounded fighters, welcoming refugees and Jews, and also sheltering partisans (including Paul Éluard, Georges Canguilhem, and Tristan Tzara). Patients were "feeding refugees" (Platts-Mills 2021); as Bonnafé, put it, "we were resistance fighters in all fields, intellectuals, soldiers, psychiatrists."[18]

After the war, Saint-Alban gained a new reputation attracting radicals and revolutionaries with whom Tosquelles collaborated in the project of making the hospital a practical model to rethink the relationship between psychoanalysis, politics, and human liberation. In practical terms, the shocking number of deaths in French psychiatric hospitals during the occupation, and the traumatic experiences of French soldiers returning from prison camps shone a light on Saint-Alban, where patients had survived and innovative therapies had developed. Its social psychoanalysis became an example of new approaches to psychiatry as a transformational social practice. Radical changes in the theory and practice of psychiatric care were viewed as a necessity and some of Saint-Alban's egalitarian, community practices, including the organization of daily life, were soon being taken up throughout the country.

After his return to France from Martinique, Fanon began working with Tosquelles as a resident at Saint-Alban. Not long after this, *Black Skin, White Masks* was published and six months later, Josie and Frantz were married. They would stay at Saint-Alban until September 1953. Toward the end of his time there, Fanon co-presented three papers on electroconvulsive therapy (ECT) at a conference with his colleagues Tosquelles, Maurice Despinoy, and Walter Zenner.

Fanon believed institutional psychotherapy to be a critical, humanistic psychotherapy based on a fundamental belief that the patient's self-liberation could be accomplished in a socialized setting. The mission to reintegrate the patient into the social community meant that their social needs took priority, and reification and alienation created by the psychiatric institution were challenged. For Tosquelles, the hospital itself was a sick organism set up to pacify patients and create docile receivers of care. Medical therapies were simply the products of this will to control and supervise. Radically restructuring the psychiatric hospital necessitated a different attitude toward mental illness: one opposed to the practice of ostracizing the mentally ill and separating them from society. Tosquelles further believed that psychosis could not be magically accessed inside the four walls of a doctor's office, cut off from the social world; instead, just as the individual should not be pathologized, the institution was part of that pathologization and itself needed to be de-pathologized. Treating the patient and humanizing and socializing the mental institution were part of the same process that would create a new society inside the hospital. It would be accomplished by reforming social and spatial relations, treating patients as human and social beings, and thereby encouraging a sense of self in place of isolating them as controllable objects. When Fanon began his psychiatric residency at Saint-Alban, it marked "the first time" that he was "involved in a clinical situation that allowed patients to contribute to their own recovery" (Macey 2012: 149).

Although written before his time with Tosquelles, though no doubt influenced by his connections with Balvet, Fanon's argument in *Black Skin, White Masks* for a sociodiagnostic psychoanalytic approach and a sociopolitical critique of alienation is one that in some senses echoes Tosquelles' approach at Saint-Alban – viz., the need to confront double alienation, psychoanalytical and social. Institutional psychotherapy, Tosquelles would argue, walks on two legs, psychoanalysis and politics. He was not alone in this: a new generation of thinkers and practitioners were also engaging with this perspective, rediscovering a humanist Marx in his *Economic and Philosophic Manuscripts of 1844*,[19] alongside a return to Freud, encouraged by Lacan during the late 1940s and 1950s.

Fanon acknowledged Tosquelles as a mentor and considered himself "a disciple" (Cherki, 2006: 20) in a totally committed and crucial relationship. The feeling was mutual. Years later, Tosquelles remarked that "Fanon had never really left us; he continued to be present in our memory in the same way he had filled the space around him. He questioned his interlocutors with his body and his voice" (quoted in Cherki 2006: 20).

In June 1953, Fanon passed his "Medicat," required by all major psychiatric hospitals. In a letter to Maurice Despinoy, he said he had applied for a position in Guadeloupe but felt he was at a "slight disadvantage," being ranked 13th out of 23 of those who had passed their exams. The list of available positions included Blida in Algeria, and Pontorson, Aurillac, Lannemezan, Aix-en-Provence, Auch, and Rennes in France. Fanon was interested in a position in Africa, where anticolonial agitation was fermenting. He applied to Blida-Joinville and also wrote a letter to Léopold Senghor inquiring about a position in Dakar. Senghor never responded[20] and Fanon decided to take a temporary position at the psychiatric hospital of Pontorson (in Normandy) in September 1953. The introduction of some institutional psychotherapy principles at Pontorson immediately caused a stir. His application to take "inmates" shopping at the local market was denied by the head of the hospital. The following morning, the patients, who were assigned all the manual labor at the hospital, called a strike, which ground the hospital to a halt. Management quickly decided to get rid of the young psychiatrist as soon as possible. Fanon's temporary appointment lasted two months: he moved to Blida-Joinville Psychiatric Hospital in November.

Fanon's interest in psychoanalytic theory continued after the publication of *Black Skin, White Masks*, first in the context of Tosquelles and Saint-Alban, and then at Blida-Joinville, and later at the hospitals in Tunisia, Razi and Charles Nicolle. At Blida-Joinville, Fanon continued to read political, medical, and psychoanalytical texts, extensively and vivaciously. He organized and encouraged study groups of Freud's works among the nursing staff; Cherki (2006: 90) writes of gatherings in the dormitory reading and discussing Freud's *The Wolf Man*). Fanon also developed the psychiatric, psychoanalytic, and neurological holdings in the library and subscribed to the major journals. "He was engaged in a continuous dialogue with the interns," remembers Cherki, "and would talk with them for hours on end, if not at a patient's bedside, then in the library, or during the scheduled discussion sessions that dealt primarily with psychopathology" (2006: 90). All this activity continued in Tunis, where his interest in the writings of Melanie Klein and Sándor Ferenczi is noted in his last medical publication on day hospitalization. He had instructed a staff member to hunt down everything by Ferenczi that had been translated into French.

When *Black Skin, White Masks* was published in 1952, it didn't attract much attention; it was only after its 1967 publication in English in the US that it became widely read and more widely translated. Its basis as a foundational work within academic postcolonial studies came in the 1980s and turned mostly on the question of identities and the ambivalence and "fissiparousness" (breaking into pieces) produced by the racial gaze. Fanon's foundational question in the book is "What does the Black want"? The answer given by Black Lives Matter is that Black life should be recognized as human. It is a demand not a request; as Fanon puts it, "there is no other solution but to use every means available to *reestablish your weight as a human being*" (2004: 221). It is a demand that gestures to a radical humanism, in its imminent critique of White liberal humanism. As Keeanga-Yamahtta Taylor argues: "Black liberation is bound up with the project of human liberation and social transformation" (2021: 194). And it has a history, like the placard "I am a Man" from the 1968 Memphis sanitation workers strike, which began after two workers were killed when they had to shelter in a garbage truck because of segregation laws. Mattering is a necessary reaction and demand that results from living in a society where Black life does not matter, or is seen as a *threat* to that very society, which is racially coded across time and place. That was the fate of Trayvon Martin, the 17-year-old African American youth who was shot by George Zimmerman, a neighborhood watch coordinator in a gated community where Martin was visiting his father in 2012.

Not fully human, Blacks are objects that are seen as creating fear and are deemed corrosive to moral values (Fanon 2004: 6). In this sense, Black life is policed, criminalized, and incarcerated into a proverbial "zone of nonbeing." But it is from this extraordinarily arid region, Fanon argues in *Black Skin, White Masks*, that a genuine new departure can emerge.

# 3

# Black Skin, White Masks

Nothing is *known* that is not in *experience*, or, as it is also expressed, that is not *felt to be true*.

Hegel, *The Phenomenology of Mind*

## Introduction

Reading Fanon's *Black Skin, White Masks*, one is confronted by its context and its seeming timelessness. It is radically critical and open, engaging a wide range of thinkers of the time. Fanon employs Freudian, Jungian, and Adlerian thinking to discuss language, objectification, and desire, and finds them both useful and wanting. Although highly critical of Octave Mannoni's just published work *Prospero and Caliban*, he agrees that the "colonial situation ... brings about the emergence of a mass of illusions and misunderstandings that only a psychological analysis can place and define," arguing that "the analysis we are undertaking is psychological" (2008: 66, xiv).

The longest chapter, "The Black Man and Psychopathology," engages contemporary Freudian theory and analyses the cultural fetishism and phobia of the Black man's sexual power in popular culture. Thinking through his own lived experience (in Martinique and in France) he critically employs Sartre, Merleau-Ponty, and Hegel, and, underscoring the importance of Black consciousness, turns to negritude writers, including Senghor and Césaire and also Black American novelists Richard Wright and Chester Himes, whose works had just been published in France. The book connects Black lived experience with a sociodiagnosis of racism that affects all social relations.

*Black Skin, White Masks* is also part of what Fanon calls the French drama. It begins with the educated Antilleans who leave Martinique for the "motherland," France. Having internalized French culture and the racism inherent in it, they believe that they are French and civilized and, if not White, they are at least not Black like the African. At the heart of the book is an understanding of the pathologization of the Black in European culture, unthinkingly reproduced by Whites and also by Blacks. Because the individual cannot be separated from the social problematic of *Black Skin*, Fanon argues that it is necessary that a psychoanalysis of the neurosis produced by a racist social system is sociodiagnostic. In addition to Freud's focus on the individual's history, Fanon emphasizes the importance of the social world in understanding a patient's mental health.

A decade after *Black Skin, White Masks* was published, Ralph Ellison described the United States as a "nation of ethical schizophrenics" whose pathology of racism "was deeply imbedded in the American ethos" (1964: 99). It forced Blacks "into an inner world," he said, "where reason and madness mingle with hope and memory and endlessly give birth to nightmare and to dream" (1964: 100). The experience of constant division and fragmentation is a form of alienation that becomes part of everyday life. W.E.B. Du Bois had brilliantly described this "peculiar sensation" as a "double-consciousness":

> This sense of always looking at one's self through the eyes of others, of measuring one's soul by the tape of a world that looks on in amused contempt and pity. One ever feels his two-ness – an American, a Negro; two souls, two thoughts, two unreconciled strivings; two warring ideals in one dark body, whose dogged strength alone keeps it from being torn asunder. (2009: 8)

Fanon clearly poses the problem of the double consciousness, but what distinguishes his analysis from others is "the convergence of the '[B]lack problem' with desire" (Gordon 2015: 21). To begin his analysis, Fanon asks the question "What does the Black want?"[1] opening up a nihilistic syllogism:

> The Black wants to be recognized as human.
> The Black is not human.
> The Black must turn White or disappear. (2008: xii–xiv)

While the White, he adds, "is desperately trying to achieve the rank of the human," they remain "locked in their Whiteness" (2008: xiii–xiv) and cannot become human; meanwhile, the destiny for the Black is to turn White or disappear. Fanon explains later that the Antillean's every action "is dependent on 'the Other' – not because 'the Other' remains their final goal but simply because it is 'the Other' who asserts them in their need to enhance their status" (2008: 187). The White/Black racial structure is Manichean and dualistic, "two poles of this world, poles in perpetual conflict" (2008: 27), but these cannot be understood in isolation from one another. Fanon calls this "double narcissism" – the White "locked in their Whiteness" and the "Black in their Blackness" – and says his work will "endeavor to determine the tendencies of this double narcissism and the motivations behind it" (2008: xiii–xiv).

The source of tension is an open secret. The racial structure is a social structure. And while the "inferiority complex" can be initially ascribed to economics, this is not Fanon's primary focus. Acutely aware of the material environment of psychic life, he believes "only a psychoanalytic interpretation of the Black problem can reveal the affective disorders responsible for this network of complexes . . . inherited from childhood" (2018: xiv).

How can "depersonalization on a collective level" (2004: 219) be broken? This is the existential question that frames Fanon's work. He answers it straightforwardly: it requires the utter destruction of the morbid universe of all racism. And to do so requires a thorough *social* diagnosis "on the subjective and objective level." By analyzing the "massive psycho-existential complex . . . we aim to destroy it" (2008: xiv–xvi). Evoking Marx, he adds: "How can we possibly not hear that voice again tumbling down the steps of History: 'It's no longer a question of knowing the world, but of transforming it'" (2008: 1).

## The journey

Fanon begins *Black Skin, White Masks* by arguing that the Black, is a "nonbeing," importantly adding that it is from this zone that "a *genuine* new departure can emerge" (2008: xii; my emphasis). But because most "cannot take advantage of this descent into a veritable hell," Fanon will take us on the journey, intending to enlighten as we follow him.

There are two points worthy of consideration. First, there is a journey, or what Fanon calls a "descent" or a going down into a "veritable hell," and second, since most Black people cannot take advantage of this descent, he takes us on this mission as *his* mission. Lewis Gordon suggests that there is a connection here with Dante's *Inferno*, arguing that Fanon is akin to Dante's Virgil, "the cooled" guide who "plans to take us through the mediations offered to the [B]lack. As such, he functions as Virgil guiding us through a world that many of us, being 'imbeciles,' need but often refuse to see" (2015: 23). It is worth underscoring the adjective "cooled" as well as my insistence on the reader being patient. The idea of a mission to a "veritable hell" also resonates with the war experience as existential. Fanon says the book should have been written three years earlier, but the "truths made our blood boil" (2008: xiii). Now he can speak without shouting.

Fanon's virulent dissent and his descent, not only his experience of being underground but also the discovery of new elements in that journey, are what will allow a "*genuine* new departure." The idea of a journey and, indeed, the book as a journey (he says later that the book is "a mirror with a progressive infrastructure where the [B]lack can find the path to disalienation" (2008: 161)) engages the reality of this zone of nonbeing. Writing about this zone, *Black Skin, White Masks* does not provide a univocal answer; rather, it is a challenging journey with false turns and dead ends, highlighting its insufficiencies. The apparent clarity of the zone of nonbeing is itself part illusory and cannot be taken as anything other than opaque. The zone is also veiled and masked. And if genuine disalienation were that simple, Fanon would have said so. He asks us to travel carefully with him, wary of zealousness (2008: 137).

*Black Skin, White Masks* is indirectly biographical, containing quite a few anecdotes and stories used to elucidate his analysis. That he takes himself as the subject of racist objectification on a train in the chapter "The Lived Experience of the Black" is not Fanon's point. Rather, it is Fanon as a Black passenger whose very presence is the cause of anxiety for a young White child who has not yet, like his mother, developed a bourgeois civility to navigate the situation. For Fanon, the train, the space of modernity and movement, is transformed into a space of non-movement. Thingified and dehumanized, he is projected into the zone of nonbeing. "Locked in this suffocating reification," Fanon writes, "I appealed to the Other . . . [But] the Other fixes me with their gaze, their gestures and attitude, the same way you fix a preparation with a dye" (2008: 89). As Paget Henry puts it "we encounter this zone of nonbeing in extreme states of ego collapse" (2000: 89).

As to scientific objectivity, Fanon says any such claim would be dishonest, "since the alienated and the neurotic were my brother, my sister, and my father" (2008: 67, 200). His insistence on a sociodiagnosis leads him to conclude, perhaps including himself, that "it is not one individual Antillean who presents a neurotic mind-set; all the Antilleans present this. Antillean society is a neurotic society. Hence we are referred back from the individual to the social structure" (2008: 188). The flaw "lies not in the 'soul' of the individual, but in the environment." This is the basis of Fanon's call for social action, but at the same time he is aware that while Blacks are "a victim of White civilization," they have also gradually assimilated Europe's "prejudices, the myths, and the folklore" and "after having been a slave of the [W]hite man, [Blacks] enslave themselves" (2004: 167). In other words, the Antillean "lives an ambiguity" that is "extraordinarily neurotic," knowing they are Black and realizing that being Black is "a result of being wicked, spineless, evil, and instinctual." The origin of "the Antillean's negrophobia" is found "in the collective unconscious [B]lack = ugliness, sin, darkness, and immorality," where "everything that is the opposite of this Black behavior is White" (2008: 168).

Traveling deeper, Fanon argues that "any neurosis, any abnormal behavior or affective erethism [a state of extreme irritability] in an Antillean is the result of their cultural situation," and what he calls a "cultural imposition," and he gives several examples of reactions of Antilleans watching films. The following are two, probably biographical, examples. The first focuses on the different experiences of watching a Tarzan movie in Martinique and in France. In Martinique, the young Antillean identified with Tarzan against the Africans. But in France, "things are not so clear-cut" because, seeing him, "the [W]hite moviegoers automatically place him among the savages on the screen" (2008: 131n.15). The second is about watching a documentary about Africa in Fort-de-France which triggers "hilarity from the young Antilleans." Perhaps "this exaggerated response betrays a hint of recognition," Fanon wonders, but in France "the Black who watches this documentary is literally petrified. Here there is no escape: he is at once Antillean, Bushman, and Zulu" (2008: 131n.15).

After stating that neither Freud, Adler, "nor even the cosmic Jung" considered "the [B]lack ... in the course of his research. And each was perfectly right," Fanon turns to Jacques Lacan's mirror stage (when a baby can identify with their image in a mirror). Fanon suggests "the true 'Other' for the White is and remains the Black, and vice versa." But for "the White ... 'the Other' is perceived as a bodily image, absolutely as the non-ego, i.e., the unidentifiable, the unassimilable" (2008: 139n.25). He then reflects on his education, a French education with French textbooks in a classroom filled with images from France. It was an education for assimilation where, in theory, the Antillean became a French citizen. Reading French compositions by 10–14-year-old Antilleans on the subject of the summer holidays, Fanon finds they write "like genuine little Parisians ... and time and again the following phrase is repeated: 'I like going on vacation as I can run through the fields, breathe in the fresh air, and come home with pink cheeks.' It is obvious we are hardly mistaken when we say that the Antillean cannot recognize the fact of being Black" (2008: 140n.25) The Blacks were Africans and the Antilleans were not. Fanon was perhaps 13 when Senegalese soldiers "were passing through Martinique, coming from French Guiana." He "scoured the streets for a sight of their uniforms, the red tarboosh and belt, that we had heard so much about." And then his "father even went so far as to pick two of them up and bring them back home, much to the delight of the family" (2008: 140n.25).

Fanon sums up: "I'm a White man. Unconsciously, then, I distrust what is Black in me, in other words, the totality of my being" (2008: 168). *Black Skin, White Masks*, will seek to analyze these "alienated (mystified) Blacks and . . . no less alienated (mystifying and mystified) Whites" (2008: 12).

One question that has concerned biographers is Fanon's relationship with his wife Josie, who was a European White woman. David Macey, for example, argues that, since he is speaking this book to Josie, Fanon is freely associating when he says: "When my restless hands caress those [W]hite breasts, they grasp [W]hite civilization and dignity and make them mine . . . I marry [W]hite culture, [W]hite beauty, [W]hite [W]hiteness" (see Fanon 2008: 45; translation altered). "But he does not ask the young *Lyonnaise* who is with him?" (Macey 2012: 132). Fanon himself answers later in the book: "I don't get the feeling I have given up my personality by marrying some European woman" (2008: 179), indicating that marrying across the color line did not mean that he was pathologically trying to escape his own color. Macey also assumes that Frantz and Josie didn't discuss the burning issue of being an interracial couple in a racist society like France.

But Josie Fanon, at least, responded to similar claims in an interview at Howard University's African American Center in

1978. The interviewer asks: "Some critics say there is a fundamental contradiction between Fanon's works, what he stood
for, and the fact that he married a White French woman. How
do you answer these critics?" Josie replied:

> It is my opinion, and I believe that it was also his – otherwise
> he would not have contracted nor remained in this inter-
> racial marriage – that there was no contradiction. In his
> works, he states clearly that it is through a revolutionary
> process that we can understand and resolve racial problems.
> Otherwise, we find ourselves in dead-end situations that are
> impossible to resolve – the sort that we can never put to
> rest. For example, critics can reproach a [B]lack American
> for marrying an Arab woman because her skin is lighter than
> his is and so on, and so on. In a certain phase of the struggle,
> such a position can have for a time a positive and benefi-
> cially unifying effect. However, it remains a limitation. We
> are not going to limit each other to race! Otherwise, where
> is the revolution? (Filostrat 1978)

## "The Black and Language"

It is not surprising that Fanon begins *Black Skin, White Masks*
with a discussion about the importance of language given that,
for him, language is not only experienced but also felt. The
body is not only the carrier of memory and trauma, but is also
expressive of it through language. For Fanon, there was no
disconnection, underscoring his attitude and integration of
phenomenology and psychiatry; he writes: "We would like
to heat the carcass of Man and leave . . . Man freed from the
springboard embodying the resistance of others and digging
into his flesh in order to find self-meaning" (2008: xiii). So
here, in a few lines, we have Fanon making the connection

between reflection and body experience essential to finding "self-meaning." He wants language to express a refusal to separate feeling, physical and cerebral, and thinking and activity; intimately connecting mind and body. He demands that we keep our minds and bodies critically open to the human condition, as he puts it on the last line of the book, as a "final prayer," "O my body, always make me a man who questions!"

Fanon's voice in *Black Skin, White Masks* is polyvocal and "never singular" (Swartz 2018: 57). He doesn't simply speak for himself; what makes the book difficult is that, when he speaks, he is often ventriloquizing.

Fanon's decision to begin with a discussion about language was motivated by the radical insight that, in the colonies, language speech carries a weight. It assumes that culture works and functions as an instrument of physical and mental domination and subjugation. The quest to master the French language is a quest to be recognized as White, to have White credentials. And Fanon uses the word "fissiparous" to express this divided self (Laing 1965) not only as division but as a literal breaking apart, which is manifested in modes of expression, tones of voice, and behavior. "The [B]lack possesses two dimensions: one with fellow [B]lacks, the other with [W]hites. A [B]lack behaves differently with [W]hites than with another [B]lack" (2008: 1; translation altered). He speaks of his turn to psychoanalysis using the analogy of a machine misfiring and thinking at the level of failure.[2]

The problem Fanon is addressing around the Black and language is put in terms of two hypotheses expressing the syllogism above. First, "the more the [B]lack Antillean assimilates the French language, the [W]hiter they become i.e., the closer they come to becoming a true human being . . . [in] possess[ing] a language [they possess] as an indirect consequence the world expressed and implied by this language" (2008: 2). And second, "All colonized people – in other words,

people in whom an inferiority complex has taken root, whose
local cultural originality has been committed to the grave –
position themselves in relation to the civilizing language:
i.e., the metropolitan culture. The more the colonized has
assimilated the cultural values of the metropolis, the more
they reject [B]lackness and the bush, the [W]hiter they will
become" (2004: 3).

Since one who possesses a specific language indirectly possesses "the world expressed and implied by this language,"
language has enormous power, and possession of it affects
status, being, and bodily experience. For the colonized, language is lived in the flesh and inscribed on the body. The
importance of language means that "every colonized subject
. . . always has to justify their stance in relation to language"
(2008: 2). The relationship is a fleshy, aural, and visible one,
since Black people have to "wear the livery" that Whites have
fabricated for them. Fanon highlights the importance of seeing
and hearing this fabrication performed by stereotypical Black
characters in comics and films. In children's comics, "all the
Blacks are mouthing the ritual 'Yes, boss'." And in American
films that are "dubbed in French . . . the grinning stereotype
*Y'a bon Banania*" appears. In one of these films, the 1943 *Crash
Dive*,[3] "there is a [B]lack guy on a submarine speaking the most
downright classic dialect imaginable. Furthermore, he is a true
nègre, walking behind the quartermaster, trembling at the latter's slightest fit of anger" (2008: 17). Fanon is convinced that
"in the original version he did not have this way of expressing himself" and then wonders: "And even if he did I can't
see why in a democratic France, where 60 million citizens are
colored, anyone would dub the same idiocies from America?"

The same stereotype across a number of films is the same as
the Black man on the packet of the breakfast cereal *Banania*:
"Always at your service. Always deferential and smiling. Me
never steal, me never lie. Eternally grinning *y'a bon Banania*"

(2008: 162). Fanon is referring to the advert of Banania represented by the smiling Senegalese soldier wearing a red felt cap with a blue tassel depicted on the tins of the chocolate/banana breakfast food. "Y'a bon Banania" is a caricature of an African saying *c'est bon*. Still popular, the cereal first appeared in 1917 and the company only abandoned the phrase "Y'a bon" in 1977. The figure's face, slowly changed into the cartoon rendering of an African boy that appears in its logo today, still wears a red cap, a wide grin, and large eyes. In the first English translation "Y'a bon" was translated as "Sho good eatin'." Aunt Jemima and Uncle Ben in the US had a similar stereotypical smiling Black mammy (Auntie) and smiling Black server/cook (Uncle), which have only recently been removed from these products. Brought over to the UK from the US, the "Golliwog" became the "most popular Black type" of the early twentieth century (Pieterse 1995: 156), becoming Robertson's company trademark in 1910. It wasn't until the 1980s that antiracist campaigners targeted the image. Insisting it was part of "our national tradition," the company renamed it Golly and only officially withdrew it in 2002, while still insisting that it had nothing to do with racism.

Whatever their specificity, the films project the same stereotypical images reproduced by and through language. Fanon argues that the Black is forced to speak "petit nègre"[4] and is tied to an image, ensnared, and imprisoned as the eternal victim of "an essence, a visible appearance" (2008: 18), whose meaning is imposed by colonial/racist/capitalist society. If language can be considered a prison house, then speaking "petit nègre" is its expression.

While the Whites are asking the Blacks to be good nègres, the Black person who quotes Montesquieu is suspect. In Paris, Fanon argues, "they threw one out [who] had the cheek to read Engels" (2008: 162). Likewise, the Black who quotes Marx is a threat, having the audacity to turn against their White benefactors (2008: 18). Thus a Black person who speaks French, according to White standards, is a "sensation," and, while praised, is also untrustworthy. In the colonies it is said among the small middle class that to speak French will open doors; it is a way to get on in the White world. Educated in French, speaking French at home, Fanon had "adopted the cultural tool of language." And thus when he gave a lecture on poetry in Lyon, a French friend said to him, "Basically you are a [W]hite man" (2008: 21). Language reflects not only education but status. In the Antilles, the more "perfect" (that is French French) one speaks, the higher the status. But the Black person could be heard but not seen. For French French was White French, and once seen something else happened. The French speaking Black is first Black. Thus Fanon asks why the surrealist Marxist writer, André Breton, should say that Césaire is a "[B]lack man who handles the French language unlike any [W]hite man today" (see 2008: 22). The White poet is a poet. Why does the poet need to be identified as Black?

The little White boy who says, on seeing Fanon, "look Mama, un nègre" is just one example. When the White professional, be they teachers, doctors, physicians, or psychologists, speak to Black and Arab people, they modulate their voices. These often-fleeting daily interactions are tainted with paternalism and express the subtle violence of the "linguistic drama":

A White talking to a person of color behaves exactly like a grown-up with a kid, simpering, murmuring, fussing, and coddling a child and starts smirking, whispering, patronizing, coddling ... Consulting physicians know this. Twenty European patients come and go: "Please have a seat. Now what's the trouble? What can I do for you today?" In comes a Black or an Arab: "Sit down, old fellow. Not feeling well?

Where's it hurting?" When it's not that, it's "You not good?"
To speak *petit nègre* to a Black [person] is insulting ... the
ease with which it classifies and imprisons [the patient] at a
primitive and uncivilized level – that is insulting. (2008: 15)[5]

On a similar theme, Fanon observes that "it is said that the
Black person likes to palaver," and when he pronounces the
word "palaver," he sees "a group of boisterous children"
(2004: 10). Thus, the idea that a Black likes to palaver "is
only a short step to a new theory that the Black is just a child.
Psychoanalysts have a field day, and the word 'orality' is soon
pronounced" (2008: 10).

In a key passage that heralds the role that the body and
the senses hold in his analysis of alienation, Fanon gives a
description of a young Martinican practicing the pronunciation of the French "r." Struggling with his own tongue – a
"lazy organ," the tongue, just as Blacks are always described
as "lazy" by colonists, practicing in their rooms making "every
effort not only to roll their r's, but also to embroider them"
(2008: 5; translation altered). The daily training of the body
to achieve good pronunciation is an application for admission
to the White world, an application for recognition. But what
is being striven for does not result in a happy outcome; rather,
it becomes the symptom of an authentic pathology. Anxious
not to correspond with the Black who swallows their r's, the
young Martinican makes use of a great many of them but
doesn't know how to divide them, says Fanon, "On arrival in
Le Havre a Martinican goes into a café and calls out with great
assurance: 'Waiterrr? Bwing me a dwink of beerrrr!'" (2004: 5)

A central aspect of Fanon's analysis is the changing personality of those traveling to and from the metropole. The
Antillean entering France literally mutates as their psyche
changes. They had left Fort-de-France, a town described by
Césaire as a "mute, baffled" town without movement, for a

France where life happens. They shout bye-bye (a popular Creole love song) on their departure. Leaving France, they bring back with them the aura and power of the words Paris, Marseilles, the Sorbonne, and they return to Martinique deified (2008: 3). The radically reformed returnee walks ashore with their head held high. Their phenotype undergoes a definite mutation which says, "evolved" and "full of themselves" (2008: 3). And, at the same time, the returnee presents a new pathology: "I must watch my diction because that is how they will judge me. They will say I can't even speak French properly" (2008: 4)

The Antillean in France is faced with two options – either support a White world with the help of French or reject Europe by speaking Creole. The returnee is faced with the same options, either speak Creole signifying that things haven't changed or speak French and indicate that it is the European who has come back, speaking "like a White man" (2008: 5).

Both options are alienating, Fanon argues. A third option is perhaps suggested by this quote from the surrealist radical writer and *Les Temps Modernes* editor Michel Leiris (who later supported the Algerian liberation struggle): "in the Antillean writer there is a desire to break with the literary forms associated with official education, such a desire striving toward a freer future, would not assume the appearance of folklore" (2008: 23) but this would require a rupture, a revolution, opening up the language to new meanings.

## The possibility of love among the races

Out of the [B]lackest part of my soul, through the zone of hachures, surges up this desire to be suddenly [W]hite.[6]

Fanon, *Black Skin, White Masks*

Chapters 2 and 3 of *Black Skin, White Masks,* "The Woman of Color and the White Man" and "The Man of Color and the White Woman," ask the question of the possibility of loving relations between Blacks and Whites by tracing "its perversions" (2004: 24). We are back into Freudian territory, provocatively introduced by Fanon's statement that "by loving me, [the White woman] proves to me that I am worthy of a [W]hite love. I am loved like a [W]hite man. I am a [W]hite man . . . I espouse [W]hite culture, [W]hite beauty, [W]hite [W]hiteness" (2008: 45). The attempted ontological transformation is expressed sexually: "Between these [W]hite breasts that my wandering hands fondle, [W]hite civilization and worthiness become mine." The desire is paramount among Antillean men, Fanon adds, whose "main preoccupation on setting foot in France was to sleep with a [W]hite woman. Barely off the ship in Le Havre, they head for the bordellos" (2008: 54).

The chapters are based on Fanon's discussion of Mayotte Capécia's semi-autobiographical *Je suis Martiniquaise,* published in 1949 (and awarded the Grand Prix Littéraire des Antilles)[7] and the 1947 semi-autobiographical work by the Goncourt prizewinner, René Maran, *Un Homme pareil aux autres.* Alongside Capécia, Fanon also refers to Senegalese writer Abdoulaye Sadji, whose novel *Nini* had been excerpted in *Présence Africaine.*[8] Sadji's novel is set in Saint-Louis, an island in the Senegal river (now Guet Ndar), which boasted a large mulatto population.[9] What connects the two novels is their shared compulsion to gain entry to the White world. The behavior in both is "similar to an obsessional neurotic . . . in the very thick of a situational neurosis" (2004: 42).

While Fanon was highly critical of Capécia's novel, he felt no need to subject it to a psychoanalytic critique because it speaks for itself in terms of the Manichean racial drama of Martinique. The same could be said about René Maran (Jean

Veneuse in his 1947 novel). Veneuse is a neurotic whose wish for White love expresses a sadomasochistic desire. Fanon refers to a recently published work by the Swiss child psycho-analyst Germaine Guex, *The Abandonment Neurosis* (1950), to discuss Maran's Jean Veneuse who, in Fanon's view, is a clas-sic case, "nothing more or less than a [B]lack abandonment neurotic . . . [who] needs to be released from his infantile fan-tasies" (2008: 61). In this case, Veneuse is not "representative of the [B]lack-[W]hite experience" but "represents a certain way for a neurotic, *who happens to be [B]lack*" (2008: 62; my emphasis).

Since Fanon's approach is sociodiagnostic, he does not place this individual neurotic outside the social environment. While Veneuse might benefit from psychotherapy, it would be equally objective to extend "Veneuse's attitude," namely how his infantile fantasies are expressed through a desire for White love, "to the man of color in general" (2008: 62).

Both Capécia and Maran are playing out Fanon's answer to the question he posed in his introduction to *Black Skin, White Masks*: "What does the Black want?" To which Fanon answered: "To be White." Put in the racial, colorist, colonial context of Martinique and Saint-Louis, the position of the mulatto woman is simple. The goal is to Whiten the race and resist "slipping back."

Capécia's novel is set in a recent past that Fanon would remember well: the Pétainist naval occupation of Martinique under Admiral Robert. André, Capécia's lover, is a White officer who admires the admiral and soon becomes the chief of aviation on the Island. He lives with Capécia for two years, "following the manuals along the lines of Dr. Barot's *Guide pratique de l'Européen dans l'Afrique Occidentale* . . . 'a temporary union with a well-chosen native woman'" (Sharpley-Whiting 1998: 41). Although the mulatto woman's desire is to marry a White man, she knows all too well that "a colored woman is never quite respectable in the eyes of a [W]hite man – even if he loves her." Asking herself whether André is handsome or ugly, Capécia explains: "All I know is that he had blue eyes, blond hair, and a pale complexion and I loved him" (quoted in Fanon 2008: 25). For Fanon, she could have just said: "I loved him because he had blue eyes, blond hair, and a pale complexion."

Capécia's inferiority complex, Fanon's explains, is felt historically, economically, and spatially. From childhood, her desires were "turned toward Didier, the boulevard of Martinican dreams." Didier, she explains, is "the elegant section of Fort-de France, where the 'Martinican Békés' [descendants of European settlers]," live. Fanon agreed with Capécia's description of the racial economy. The "'Martinican Békés' ... were not pure [W]hite, but often very rich (it is accepted that one is [W]hite if one has a certain amount of money)" (quoted in 2008: 26) was translated in *Les Damnés de la terre* as: "you are rich because you are White, you are White because you are rich" (2004: 5). Capécia understands this. She doesn't want money but recognition of a bit of Whiteness. When her White lover, André, slips a ring on her finger, she responds angrily: "You treat me like a prostitute!" Later, when she finds money in her purse, she gets angry with André, telling him: "I do not sell my love and my services." What does Capécia want? "She asks for nothing," argues Fanon, "except for a little Whiteness in her life" (2008: 25).

In another example, Mactar, an educated Black man in Sadji's *Nini*, wants to marry a mulatto woman. Mactar has proposed to Nini, who, he says, "will radiate light to the darkest corners" and is "too civilized and refined to reject brutally this offer of love" (Fanon 2008: 37). Will she ignore the color of her lover? Absolutely not. Interracial love between a mulatto woman and a Black man was unacceptable in the colorist caste hierarchy of Saint-Louis. A few extracts from

*Nini* allows Fanon to discuss his delusion. Nini considers the proposal an insult, "an offence to her '[W]hite girl's honor'" and she will make him understand that "'[W]hite skins' are not for bougnouls."[10] Her decision is social not individual, one affecting the standing of "the entire mulatto caste" who want "not only to become [W]hite but also to avoid slipping back" (2008: 37). Outraged, the "mulatto caste" want him dismissed from the civil service for the "moral havoc he has inflicted" (2008: 38). How should such a "breach of principle be punished?" asks Fanon. The answer is obvious: "castration" (2008: 39). On the other hand, when there is a proposal of marriage by a [W]hite man to a mulatto woman, there is jubilation: "overnight the mulatto girl had gone from the rank of slave to that of master." She had become White. Her ability to become White by marrying a White man "meant that all the mulatto Ninis, Nanas, and Nenettes lived outside *the reality* of their country," as they become "obsessed with the dream of being wedded to a [W]hite man from Europe" (2008: 39). Deep down they "want to evolve," writes Fanon, and the same process can be seen whether it is Capécia or Nini. Fanon calls it an "affective erethism." In reaction to the woman of color's feeling of inferiority, she puts all her energy into gaining entrance to the White world (2008: 41).

Capécia and Veneuse have internalized European values and notions of civilization. For Capécia, that internalization is not intellectualized, and simply reflects the lived socioeconomic reality and color hierarchy experienced in everyday life. For her, blood lines and nearness to Whiteness do count. Finding out that she has a White grandmother gives her a new sense of self. The fact that her mother had "[W]hite blood" made her appear to Capécia "prettier than ever, more refined, more distinguished." Expressing the logic of her blancophilia and negrophobia, Capécia reflects what "every woman in Martinique knows." She asks: "If [her grandmother] had mar-

ried a [W]hite man, would I perhaps have been all [W]hite? . . .
Would life have been less difficult for me?" (quoted in Fanon
2008: 29). Capécia operates in a Manichean world of color:
White is good, Black is bad. Every judgment and every action
is mediated by this lived experience and its rationalization.

Fanon describes Capécia's novel as "delusional" and views
her negrophobia and desire for lactification as reflections of
Antillean society; "The crux of the problem" for her "is not to
slip back among the 'nègre' rabble" (2008: 30). His research
includes talking with young women from Martinique who are
students in France. They "confess in lily-white innocence that
they would never marry a [B]lack man" and make necessary
plans to avoid meeting them (2008: 30, 33). Capécia had also
moved to France and published a second book, *La Négresse
blanche*, which takes up her story. Living in France with her
son François (perhaps named for France) she remains ada-
mantly negrophobic: "I've never slept with a Black man," she
says; "I'm afraid of them" (1997: 162).[11]

In contrast to Capécia, in Maran's book Veneuse's internalization of White values is intellectualized. He was born
on a boat heading to Martinique, where he lived until the age
of seven. He was then abandoned by his middle-class parents
and sent to a boarding school in Bordeaux. He lived a solitary
life where his best friends were books (Fanon 2008: 46) and
becomes, in Germaine Guex's terms, "a prisoner of himself"
(quoted in Fanon 2008: 59). Later, serving "the motherland,"
he follows his father into the French colonial service. He is a
European who is Black and nothing like a nègre (2008: 46).
He is a colonial *évolué* now living in France, and has fallen
in love with a White woman, Andrée, the daughter of the
poet Louis Madelle. She loves Veneuse, but does she really?
He obsessively needs to be reminded, asking Andrée: "despite
my color, would you agree to marry me if I asked you?"
(2008: 58)

Fanon is as critical of Maran's book as he is of Capécia's. It is an "attempt to have any contact between the races depend on a constitutional morbidity" (2004: 61) that is constituted as the physiognomy of racial others. The racial social order constitutionally defined by innate and hereditary characteristics.

## "The So-Called Dependency Complex of the Colonized"

Octave Mannoni was a civil servant in Madagascar, working as director general of the information service before returning to liberated France in 1944 after almost 20 years. Back in France, he underwent analysis with Lacan before returning to Madagascar in 1947. His return coincided with the anticolonial revolt and resulted in the publication in 1950 of a major work on psychology and colonialism: *Psychologie de la colonisation* (*Prospero and Caliban: The Psychology of Colonization*). In the 1965 foreword to the book, Mannoni tells us that he had carried out a number of ethnographic studies before the war, but *Prospero and Caliban* presented a significant change in focus, reflecting a wish to get behind the ethnographic.

Fanon first came across Mannoni's work in articles published in the journal *Psyché* in 1947 and 1948.[12] Mannoni's attempt to develop a psychoanalytic explanation of the colonial situation seemed to jibe with Fanon's project. Mannoni states that the colonial "problem" is "one of the most urgent ... [in] the world today – and France in particular" and that "only psychology can explain how and why a colonial situation degenerates into error and illusion and this is precisely the job psychoanalysis should perform" (1990: 198).

Fanon might well have agreed with Mannoni, who wrote that "it is not really necessary for us to find a psychological explanation for the facts of colonization; what we need to know is why we perceive these facts in a distorted fashion" (1990: 198). Fanon might also have agreed that "this is precisely the job psychoanalysis should perform in the study of such situations. Psychologically, then, errors of perception in colonial matters may well be, as Jung suggests, the result of the projection on to the object of some defect which is properly attributable to the subject" (1990: 198). Fanon references Jung in a similar way in *Black Skin, White Masks* and might concur with Mannoni that Jung's "projection is not quite as he describes it . . . What we project on to the colonial inhabitant, in fact, is not our 'mental derangement,' but our most elementary and deeply-hidden fears and desires" (1990: 198). In addition, Fanon endorses "that part of Monsieur Mannoni's work which demonstrates that the [W]hite colonial is driven only by his desire to put an end to a feeling of dissatisfaction on the level of Adlerian overcompensation" (2008: 65) but he cannot abide Mannoni's insistence of a latent inferiority complex that antedates colonization. And while Fanon calls Mannoni intellectually honest, he qualifies it, "having experienced firsthand the ambivalence inherent in the colonial situation, [he] has managed to grasp the psychological phenomena – albeit, unfortunately, too exhaustively" warning, "we should not lose sight of reality" (2008: 64).

The first sentence of *Prospero and Caliban* invokes Alfred Adler, arguing that the "inferiority complex of the colored peoples . . . is no different from the inferiority complex pure and simple as described by Adler" (1990: 39). This is the basis of his psychology of colonization. In short, his argument is that, just as the colonizer overcompensates for an inferiority complex that is the result of feelings of abandonment, so the colonized, mired in a dependency complex, are also prone to feelings of abandonment. Fanon views this as an inversion that de-historicizes and essentializes the inferiority complex, which is a product of colonial domination. For Mannoni, on the other hand, colonialism is normal, a "natural" result of an inferiority complex of the colonized and a superiority complex of the colonizers. Rather than colonialism producing inferiority complexes, Mannoni argues that such a complex already existed and is being played out in relations between the colonizer and colonized rather than being produced by them. In other words, the whole system of colonization and racialization is abstracted from Mannoni's analysis. In response, Fanon called Chapter 4 "The So-Called [*prétendu*] Dependency Complex of the Colonized."

One crucial difference between Mannoni and Fanon is Fanon's argument that the colonized are made to feel inferior by colonial rule, whereas Mannoni argues that it is the Malagasy's dependent *being* that welcomes colonization. According to Mannoni, the colonizing Europeans take the place of the revered ancestors and the colonized are colonized because they are dependent. In fact, the colonized "unconsciously expected – even desired" such a development (1990: 86). Thus, the submissiveness of the Malagasy was inherent in their culture and redirected toward European colonizers:[13] "To my mind," argues Mannoni, "there is no doubting the fact that colonization has always required the existence of the need for dependence. Not all peoples can be colonized: only those who experience this need" (1990: 85). So it is in the colonies that each population realizes its allotted place, Prospero or Caliban. "As we have seen," Fanon sarcastically responds, "the [W]hite man is governed by a complex of authority, a complex of leadership, whereas the Malagasy is governed by a complex of dependency. Everyone is happy" (2008: 65).

For Mannoni, this dualism of inferiority and the dependency is also at the root of the 1947 rebellion, which he argues, was a result of the colonized fear of abandonment, and thus the solution is not political independence but rather a controlled process in which a newly enlightened colonial regime brings the Malagasy slowly toward independency. Such a solution can be engineered only by metropolitan France, he argues, "unquestionably one of the least racially minded countries in the world" (1990: 110).

Applying a classical psychological typology onto the Malagasy enables Mannoni to portray the Malagasy as the child of Europe. "The fact that when an adult Malagasy is isolated in a different environment he can become susceptible to the classical type of inferiority complex proves almost beyond doubt that *the germ of the complex was latent in him from childhood*" (1990: 40, quoted in Fanon 2008: 66; my emphasis). Thus, in a time of crisis, the Malagasy's main concern was "not to feel abandoned" (1990: 49).

Faced with colonization, the Malagasy, according to Mannoni, transfer their sense of dependence onto the colonizer, who become a type of father figure. But who are these colonizers? According to Mannoni, they are often abandoned by their parents and wish to overcome that abandonment by a superiority complex that can be expressed in their domination of the colonized. This, he says, is the "psychology of colonization."

While Fanon might have agreed with the deep connection Mannoni sees between racism and sexual guilt, he thinks Mannoni's linkage of "sexual excitement ... with violence and aggressiveness" (quoted in 2008: 143) is a "dangerous misunderstanding." General Gallieni's brutal "pacification" of Madagascar (after 10-years of anticolonial resistance at the turn of the twentieth century) included French soldiers taking young women as "temporary wives." Mannoni claims that these relations between colonial soldiers and their "temporary wives" were "healthy" and unmarred by complexes. The truth was, of course, quite different and the "pacification" of Malagasy resistance was a fruitful site for racialization to quickly develop. For Fanon the French soldiers had no respect for the young Malagasy women they slept with, and he adds a reference to colonial Algeria where he would shortly be living, "The fact that Algerian colonists sleep with fourteen-year-old housemaids in no way demonstrates a lack of racial conflicts in Algeria" (2008: 29n.5).

## The 1947 revolt

Mannoni's liberal colonialism, manifested in a project of slow decolonization, mirrored his psychological idea of dependency. Politically, the project was based on the revival of the village councils taken over by the French colonial administration in an attempt to avoid granting independence. Such a view of mixing the "traditional" and the "modern" was a typical colonial form of rule (the "indirect rule" of mapping colonial administration on top of traditional forms of rule perceived to be compliant) often restructured by colonial taxation and forced labor. Mannoni's liberal colonialism provided an important context for his psychology of colonization. In his view, the rebellion resulted from the authorities, loose talk about self-determination and the liberalization of colonial rule (including the end of forced labor). Ignoring what Malagasy nationalists were arguing, Mannoni searched for unconscious causes. For him, the feeling of abandonment provided an answer to why thousands of Malagasy would be willing to die for freedom. In line with inferiority/superiority complexes, these feelings, in his view, engendered a massive (childish) rage against the colonial system and a massive overreaction by the colonizers. In his penultimate chapter, "What is to be done?" Mannoni suggests that the solution to the problem lies in the proper education and the development of a new enlightened colonial administration.

At the end of World War II, laws forbidding political activities were relaxed and independence became radically articulated with many of the returning veterans becoming hardened nationalist militants in response to colonial intransigence. The French bombing of Sétif, Algeria, took place after a demonstration of 5,000 people celebrating the end of the war and demanding independence was attacked by the gendarmerie. On the Gold Coast (Ghana) a turning point was reached when three veterans were shot by colonial police after they tried to deliver a petition to the governor. In Madagascar, the armed insurrection began on March 29, 1947 after the Fourth Republic in France rejected calls for independence.

## The interpretation of dreams

Mannoni includes six dreams as an epilogue to the first part of *Prospero and Caliban*. He informs us that the dreams have come from different sources, "but in the main they have been collected in schools in the form of French homework" (1990: 91n.2). Even though he attached great importance to the choice of words, he was not concerned that the dream recollections were written in French, the students' second language.

Mannoni gives very little background to each dream, seeming to be content with symbolism, dominated by notions of protection and danger, associated with the mother and the more symbolically richer father: Mother = tree = security; Father = rifles/bull's horns = phallus = sexual danger = Senegalese troops = lack of protection. But what is particularly striking about these symbolic equivalences is his insistence that even though the dreams "were recorded at the time of public disturbance ... their authors had seen nothing of the disorders and knew nothing of the disorders" (1990: 89). Fanon, in contrast, considers the dreams had everything to do with the situation. His approach was to begin with manifest rather than latent dream content. We must put the dreams in their time, he insists, "and this time is the period during which eighty thousand natives were killed" (2008: 84).[14] What is central to Mannoni's dream analysis is the Malagasy's supposed need for routine and security, which is nothing but the routinization of colonial rule – namely, the pacification of Madagascar. Fanon characterizes Mannoni's psychology of colonialism as the need for the colonized to remain in place.

Dream symbolism allows Mannoni to quickly shift from the figure of the Senegalese soldier to the "deeper image of the father" (1990: 89) and typically views the soldier's rifle as phallic. In contrast, Fanon argues that the Senegalese soldier's rifle is not a penis, but a real rifle. And while he states that "Freud's discoveries are of no use to us whatsoever," what is as stake is less a dismissal of Freudian dream interpretations than Mannoni's a priori dream symbolism recorded during a bloody episode of colonial repression about which Mannoni makes no mention.

For Fanon, the massacre of 1947 is the determinant. The Senegalese soldier is not the smiling consumer of the Banania breakfast cereal, but part of the military intelligence terror machine. It is the reality of torture (and Senegalese soldiers were often used as torturers) that often haunt the dreams. France and Britain were signatories of the UN's Universal Declaration of Human Rights in 1948, which included a commitment to prevent genocide. This hypocrisy was no doubt on Fanon's mind with the slaughter of the Malagasy. In a long footnote, he informs readers of a testimony at a trial in Antananarivo (Tananarive). In the testimony, the accused, Rakotovao, spoke of torture including repeated waterboarding and beatings by Senegalese soldiers at police headquarters. In the trial testimony, we are informed that a Monsieur Baron (one of the interrogators) told the accused that he was being sent to a room "where you can think." A Senegalese soldier was ordered to waterboard him to teach him "to accept what I have just asked." "When one read such things," Fanon concludes, "it certainly seems that M. Mannoni allowed one aspect of the phenomena that he analyzes to escape him: the Black bull and the Black men are neither more nor less than the Senegalese in the criminal investigation department" (2008: 85n.30).

Fanon's critique of Mannoni's a priori dependency continues his work on "The 'North African Syndrome" a syndrome based on the idea that "the North African is a-man-who-doesn't-like work" (Fanon: 1967: 6) and a French medical staff who have an "a priori attitude." The patient is fixed within narrow diagnostic categories, even if this is informed by a so-called sociocultural approach. It is, to use the language of *Black Skin, White Masks*, a cultural imposition based on the idea of Europe as the pinnacle of civilization. This is also reflected in the Algiers school of psychiatry, whose *Alphabetic Manual of Psychiatry* was published in 1952 and repeated familiar concepts – "primitive mentality," "lack of intellectual curiosity," "criminal impulsiveness," "not infrequently bestiality" – as characteristics of the Arab. Such terms were typical across colonial psychiatry (see Gibson and Beneduce 2017: 95–119). J.C. Carothers, a psychiatrist at Mathari Hospital in Nairobi, Kenya, whom the World Health Organization considered "the most internationally renowned ethnopsychiatrist with clinical experience at the time" (Gibson and Beneduce 2017: 103), wrote a British Government paper on the so-called Mau Mau revolt in 1954 arguing, similarly to Mannoni, that the roots of the revolt were based on an envy of White power, with Africans showing no gratitude for the colonial civilizing mission. Revolt, in other words, was a symptom of the organic-psychological failings of the colonized.

Whether it was Mannoni or Porot and Carothers, these hegemonic ideas were predicated on notions of racial inferiority; that the Algerian, Kenyan, and Malagasy were quite simply at a lower stage of psychological development and rebellion could be automatically connected with the failings of the colonized, and not to the actions of the colonizers. When Mannoni tells his readers that the Malagasy should accept and "remain in the place assigned to you," Fanon disagrees (2008: 198).

## "The Lived Experience of the Black"

Chapter 5, "The Lived Experience of the Black," has been the most widely discussed chapter of *Black Skin, White Masks*. It was first published as a stand-alone article in a volume of *Esprit* in May 1951, in which it was titled "La Plainte du Noir" (the complaint or lament of the Black). Fanon says that the Black in this chapter has nothing in common with those whose desires and actions are directed toward becoming White.

The chapter begins with Fanon recounting his experience of objectification on a train. He had been thinking his own thoughts when suddenly he is frozen by the White child's words that disrupt his self-image and certainty in space: "Look, un nègre!" Having come "into this world anxious to uncover the meaning of things," he is immediately objectified and denied the freedom of a being in motion, locked into a "suffocating reification" (2008: 89). "Sale [dirty] nègre!":' these opening words of the chapter mirror the title of the famous poem by Haitian communist negritude poet and novelist Jacques Roumain, with its reference to "les damnés de la terre." The child points at Fanon, calling to their mother, "I'm scared"' (2008: 91). Fanon is a phobic object.

Fanon begins the chapter as an "I" and soon finds out that there is no "I" or "we"; rather, he is a thing among other things. This is the "fact of Blackness" or "the lived experience of the Black" (the first is Markmann's 1967 translation, the second the literal translation of the chapter title).[15] The movement of the chapter reflects Fanon's critical mind in motion, intimately connected with his bodily experience where being seen as Black is the determinant, fixing and walling him in.

Fanon insists that a definitive structuring of self and the world "creates a genuine dialectic between my body and the world" (2008: 91). The White racial gaze subverts this dialectic, carrying an imposition that makes it difficult for racialized people to elaborate their "body schema" because "all around the body reigns an atmosphere of certain uncertainty" (2008: 90, 92). Rather than construction of the self "as a body in a spatial and temporal world," a schema is imposed, a "historical-racial schema," where the body schema gives way to "an epidermal-racial-schema" a racialized skin (2008: 91): "My [B]lackness, my ethnic features; deafened by cannibalism, backwardness, fetishism, racial stigmas, slave traders, and above all, yes, above all, the grinning *Y'a bon Banania*" (2008: 92).

Fanon begins the chapter stating that he came into the world seeking recognition, which connects with his critique of Hegel's master/slave dialectic, which he discusses in a later chapter.[16] With Hegel, the struggle results from the desire of independent self-consciousnesses to gain recognition from the other. In Fanon's analysis this ground is closed off, making "any ontology . . . impossible in a colonized and acculturated society." Thus, he agrees with Césaire's response to acculturation, or what we might consider the rhetoric of the post-racial with its assumed but unrealized equalities: "Accommodate me. l am not accommodating you!" (1995: 101). As Fanon put it, since it ignores lived experience, "ontology does not allow us to understand the being of the Black."

Fanon's reflections on and conceptualizations of the Black's lived experience begin as soon as they become aware of the

White gaze. Discussing Sartre's *Anti-Semite and the Jew*, he finds an analogy with Sartre's idea that the anti-Semite makes the Jew, and praises Sartre's writing as "some of the finest we have ever read . . . because the problem they raise moves us to the very core" (2008: 154).[17]

Unlike the Jew, however, "I'm not given a second chance." Overdetermined from the outside, he can't escape. "I am a slave not to the 'idea' others have of me, *but to my appearance*." Fanon crawls along learning to "arrive slowly in the world . . . The [W]hite gaze, the only valid one, is already dissecting me. I am fixed" (2008: 95). "I slip into corners," Fanon continues, "I was walled in . . . I was hated" (2008: 95–7).

In a society where Blackness is a source of fear, and Whiteness is the measure of "civilization," it is not surprising that Whitening becomes the ego ideal: "Don't pay attention to him, Monsieur," the White mother says to Fanon of her child. "He doesn't realize that you're just as civilized as we are" (2008: 93). But what the child expresses is the social truth. Fanon is Black and wherever he goes he is already marked. His "logical" response is reasonable, reason is his only weapon, and he resolved to defend himself. "Like all good tacticians," he remarks, "I wanted to rationalize the world and show the [W]hites they were mistaken" (2008: 98). It seemed like a good tactic but *reality* made it impossible. He is up against something irrational. He had tried to go unnoticed, but everywhere he went the White world was waiting for him reminding him he was Black. White liberals told him that they were "fans of Black people" while warning their friends to be careful what they say: "he's very touchy" (2008: 96). Before opening his mouth, the racial schema is expressed. When he walked into a room, reason walked out. While "everyone was in agreement with the notion: the nègre is a human being," when it came to sexual relations "the [W]hite man remained uncompromising. Under no condition did he want any intimacy between the races" (2008: 99).

Objectification and reification, internalized from a young age, are often expressed in the destructuring of the body, where self-loathing and self-deception are constantly present. Fanon thus describes himself as a constantly questioning body with long antennae (2008: 96). "If I had to define myself," he adds, "I would say I am in expectation; I am investigating my surroundings; I am interpreting everything on the basis of my findings. I have become a sensor" (2008: 99). Having been denied recognition, there was only one answer: "to make myself known" (2008: 95).

Confronted by what Fanon calls "affective ankylosis" and "affective tetanization" as the effects of anti-Black racism on the body schema (ankylosis is a medical term for abnormal stiffening and tetanization for contraction), "I made up my mind to shout out my Blackness." Taking himself as the subject of the questioning body, and underscoring how the work of questioning comes from critical self-reflection on lived experience, the "certain uncertainty" means questioning everything, even norms that he didn't actually question. It is this that gives "The Lived Experience of the Black" an aliveness as new generations confront him with new questions about reification, objectification, and identity.

In making himself known, Fanon secretes a race "under the weight of one basic element. Rhythm." Of course, he had already read Césaire's *Notebook*, as well as articles in *Présence Africaine*, Léopold Senghor's *Anthologie de la nouvelle poésie Nègre et Malgache de langue Française* (*Anthology of New Black and Malagasy Poetry in French*, published in 1948), and other negritude writers. Although he makes more references to Césaire at a later date, saying "we would like a lot of Black intellectuals to get their inspiration from him," (2008: 164), he doesn't especially single him out here. Rather, he argues that since his attempt to reason with the world was rejected, he "resorted to irrationality" (2008: 103). As he puts it in *L'An V de la révolution algérienne*, "the White creates le nègre, but it is le nègre who creates negritude" (1965: 47, 2011: 284). And this creation means embracing and working through the contradictions including Senghor's statement, "Emotion is nègre as reason is Greek" (2008: 106). Here he lets it stand without comment. Whatever his questions (see 2004: 105–6), he realized that he had no choice but to commit to it all. Logically, he delves deeper, discovering Black civilizations, city-states, universities, architects, and empires, and he quotes from Césaire's introduction to Schoelcher's *Esclavage et colonisation* (*Slavery and Colonization*): "The [W]hite man was wrong . . . I was not a primitive or a subhuman; I belonged to a race that had already been working silver and gold 2,000 years ago" (2008: 109).

It is negritude, as negation and as creation, that moves him. Césaire, he says, had "agreed to see what was happening at the very bottom," explaining that he had prepared us with his *Notebook of a Return to My Native Land*, choosing "the upward psyche" (Fanon 2008: 172). We have already discussed how important Césaire's poem was to the younger Fanon, who knew it off by heart, and it remains important in *Black Skin, White Masks*, where he later excerpts the final two pages of the poem, heralding movement and self-movement:

Embrace . . .
Our multicolored purities
And bind me, bind me without remorse
Bind me . . . bitter brotherhood . . .
Rise, Dove
Rise
Rise
Rise
I follow you, imprinted on my ancestral white cornea

Rise sky-licker
And the great black hole where I wanted to drown a moon
    ago
This is now where I want to fish the night's malevolent
    tongue in its immobile revolution.
                                        (Quoted in 2008: 172–3).

But then, no sooner had Fanon tried to claim negritude, "they snatched it away from me" (2008: 111). Who and what did this? It was Sartre – a friend, he says, who had undermined him. How could this be?

Sartre had written an important 50-page introduction to Léopold Senghor's anthology, which he called "Orphée noir." It represented a serious attempt to engage negritude as a radical political-aesthetic movement. In it, Sartre shares a great appreciation for Césaire as a revolutionary poet, considering the movement in his negritude as a "becoming" (1965: 57). It has its basis in a specific historical situation based in a "sense of revolt and love of liberty," declares Sartre (1965: 57). But after this there is something much "more serious," as Fanon notes:

> Negritude appears as the weak stage of a dialectical progression: the theoretical and practical affirmation of [W]hite supremacy is the thesis; the position of Negritude as antithetical value is the moment of negativity. But this negative moment is not sufficient in itself and the [B]lacks who employ it well know it; they know that it serves to pave the way for the synthesis or the realization of the human society without race. Thus Negritude is dedicated to its own destruction, it is transition and not result, a means and not the ultimate goal. (2008: 112–13)

Fanon's critique of Sartre leads us back to his conception of the dialectic of Black consciousness based on reflexive lived experience. Sartre's idea of "historical destiny," Fanon argues, has destroyed "Black impulsiveness" (2008: 112). "Consciousness committed to experience," Fanon was reminding Sartre, "has to know nothing of the essence and determination of being" (2008: 113). Rather than being allowed to lose himself in negritude and find his own critical attitude to it, the script was already written.

Fanon's critique also highlights the external and mechanical character of Sartre's dialectic, Fanon reminds him that consciousness had to learn for itself and not be told beforehand:

> I did not create a meaning for myself; the meaning was already there, waiting. It is not as the wretched nègre, it is not with my nègre's teeth, it is not as the hungry nègre that I fashion a torch to set the world alight; the torch was already there, waiting for this historic chance. In terms of consciousness, [B]lack consciousness claims to be an absolute density, full of itself. (2008: 113)

Fanon thereby sees Sartre's position as that of a patronizing school teacher telling him: "You'll change, my boy; I was like that too when I was young . . . You'll see, you'll get over it" (2008: 114). Sartre allows Black self-organization only for a moment, the moment of "anti-racist racism" waiting for the "objectivity" of the proletariat to enter the scene (see Sartre 1976: 18–19). For Fanon, Black consciousness is a subjectivity that has become an objective "in itself" (2008: 114). Thus, Sartre already had a conclusion waiting – class universalism – without thinking through how the wealth of Black consciousness fundamentally gives content to and changes the form of universalism.

Through different negritude poems, Fanon explains that Black experience is ambiguous, but Sartre kept reminding him that negritude was "nothing but a weak stage," forgetting, Fanon sums up, "the Black suffers in their body quite differently from the White" (2008: 116).[18] The suffering Fanon describes is total. He speaks of being bombarded from all sides, hemmed in, fixed, fragmented, and being locked into thinghood. "Where do I fit in?" he asks, adding: "Where should I hide?" (see 2008: 93). Reified, he explodes and has to construct "another me." And Sartre is denying "another me," that is to say, one who can make their own experiences and fashion their own life.

While Fanon "didn't want to know" what Sartre was telling him, he now knew and that knowledge was shattering: "My shoulders slipping from this world, and my feet no longer felt the caress of the ground. Without a [B]lack past, without a [B]lack future, it was impossible for me to live my [B]lackness. Not yet [W]hite, no longer completely Black, I was damned" (2008: 117).

So rather than simply coming around to "Sartre's way of thinking," as some critics argue, Fanon ends the chapter full of anguish. Taking examples from Chester Himes's *If He Hollers Let Him Go* and films like the award-winning *Home of the Brave*, which was released in France as *Je suis un nègre* (Briefel 2015: 152), Fanon says that, for Blacks, there seems to be no exit. "I can't go to the movies without encountering myself," he reminds us and reacts to the soldier in *Home of the Brave* who "tells my brother," "Resign yourself to your color the way I got used to my stump; we're both victims" (see 2008: 119).[19] Fanon had begun his chapter reaching out to the world and experiencing a rejection from the White world that had "amputated my enthusiasm" (2008: 94). At the end of the chapter, he rejects the "cultural pluralist" message of the film with its message that the US is no home of the brave reinventing the dialogue of the "Black soldier "in a moment of critical creativity" (Garcia: 2006: 56), refusing "with all my being to accept this amputation" (2008: 119).

Fanon ends the chapter weeping, yet his anguish takes many shapes and does not end in passivity, which is why he refers to Richard Wright's *Native Son*, which, Lou Turner argues, "made Fanon aware" that for Whites to understand Blacks "a revolution must occur in *their own* lives" (2008: 156). Throughout *Black Skin, White Masks*, Fanon unites the phenomenological and the psychoanalytic with the necessity of personal enlightenment and social action. To feel means that "once [the Black] has discovered the White man in himself, he kills him" (2008: 174).

## "The Black Man and Psychopathology"

At the beginning of Chapter 6, "The Black and Psychopathology," Fanon tells us that an in-depth study ought to be conducted along two lines: a "psychoanalytic interpretation of the [B]lack lived experience" and "a psychoanalytic interpretation of the [B]lack myth." But because "the facts are much more complicated . . . reality prevents us from doing so" (2008: 129). Later, he argues that "to understand the racial situation psychoanalytically, not from a universal viewpoint, but as it is experienced by individual consciousnesses, considerable importance must be given to sexual phenomena" (2008: 138). For Fanon, these individual experiences and complexes reflect real material and social conditions. Thus, he immediately adds to Freud's emphasis on the family and what might be considered the interior and private world of the necessity of a sociodiagnosis. It is this that continues to make the work timely, namely, ways in which a host of information and propositions "slowly and stealthily" work their way into popular media – "books, newspapers, school texts, advertisements, movies, and radio" – shaping the community's vision of the world (2008: 130–1). For Fanon, mass culture like Tarzan and Mickey Mouse are written by "White men for White children" and he adds: "We would like nothing better than to create magazines and songs ... and special history books ... especially designed for Black children" (2008: 127). This battle is ongoing in schools as well as in popular media.

As we have seen, to Freud's body-ego[20] Fanon adds the epidermal schema, a social construction continually woven out of thousands of myths and anecdotes. For Fanon, the importance of the sociogenic emphasizes the colonial and racist social structure that forms the Black person's experience and social relationships. Thus, he argues, "we preferred to call this chapter 'The Black Man and Psychopathology'" emphasizing not a psychoanalysis of the Black man but rather an analysis of the pathologization of the Black man. Freudian analysis plays an important framing role in the image of the Black man as a fantastic biological sexual power, and one could conclude from Fanon's analysis that European (White) sexual fantasy is organized around racism and negrophobia.

The unconscious image of the Black as evil and sexual becomes the subject of the chapter, and Fanon keeps returning to how it plays out in reality, wondering whether Freud, Jung, and Lacan help us understand this. His answer is both yes and no, and thus throughout the book he keeps on coming up against dead ends, sure that the whole rotten social structure needs shaking up and aware that the liberation of the Black's mind and the clarification of thinking is absolutely essential to any project of disalienation.

Chapter 6 is perhaps the most controversial one in Fanon's book; even though every chapter is difficult in its own way, this one is especially difficult for those without a background in Freudian theory. The only direct quote from Freud (2008: 122–3) comes from the first and second lectures of his 1909 *Five Lectures on Psychoanalysis*,[21] where Fanon argues that "we too often forget that neurosis is not a basic component of human reality" (2008: 130).[22] Fanon returns to Freud, asking: "Has the young [B]lack child seen his father beaten or lynched by the [W]hite man? Has there been a real traumatism? To all these questions our answer is no. So where do we go from here?" (2008: 124). If for (the 1895) Freud, "there is determined Erlebnis at the origin of every neurosis" – even if the "first trauma [is] ... expelled from the consciousness and memory of the patient" (Freud quoted in Fanon 2008: 123) – then the event for the Black is "the traumatic contact with the [W]hite" (2008: 164).[23]

An honest answer to the question of a real traumatism would have to call on the notion of "collective catharsis," by which Fanon means "an outlet whereby the energy accumulated in the form of aggressiveness can be released" (2008: 124). In the early 1950s, examples of these "outlets" were found in popular culture, such as stories, comics, and films.[24] Fanon gives examples from Tarzan and Disney, where "the Devil, the Wicked Genie, Evil, and the Savage" are always represented by Blacks or American Indians. Since they always identify with the good guys, the Black child, just like the White child, becomes an explorer, an adventurer, and a missionary "who is in danger of being eaten by the wicked nègres" (2008: 124–5). In the Antilles, the young Antillean identifies with "the civilizing colonizer, the [W]hite man" and bringer of "lily-white truth" (2008: 126). Subjectively, the Black child adopts a White attitude and "gradually, an attitude, a way of thinking and seeing that is basically [W]hite, forms and crystallizes in the young Antillean. Whenever they read stories of savages in their [W]hite schoolbook they always think of the Senegalese," and, writing about what they will do in the summer holidays, "they reply like genuine little Parisians" (2008: 140n.25). The fact is, Fanon concludes, Antilleans do not see themselves as Black. "The nègres live in Africa. Subjectively and intellectually the Antillean behaves like a [*W*]*hite*." On home ground, the Antillean child is French and "life follows more or less the same course as that of the White child" (2008: 127), but once they get to Europe "the real White man" (2008: 169) is waiting, and when they hear Europeans talk about *les nègres* they will immediately "know they're talking about Antilleans as well as the Senegalese." Psychoanalytically, this is discussed in a long footnote on Lacan's "mirror stage."

In the Antilles, Fanon argues, the Antillean child's mirror image is always neutral, the imago of the self and other is perceived in White terms. The mirror does not give the Antillean child an image (however fantastical) of the unified self, but a delusional one of Whiteness as the child gradually assimilates the prejudices, folklore, and myths from Europe. Thus, Fanon finds Jung's collective unconscious suggestive if it can be considered "the repository of the trace effects of a specific culture and history" (Cherki 2006: 121)[25] rather than the "primitive" and "uncivilized" that Jung claimed to have found in the collective unconscious of the Pueblo Indians and Kenyans. The idea of the primitive savage and the bad nègre, as part of the collective unconscious, is cultural and acquired. "Beautiful Black child," Fanon adds, are adjectives that "literally don't go together" because "the color Black symbolizes evil, sin . . . shameful feeling, base instincts" (2008: 167). Thus, in Jung's terms, the animus of the Antillean is White. But this cultural imposition is unknowingly created: "I am a [B]lack man – but naturally I don't know it, because I am one. At home my mother sings to me, in French, French love songs where there is never a mention of [B]lack people. Whenever I am naughty or when I make too much noise, I am told to 'stop acting like un nègre'" (2008: 168).

For Fanon to understand the pathologization of the Black man psychoanalytically meant understanding the racial-fetishistic character of "how quickly we switch from 'handsome young [B]lack man' to 'young colt or stud'" (2008:

145) in the film *Mourning Becomes Electra*. As we shall see, a remarkable sexual power is attributed to the Black man, which is represented repeatedly in the exoticization and fetishization of Black bodies. And yet, at the same time, we need to keep in mind when this work was written.[26] To talk about the Black man as a phobogenic object, the Black man as purely biological, the Black man as an object creating fear, and reducing the Black man to an object of sexual power in 1952, is to immediately remind us of the torture and lynching of the 14-year-old Chicagoan Emmett Till in 1955, accused of whistling at a White woman while visiting family in Mississippi.

While Fanon disagrees with Lacan and Freud about the universality of the Oedipus complex, he does not question the applicability of the complex to Europe. In other words, looking at his discussion of Br'er Rabbit and the stories of Uncle Remus (stories that were made into Disney films), Fanon quotes extensively from the writer and critic Bernard Wolfe, whose Freudian analysis, "Uncle Remus and the Malevolent Rabbit" was published in *Les Temps Modernes* in 1949. There is fear and admiration in the White child's attraction to Br'er Rabbit, and "in order to protect him from unconscious masochism," argues Fanon, the White author had to remove aggressiveness from these stories. What is this unconscious masochism? In Freudian terms, it is the interiorization of the guilt of sadistic pleasure projected onto the Black, a "Christian and democratic guilt," argues Wolfe (quoted in Fanon 2008: 152). Searching for the "Black man's love," he found it in Remus's grin, writes Wolfe, while all the time "searching for his hatred of the [B]lack man (Bre'r Rabbit) and reveled in it in an orgy of unconscious masochism" (quoted in Fanon 2008: 153). Fanon offers another solution: "First of all sadistic aggressiveness toward the [B]lack man, then a guilt complex because of the sanction by the democratic culture of the country in question that weighs heavily against such behavior. Such aggressiveness is suffered by the [B]lack man, hence masochism." While the answer might appear false because there are no "signs of conventional masochism," Fanon argues, "the situation is not conventional. In any case, it's the only way to explain the masochistic behavior of the [W]hite man" (2008: 155). The unconscious masochism, the pleasure of suffering, is in response to the sadistic (and erotically sadistic) punishment of the Black man. Violating the White liberal notions of civilization and democracy produces guilt. So the democratic culture of the US operates as a kind of super-ego on the sadistic aggressiveness toward the Black man producing guilt in the White. But (and this is essential) the White's desire to hurt the Black is, in fact, not impeded, indicating how the goals of American democracy are impossible (Musser 2014: 47). Because racism is objective and structural, "democratic guilt" does not impede it. On the other hand, democratic guilt puts Blacks in demand as books on racism "become best sellers" (2008: 153).

Engaging the dialectic of Freud's *Civilization and Its Discontents*, the cost of which Freud says is sexual repression, Fanon adds, "the civilized [W]hite man retains an irrational nostalgia for the extraordinary times of sexual licentiousness orgies, unpunished rapes, and unrepressed incest. In a sense, these fantasies correspond to Freud's life instinct" (2008: 143). And importantly, projecting "these desires onto the [B]lack man," Whites behave "as if the [B]lack man actually had them" (2004: 143). One cannot have a hard-on everywhere, but that is precisely what is projected onto the Black man. The projection provides an answer to the question: Can the White behave in a sane manner toward the Black? The answer is no because wherever they go the Black symbolizes "the biological" (2008: 146, 150).[27] This cultural imposition, Fanon argues, also accounts for the White woman's negrophobia, a fear combined with sexual revulsion and fantasy that they might do "immoral and shameful things" to her (2008: 134). Contact alone, Fanon says, is enough to arouse anxiety expressing an ambivalence of fear and desire (2004: 134).

This leads us to one of the most controversial sections of the chapter involving Fanon's discussion of Helene Deutsch and Marie Bonaparte, whose recent books, *The Psychology of Women* and *Female Sexuality*, Fanon says, "followed up and in a way carried to their ultimate conclusion the ideas of Freud on female sexuality" (2004: 155). Freud's idea of the unconscious as a psychic agency with its own means of repression (primary process[28]) is entertained by Fanon in terms of fantasy and phobia. Wondering about "certain failures or certain fixations," Fanon presents Deutsch's and Bonaparte's strictly Freudian view to investigate and offer an explanation of the fantasy, "'A [B]lack man is raping me,'" from, he adds, "a heuristic point of view, *without basing it on reality*" (2008: 155; my emphasis).[29] It is important to recall, argues Diana Fuss:

> that Fanon constructs his reading of this particular fantasy during a period when fabricated charges of rape were used as powerful colonial instruments of fear and intimidation against [B]lack men. Fanon's deeply troubling comments on [W]hite women and rape are formulated within a historical context in which the phobically charged stereotype of the violent, lawless, and oversexed nègre puts all [B]lack men at perpetual risk. What we might call Fanon's myth of [W]hite women's rape fantasies is offered as a counternarrative to "the myth of the [B]lack rapist." (1999: 311)

In Freud's essay "A Child Is Being Beaten" fantasy plays a role as organizer of experience. The fantasy, argued Freud, has feelings of pleasure attached to it and is thus often reproduced. It can become an obsession, which is not easily confessed because of the association with shame and guilt. In

"A Child Is Being Beaten" the first fantasies are entertained early in life before school age. Then, at school, seeing other children beaten by a teacher, the experience is called back. At a later age, culture helps produce a wealth of fantasies and auto-erotic satisfaction. Who is the child being beaten? asks Freud. The one indulging the fantasy or the one watching? An enquiry of the gender of the child, says Freud, brought little success. And, it was difficult to describe the fantasy as sadistic or masochistic. Freud suggests that competition and resentment fuel the first phase of the fantasy: the pleasure is connected to the father beating a rival child who is hated. It is an Oedipal expression.[30]

The child views the father beating a rival whom the viewer hates. But this elemental sadism expressed in looking is repressed. There is guilt, but also fantasy and masochism, and also something else: the sadistic pleasure in the threat of dismemberment of the accused. Fanon explains:

The little girl sees her father, a libidinal aggressive, beat a rival sibling. The father, now the focus of her libido, refuses in a way to assume the aggressiveness that at this stage (between the ages of five and nine) the girl's unconscious demands of him. At this point, this unfounded, liberated aggressiveness is seeking a cathexis. Since the girl is at the age when children plunge into their culture's stories and legends, the [B]lack man becomes the predestined depository of this aggressiveness. If we penetrate the labyrinth farther, we discover that when a woman lives the fantasy of rape by a [B]lack man it is a kind of fulfilment of a personal dream or an intimate wish. (2004: 156)

But, adds Amber Musser, "the fantasy is not about a fear of the [B]lack man but about the [W]hite woman's subconscious desire to hurt herself" (2014: 48). It is a kind of fulfillment of an intimate wish based in a "cultural treasure house of images concerning [B]lackness" (Doane 1991: 221). The fantasy is being destructed, argues Fanon – "I want the [B]lack man to rip me open as I would do to a woman" – and it is also a kind of intimate wish represented by the culture's stories (in "A Child Is Being Beaten," Freud had mentioned the beating scenes in *Uncle Tom's Cabin*) and legends where the "[B]lack man becomes the predetermined depository of this aggressiveness" (2008: 156).[31] The woman "wishes violence on her body" and the Black man's sexual power "offers the possibility," argues Musser. But, she adds, le nègre "does not serve as a superego for the woman" (2014: 48, 49). Rather, emphasizing Fanon's sociodiagnosis, White society is the superego and this needs to be kept at the forefront of whoever says rape says Black man.[32]

The fear of the [B]lack man is connected with the fantasy of doing immoral and shameful things connected with the double-Oedipus complex. For Fanon, we have to keep in mind that phobia is understood from the standpoint of the imago and the fantasy. The imago of the Black man is a phallus, a tremendously powerful biological force. This leads us to the second problematic. "And from this standpoint the negrophobic woman is in reality merely a presumed sexual partner," he argues, "just as the negrophobic man is a repressed homosexual" (2008: 135). To understand this, let's remember what the Black man is here. A fantasy, a biological object among other objects. Fanon takes a long excerpt from Michel Cournot about the enormous size of a Black man's penis.[33] And suggests that if "we read this passage a dozen times" (2008: 147), the Black man is occulted. He is turned into a penis so large and powerful that the man has become invisible. A sex worker Fanon had spoken to about the fantasy of sex with a Black man told him a story of a woman who went mad after having sex with a Black man. The idea sent the sex worker searching for a Black man. In reality the "delirium of orgasm escaped her" (Fanon 2008: 149). The fantasy was, of course, much more powerful.

In the fantasy discussed earlier, the White woman takes over the Black man's imagined sexual power and imagines herself in control of that biological thing "with violent, carnal desires, which she then imagines being turned on herself and importantly also turned on another woman" (Musser 2014: 48). Thus the woman's imagined punishment of another woman operates at the hands of the Black man, or, more literally in Cournot's terms, the enormous penis. In her fantasy, the Black man thus becomes a puppet of her psyche, mediating White society's patriarchy reflected in its culture and legends. Which is to say that the fantasy articulates the patriarchal White master's phobia of the White woman being violated by the appearance of a Black man. The White father has not been replaced by the Black man; rather, it is the White man's fear of lost virility that is symbolized by the Black man "at the intangible gate leading to the real of mystic rites and orgies, bacchanals and hallucinating sexual sensations" (2008: 154).

Fanon is critical of the universality of the Oedipus complex, but rather than following his "subversion" of the Oedipus complex (Thomas 2007: 87), he has what Lewis Gordon calls a "manhood project" in his shockingly orthodox heteronormative attitudes, which can be seen when he writes: "I have a confession to make: I could never bear hearing a man say of another man 'How sensual he is!' without feeling nauseated. I don't know what the sensuality of a man is" (2008: 178). What accounts for this regression to hegemonic European and colonizing sexualities? The context is Michel Salomon's piece "D'un juif à des nègres," published in *Presence Africaine* in 1948. Fanon quotes him writing of the "aura of sensuality" that the Black man "exudes" through hair and skin, as well as the "extraordinary stamina of the Black man" (quoted in Fanon

2004: 177–8). Fanon asks Salomon how many nights have you "been subjected to the image of the biological-sexual-sensual-genital nègre"? Fanon's anger "conveys an affect (revulsion, dégout, nausée),"[34] argues Teresa de Lauretis (2002: 62–3), terms that he had used earlier when discussing phobia.[35] This is the context for Fanon to announce his heterosexuality, telling the dermatologist Michel Salomon, who had approached racial epidermalization dermatologically, in hyper-sensual terms, that his skin and hair are not "permanent sources of sexual heat" always available in the White's fantasy life.

## The failure of reciprocity and the adventures of the dialectic

> Dialectics, at all cost, got the upper hand and we have been forced to see that the Antillean is above all [B]lack.
>
> Fanon, *Black Skin, White Masks*

The ideas of recognition, pseudo-recognition, and non-recognition are important throughout *Black Skin, White Masks* and continue to be important concepts throughout Fanon's clinical and political work. Chapter 7, "The Black and Recognition," is divided into two sections. The second considers the Black and Hegel, which we will consider in greater depth; the first is about the Black and Adler. Alfred Adler was the first to theorize inferiority as a "complex," which had already been discussed in Fanon's critique of Mannoni. Adler was the founder of "individual psychology," which had a holistic view of the individual emphasizing social contexts including institutional and social relationships. Adler developed the idea of compensation and overcompensation as responses to inferiority and superiority complexes that emerge out of an individual's navigation in the family and in the social world, including an emphasis on the social origin of pathologies and neuroses. For Adler, everyone has a feeling of inferiority; it becomes a pathology when it becomes an overriding feeling with neurotic symptoms traced to overcompensation for this feeling of inferiority. Unlike Freud and Jung, Adler was a socialist. He was critical of bourgeois Viennese society; he wanted to widen the frame of the individual's psychic development to include a community perspective, which, says Hussein Bulhan, "comes closest to Fanon's psychological perspective" (1985: 77). Fanon's opinion that "the White man behaves toward the Black man, like an older brother reacting to the birth of a younger sibling" (2008: 135) is classically Adlerian.

Fanon employs an Adlerian approach to see how it works in Martinique. Here, Fanon says, echoing Adler, there is a constant comparison going on between young people meeting on the Fort-de-France streets. Taking us back to the judgments being made at La Savane, Fort-de-France's central park, in his chapter on language, the *comparaison* is now taking place on its adjoining streets, rue Schoelcher and rue Victor Hugo: "The question is always whether he is less intelligent than I, [B]lacker than I, or less good than I," Fanon sums up. "The Antillean ... is always dependent on the presence of 'the Other' ... [and] does not possess a personal value of their own" (2008: 186).

But rather than an Adlerian scenario, Fanon suggests the real difference is that the ego-ideal is mediated by an "invisible" third term (Whiteness). He calls this "*comparaison*," a creolism he uses "in the sense that the Black is continually pre-occupied with self-assertion and the ego ideal" (2008: 186), often through jokes, mockery, and banter. One can see it in action taking a walk down the streets of Fort-de-France as an Antillean meets a friend they have not seen for a number of years: "The inferiorized" wants to enhance their standing, and the other wants to remain superior. What is the origin of this narcissistic hunger for "reassurance" (2008: 187) which seems to be on familiar Adlerian ground? Fanon answers: "Adler created ... a psychology of the individual," but "the feeling of inferiority is Antillean" is social. Fanon makes it clear here that the sociogenic is *the* determinant: "If we apply in strict terms the findings of the Adlerian school, we would say that the Black endeavors to protest against the inferiority they feel historically" and socially (2008: 188). We are back to Césaire's quote, which opened *Black Skin, White Masks*; the inferiority complex is instilled by colonialism and the focus necessarily must shift "from the from the individual to the social structure" (Fanon 2008: 188).

If the Antillean is neurotic, it can only be understood because the social structure itself is neurotic. Antillean society is a neurotic society where the Black is inferior and thus "attempts to react with a superiority complex" (2008: 188). While this could be understood from the Adlerian "perspective of overcompensation," the connection with Adlerian psychology is superficial and obscures the larger structural problem: in school programs, "they desperately try to make a [W]hite man out of a [B]lack man. In the end they give up and tell him you have undeniably a dependency complex regarding the [W]hite man" (2008: 191). If Adler's idea of the inferiority/superiority complex and comparison is connected to self-assertion and the ego ideal, the Antillean inferiority/superiority complex is, Fanon argues, "topped by a third term," the White. This is the dividing line. It does not mean the Antillean compares themselves to Whites; rather, they compare themselves to their "own counterpart *under* the patronage of the [W]hite man" (2008: 190; my emphasis).[36]

Fanon's perspective is straightforward: "If there is a flaw, it lies not in the 'soul' of the individual, but in their environment" (2008: 188). Fanon's "psychology founded in a social dialectic," remarks Bulhan, allowed Fanon to guard against a "classification of 'human reality and describe its psychic modalities only through deviations from it'" (1985: 80).

Geo Ciccariello-Maher (2012) has explicated Fanon's concept of *comparaison* by focusing on George Zimmerman's motivations to defend the White community from a Black man, which led to the murder of Trayvon Martin in 2012. Zimmerman, who was characterized in the US press as "half-Latino," was policing the streets of Sanford, Florida looking for recognition. He was not looking for recognition from Trayvon Martin, whom he confronted, but from "the distant other of onlooking [W]hiteness," toward which the passage through this more proximate other (Martin) was just a stepping stone. Through his internalized idea of Whiteness and White approval, Zimmerman viewed Martin as the Black man and thus as an intruder and a threat. His reaction – as a defender of Whites – proved to himself that he acted in a way Whiteness would react. The social media hashtag, #BlackLivesMatter, was created after the acquittal of Zimmerman in 2013, and ushered in a new moment of what Fanon considers, as we shall see in the next section, the American "drama" of the continuous Black struggle against White supremacy.

## The Black and Hegel

This woman who sees without being seen frustrates the colonizer. There is no reciprocity. She does not yield herself.

Fanon, "Algeria unveils itself", *A Dying Colonialism*

In the catalogue of the failure of French humanism, Fanon turns to Hegel's master/slave dialectic (also known as Lordship and Bondage), which had become important in intellectual circles in France in the 1930s through Alexandre Kojève's seminars[37] and became the first chapter of his book, *Introduction to the Reading of Hegel: Lectures on the Phenomenology of Spirit*, published in France in 1947.[38] Fanon asks the question: how does the dialectic of recognition work in Martinique, where slavery had been abolished not by revolt but by the "generosity" of the White reformers with a decree abolishing slavery in the French Empire in 1848?[39]

Setting up the master/slave dialectic, Hegel assumes an equality between the two self-consciousnesses that both desire recognition from the other and, to fulfill that desire, each is willing to risk life in a fight to the death. Fanon posits what happens when color is added to this dialectic. He does not simply dismiss Hegel's notion of reciprocity; rather, the movement of Hegel's dialectic cannot begin because the ground of independent self-consciousnesses meeting each other in a struggle for recognition does not exist.

Hegel and the Black returns to the narcissist syllogism in the introduction to Fanon's book: because the Black is not human, the Black must put on a White mask. This is apparent in the everyday life of the Martinican, where an internalized White master mediates social relations and the value of Whiteness is the social norm. As suggested in his critique of Adler, the micro-competitiveness and feelings of superiority are mediated by the symbolic White other. The formerly colonized, still mimicking Europe, looks for recognition in its terms and values (and language): "The [B]lack is a slave *who was allowed to assume a master's attitude*. The [W]hite man is a master who allowed his slaves to eat at his table" (2008: 194; my emphasis). Here, Fanon, at his most damning, argues that even where there has been a struggle, the Antillean is doomed to repeat the drama over and over again because the upheaval reached the Black from the outside: The [B]lack was acted upon. "Values that were not engendered by the [B]lack's actions." So rather than going from "one life to another . . . The [B]lack went from one way of life to another" (2008: 194).[40]

While, in Hegel's dialectic, each is willing to risk life in the struggle, dialectical movement can only take place when one submits while the other becomes independent. The dependent consciousness, bond or slave, works for the master and, through working, which is "desire restrained and checked," transforms the external thing and begins to develop their own independent consciousness. The other, the master, becomes more and more dependent on the slave.

There are a number of important aspects of the dialectic that Fanon says do not work for the Antillean. First, the Antillean has not struggled for freedom and there is "no open conflict, between Black and White." Rather, "one day the White master recognized [the other] *without a struggle*" (2008: 191).[41] Second, Hegel argues (quoted by Fanon approvingly) that "it is solely by risking life that freedom is obtained," and it is in this risking that the "essential nature of self-consciousness" and not its "bare existence" is proved (quoted in 2008: 193). Without risking life, there is no attainment of "the truth of this recognition as an independent self-consciousness" (quoted in 2008: 194). Third, Hegel argues that by working on the object, the slave gains a "source of liberation" and independence. The opposite is true for the Black. All the White master cares about is the work the slave has been bought and bred for. "Black" becomes synonymous with slave, and the slave is quite simply a factor of production whose duration of life is calculated in terms of productiveness.

Thus, Fanon argues, rather than finding independence through working on the object, the Black finds only endless work.[42] In Fanon's scenario, rather than becoming an independent consciousness, the Antillean turns toward the master and "wants to be like the master." Discursively, this is connected to Fanon's argument about internalization of the racial gaze and its values. Where there have been struggles, they are always articulated by "values secreted by the masters . . .

always [W]hite liberty and [W]hite justice," and thus there is "no memory of the struggle for freedom" (2008: 196).

Fanon's is a harsh and unyielding critique, and the context, we should remember, is neither the Haitian revolution nor the continuous slave revolts and struggle histories but, rather, the period following the 1848 abolition of slavery. Reminding us of the argument and concern of *Black Skin, White Masks*, the Antillean remains mystified: They do "not know the price of freedom because they have never fought for it" (2008: 195). In an existential sense, the humanity of humanity is never a given, but has to be fought for and created in the fight. The Antillean, Fanon argues, is cast in a different drama than the one discussed by Hegel.

How to fight the alienation and the neuroses and willful narcissism of the White gaze which express only one conclusion, Whiteness (2008: xiv)? Fanon thus proposes that Black liberation is immanent in itself (2008: xii, 112). It seems to have an almost impossible beginning point expressed in a dialectical circularity that keeps Fanon returning to the problem of alienation and social liberation. His engagement with Hegel's master/slave dialectic keeps repeating a cycle – non-recognition opposed to recognition, bare existence opposed to desire, inessentiality opposed to subject/object, life opposed to the human world (Turner 1996: 150–2). But still it is only from this zone of nonbeing, Fanon argues, that an authentic liberation can be born.

Fanon's analysis turns not only on struggle but on the values of the struggle, which is also a question of intellectual alienation. Framed by the former master, the struggle becomes limited to a new way of life rather than the totality of a *new life*. The politics of substitution reflects this. Since there is no risk of life in this struggle, Fanon argues, the former slave cannot be recognized as independent and self-determining, and even when there is a struggle for freedom, it is framed by

White values. In other words, it is always a losing hand, and in contrast to a new life demanded in and through a particular liberation struggle, the former slave continues to look to the former master for recognition. Reciprocity fails, and, Fanon concludes, "steeped in the inessentiality of servitude," the Antillean Black is doomed sociopolitically and psychologically, doomed to continue to look to the White master.

At the same time, Fanon reminds us throughout *Black Skin, White Masks* that there is a constant struggle against "exploitation, poverty, and hunger" (2008: 199) and although often unrecognized, slaves did remain human as they struggled against cruelty, degradation, and dehumanization. Out of this zone of nonbeing, they continued to "create a world," create community, symbols, and rebellion, a freedom in marronage (Roberts 2015): "They produced ways of thinking and languages that were truly their own. They invented literatures, music . . . [and] institutions" and "developed a phenomenology of the colony" (Mbembe 2017: 48, 104). Here Fanon sets up a binary. In America, he argues, "there are struggles, there are defeats, there are truces, and there are victories (2008: 196). The American Black, who continually fights – and no quarter is given – lives in a "different drama" to the Antillean. This is *the history* of freedom struggle on the verge of the 1955–6 Montgomery Bus Boycott reflected in Richard Wright's literary and cultural work as a newly emergent consciousness.[43] In *Les Damnés de la terre*, Fanon, perhaps referring to Rob Williams's armed self-defense, writes of Black radicals in the US arming themselves. It is also the history of the present. A constant struggle where victories can be short and the reaction to them ferocious.

The dramatis personae that Fanon mentions (the Antillean and the Black American) are typologies. There is a physical and moral struggle, yet for Fanon this is exactly the problem, since the question is: what kind of life? Where the Antillean

Black seems doomed, the American Black seemingly con-
firms the Hegelian schema. Thus, we are presented with two
dramas. The difference between these two typologies is not
simply about action and struggle versus inaction and passivity.
There is action on both sides; important for Fanon are the
values engendered by action where memory and consciousness continually re-emerge to undermine the White master's
reason. Fanon's dialectic, in other words, is about the inner
determination of action and thought that "drives me out
of myself" (2008: 114). This constitutes a real revolution;
namely, a real change in cognition. In contrast, where there is
a disconnection between "life" and freedom, there is only fear
and a life not worth living, or what he calls "a death in life"
(1967: 13).

This dual movement expressed by these two typologies
could be conceptualized singularly. We could consider them
as one character (with a double consciousness) or one movement, self-opposed, where the internal engagement with
failure is critical. It is expressed in Amiri Baraka's criticism
of electoral Black Power in the US as "Black faces in high
places" (see Taylor 2021: 75). This doubleness is reproduced
in Fanon's critique of decolonization in *Les Damnés de la terre*.
While there is no doubt a class character to Fanon's critique
of the nationalist elites, the gulf between them and the mass of
people is both material and ideational: the opposition between
the colonized intellectuals who have internalized Western
values and the "the Greco-Roman pedestal" (2004: 11) and the
colonized masses' sense of "self-preservation" to reject them.
Narcissism and *ressentiment* return in the nationalist leaders'
desire to have what the colonizers have mediated through the
master's values, reducing being to having, as Fanon puts it
(2008: 27).

At the conclusion of the master/slave dialectic, Hegel argues
that by working on the external thing, the slave "gains a mind

of their own." With Hegel, this "rediscovery" of self and reflection of self into self is based not only on work, but also on the experience of fear, going as far as to say that the experience of fear of death must be "absolute" and not "merely some slight anxiety." No doubt Fanon had taken seriously Hegel's insistence that without "the initial state of absolute fear," the "mind of one's own" is "vain and futile" (Hegel 1931: 240) when he writes in his play "Parallel Hands": "Man speaks too much. He must be taught to reflect. For that, he must be made to fear." Conceptually, "Black consciousness" can be connected to having a mind of one's own and to the necessity of changing the world. This becomes the "militant's work" and "service" to the revolutionary movement in *Les Damnés de la terre*, which some Fanon scholars have seen as an expression of Fanon continuing to work through Hegel's dialectic of self-consciousness (see Zahar 1974; Turner 1996).

The dialectic is not abandoned by Fanon. Robert Bernasconi argues (2022: xviii) "that attention be given not to the former slave's work but to his or her 'negating activity'" (*mon activité négatrice*). "I demand that an account be taken of my contradictory activity," Fanon adds, "insofar as I pursue something other than life, insofar as I am fighting for the birth of a human world, in other words, a world of reciprocal recognitions" (2008: 193). The action of clearing one's head of mystification is again emphasized. At the end of the section on Hegel, Fanon argues that to be actional in "respect of the fundamental values that make the world human" requires "careful reflection" (2008: 197). The dialectics of Black consciousness expresses the importance of liberation from the internalization of White values and the racial-colonial cultural imposition. Earlier, Fanon had returned to Césaire's *Notebook*: "Through an unexpected and beneficent inner revolution I now honor my repulsive ugliness" (2008: 175)[44] and here he quotes from Césaire's play *And the Dogs Were Silent*:

We forced the doors. The master's bedroom was wide open. The master's bedroom was brilliantly lit, and the master was there, very calm . . . and all of us stopped . . . he was the master . . . I entered. It's you, he said, very calmly . . . It was me, it was indeed me, I told him, the good slave, the faithful slave, the slave's slave, and suddenly his eyes were two cockroaches frightened on a rainy day . . . I struck, the blood spurted: it is the only baptism that today I remember. (2008: 175)

## "By Way of Conclusion"

If Fanon's judgment of Hegel's dialectic of reciprocity is blocked off, indeed destroyed, by the addition of race, there is also the constant interruption of history into human thought.[45] Considering Fanon's quote from Marx's *Eighteenth Brumaire of Louis Bonaparte*, which he uses as the epigraph to the final chapter of *Black Skin*, "By Way of Conclusion," it could read: "In order to find their *own content*, the [anticolonial] revolutions" should not return to the past or look toward Europe but "have to let the dead bury the dead" (2008: 198).

Recognizing the sociogeny of psychoanalysis combined with phenomenology, Fanon called for an analysis, one that would develop into a philosophy of revolution – as much a call to question as it is a call to action. Though Marx does not directly feature in Fanon's book, the conclusion brings to the fore the character of a drama (more Marxist humanist than Hegelian) in that the idea of *being* a revolutionary is connected to a revolt against a society that exploits and dehumanizes. Fanon begins the chapter with the comment:

It is obvious – and I can't say this enough – that the motivations for disalienating a physician from Guadeloupe are

essentially different from those for the African construction
worker in the port at Abidjan. For the former, alienation is
almost intellectual in nature . . . For the latter, it develops
because they are victims to a system based on the exploitation of one race by another and the contempt for one branch
of humanity by a civilization that considers itself superior.
(2008: 198–9)

For the former, the alienation is "almost intellectual in
nature"; for the latter, it is based on a system of exploitation
and contempt. The former intellectualizes the problem, focusing on individual solutions; the latter knows that there is only
one solution, to fight. Workers Fanon had met, "never both-
ered to ask themselves about discovering a [B]lack past. They
knew they were [B]lack, but, they told me, that didn't change
a thing. And damn right they were" (2008:199). Employing
a sociodiagnosis, these Black workers have not internalized
dominant values and have not blamed themselves; their sociality expresses an elemental solidarity. This doesn't mean
that they were dismissing Black consciousness, rather, that,
for them, their Black worker's consciousness meant fighting
exploitation.

"Intellectual alienation is a creation of bourgeois society,"
Fanon adds, "and bourgeois society [has become] ossified in
a predetermined mold, stilling any development, progress, or
discovery . . . a closed society where it's not good to be alive,
where the air is rotten and ideas and people are putrefying."
Anyone "who takes a stand against this living death is in a
way a revolutionary" (2008: 199). This is why the pauperized Black workers in the sugar plantation in Martinique are
revolutionary – not because they appeal to reason but because
they understand that they have no other choice but to struggle
"against exploitation, misery, and hunger" (2008: 199). This
negativity must also negate itself, as Hegel would insist, and as

Fanon sums up on the final page of his critique of Hegel, indicating the richness of his philosophical engagements by also gesturing to Nietzsche and perhaps reminding us of "Parallel Hands" (see Arnall 2020: 52, 89):

> We said in our introduction that humanity was an affirmation. We shall never stop repeating it. Yes to love. Yes to generosity. But the human is also a negation. No to humanity's contempt. No to the indignity of the human. To the exploitation of humanity. To the massacre of what is most human in the human: freedom. (2008: 197)

Warning of reaction, Fanon concludes: "There is always *ressentiment* in *reaction*. Nietzsche had already said it in *The Will to Power*" (2008: 197). And finally, he returns to an idea of praxis: "To induce the human to be actional, by maintaining in their circularity the respect of the fundamental values that make the world human, that is the task of utmost urgency for those who, after careful reflection, prepare to act" (2008: 197).

# 4

# Fanon in Algeria

This Martinican, who was turned by his transition through French culture into an Algerian revolutionary, will remain for us a very living example of universalism in action and the most noble approach to the human that has ever been made until now in this inhuman world.

Francis Jeanson, *La Révolution algérienne*

Fanon's decision to leave France for Blida-Joinville Psychiatric Hospital in Algeria is, as Francis Jeanson suggests, perhaps one of the most consequential decisions made by an intellectual in the post-World War II world. Fanon's three years in Algeria could be considered in two periods, divided by the day when the FLN launched the war of national liberation on November 1, 1954. As Fanon argues in *L'An V de la révolution algérienne*, the first day of the revolution marks a dividing line, a Manichean period before and a radical mutation in Algerian consciousness after. The first period covers the first year of his appointment (November 1953 to November 1954), and reflects his attempts to reform the Blida-Joinville Hospital as well as the self-criticism of these attempts. The second period (from November 1954 to December 1956) builds on this critique and his growing connection to the liberation movement, culminating in his resignation from Blida-Joinville, his fulltime commitment to the revolutionary movement, and the completion of his break from France. And yet such a divide should not overlook Fanon's experience of and reaction to the racist settler-colonial Algeria expressed in daily behaviors and attitudes both in and outside the hospital,[1] as well as his education in anticolonial resistance, including his contact with the Algerian revolutionaries before the revolution.

Blida was a small city, about 30 miles from Algiers in the foothills of the Atlas Mountains. Like other cities, it contained shack settlements (*bidonvilles*) and boulevards with every exit from the colonial "city" opening onto "enemy territory" (1965: 52). Just above Blida lies Chrea, a ski resort for Europeans, which was in fact one of the first sites of armed resistance.

Blida-Joinville Psychiatric Hospital had been recently built (in 1938). It was modern and airy with vast grounds and shaded areas, but it was overcrowded with more than double the number of patients it was planned for. Muslims and Europeans were in separate wards, which were also divided by gender. The wards expressed the spatial dynamic of colonialism that Fanon famously describes in *Les Damnés de la terre*: the European wards were airy and spacious; the Muslim wards were overcrowded, airless, and cramped.

The dominant psychiatric theory at the hospital was that of the Algiers school, which was shared by the majority of the section heads, which Fanon had criticized in "The 'North African Syndrome.'" To the French, Fanon was not only a Black man from Martinique but also a *Francaouis* (a term used by *pieds-noirs* settlers for a "liberal" from metropolitan France) who, in their view, knew nothing about Arabs and would soon have to understand the "scientific proof" of the Arab's lower brain function characterized by laziness, violence, and lies.

## The Algiers school

The Algiers school of neuropsychiatry was founded by Antoine Porot, chair of the psychiatry department at the University of Algiers. Aligning with mainstream orientalist assumptions, the school repeated racist colonial ethnopsychiatric concepts which would remain in textbooks until the 1970s. Claiming that Arabs lacked moral sense, had a defective intelligence and impulsive and criminal behavior, Porot and colleagues found a constitutional rationality of inferiority in their claim that the Algerian did not have a cerebral cortex. They published *Manuel alphabétique de psychiatrie* in 1952, with entries on "Ethnopsychiatrie," "Psychopathologie des Indigènes Nord-Africains," and the "Psychopathologie des Noirs" – all repeating "the same collection of concepts and terms" (Gibson and Beneduce 2017: 102).

The year after Fanon took the position at Blida-Joinville, the FLN signaled the beginning of the national liberation struggle, with coordinated attacks on targets across the country. Initially dismissing the FLN as a bunch of criminals (in the language of the Algiers school), the French continued to dismiss the group as a criminal organization and to deny that any kind of political struggle was taking place. The Algiers school provided the easy terminology of fanaticism and deviance to describe those responsible for the "savage," "impulsive," and "blood-thirsty barbaric acts" perpetrated on Europeans.

Fanon quickly learned that it was one thing to criticize racist medical practices in France, but quite another to take on the dominant paradigms in colonial Algeria, where medicine was directly related to colonial power, and where any space for criticism was quickly shut down for "security" reasons. But his political commitments were also changing. It was in this changed political environment of Algeria in 1955 that he criticized Porot's theory, linking it with John Carothers's idea of the African as a "lobotomized European." The Algiers school deployed "an intellectual violence," argues the historian Richard Keller, "a savagery concomitant with the brutality required to police Algeria's Manichean world" (2007: 159). After three years in Algeria, Fanon would agree, writing in his resignation letter: "the Arab – permanently alienated within his own country – lives in a state of absolute depersonalization" (1967: 53). And yet, it should not be forgotten that Fanon joined Blida-Joinville Psychiatric Hospital to put into practice the challenge he set out in "The 'North African Syndrome,'" to get things done and be part of the work to "call forth the human that is before you" (Fanon 1967: 13).

As well as being a conservative psychiatric institution like the psychiatric hospital of Pontorson, Blida-Joinville was a colonial institution. A "chef de service" at Blida-Joinville could be considered part of the settler bourgeoisie. In *L'An V*, he makes the point that the doctor as a settler is primarily a landowner with a direct interest in the maintenance of the colonial order. Rather than being defined by his profession, the doctor "coyly speaks of his medicine as simply a supplementary source of income" (1965: 133–4).

It was the nurses not the doctors who were really in charge of the day-to-day running of the hospital and of taking care of the patients, some of whom were restrained and many of whom were pacified medically to keep them "under control." As Fanon wrote to his colleague Maurice Despinoy, Blida-Joinville had recently more than doubled its capacity from 1,200 to 2,500 beds, resulting in exhaustion for the staff and mistrust of the administration. The "harsh conditions ... makes every attempt at organizing collective psychother-

apy extremely difficult. I would say impossible" (2018: 349).
And yet this is exactly what Fanon would put all his energy
into. Peter Geismar claims that Fanon's first tour of a ward
under his supervision shook up all the hospital's household
arrangements:

> On his first tour of inspection of a ward in his service,
> Fanon came upon a nurse attending sixty-nine inmates, each
> strait-jacketed and chained to a bed. He told the male nurse
> to release every one of the patients. His subordinate looked
> back at him without understanding. Fanon ejaculated the
> order again in a more furious tone of voice. As the nurse
> began to unchain the inmates, other nurses in the pavilion
> collected about the doorway where they had heard the new
> doctor raving. Fanon, who had been introduced to them all
> earlier in the day at a formal reception arranged by M. Kriff
> [the director of the Hospital], looked toward them and
> inquired why they were neglecting their own duties. The
> nurses withdrew slightly but continued to stare at the doc-
> tor's unusual performance. He ignored them.
>     Fanon went to the first patient who had been relieved of
> his strait jacket. The man continued to lie in bed as though
> he were still bound there. The doctor introduced himself
> and explained that he would be available at all times for
> consultation. He assured him that there would be no strait
> jackets or chains in the future. Meanwhile the nurse was
> continuing down the row of beds and freeing patients. Not
> one stirred. Not one got out of bed. They all stared at the
> doctor as he continued to talk to each of them. The nurses
> outside the doorway stood in shocked silence. (1971: 65)

Fanon only slept three hours a night and was often still
working at the hospital in the early hours of the morning.
From his first day onward, he put an enormous amount of

energy into establishing, directing, and organizing institutional sociopsychotherapy at Blida. To do so meant not only his continued presence but also creating a committed staff (especially the nursing staff), as well as interns.

Soon after his arrival at Blida, Fanon coauthored an article on the state of psychiatric care in Algeria with the other section heads, Drs. Dequeker, Lacaton, Micucci, and Ramée (who was a student of Porot's). The article, "Current Aspects of Psychiatric Care in Algeria" (1955), published in France's leading psychiatric journal *L'Information psychiatrique*, is indicative of Fanon's organizing activity. Though the four section heads were more conservative than Fanon, the article details a situation about which they all could agree: namely, underfunding, understaffing, and massive overcrowding, which was having an increasingly detrimental effect. Fanon had also quickly garnered support from his colleagues for sociotherapy programs. Patient living conditions had improved with new collaborations that had helped develop a patient newspaper, a Moorish café,[2] film screenings, and trips.

## Sociopsychotherapy at Blida-Joinville

While the hospital administration had little interest in the daily life of the wards and the senior medical staff were not much involved in the day-to-day running of the hospital, Fanon was free to work directly with the nurses in developing sociopsychotherapy. One program was the creation of a football team, which included staff and patients making a pitch, developing a schedule of matches with local Blida teams, and being involved with refereeing – which Fanon and Dr. Lacaton took up therapeutically in the newsletter. By April 1955, there were three teams with regular training sessions, and they attracted a "considerable crowd" (see Fanon 2018: 333). One match day, an administrative official found that a number of Fanon's patients, as well as Fanon himself, were missing from the institution. He informed M. Kriff, who "telephoned the préfect's office to report the 'possibility' of what might best be described as a jail break." Of course, the bus returned with the "hospital's victorious team, which the director didn't know existed" (Geismar 1971: 67).

Fanon's work to "call forth the human that is before you" meant instituting programs of sociotherapy and challenging the cycle of agitation–restraint–agitation. He wanted to democratize the institution, beginning with removing all restraints and confronting the cycle of sadistic practices produced by the institutional directive to control the patients. Autonomy, movement, and self-determination, terms that are so important to Fanon's political thought, were fundamental to his sociopsychotherapeutic approaches.

Subjecting the institution itself to sociotherapy meant breaking down hierarchies and drawing nurses and other staff into the project. Fanon developed all kinds of programs and new therapies: he expanded the library, created a cinema club, ran reading groups, and developed a quasi-journalistic newsletter called *Notre Journal*. With the goal of having patients as contributors to record the progress of reforming the hospital, language and translation became key issues for reimagining sociotherapy.[3]

There were new occupational therapies (including market gardening and handicrafts), as well as new spaces to socialize (including the café). In short, the programs meant beginning with those formerly excluded: the patients. He wanted to change their daily life, allowing them autonomy over what might be considered minor details, such as what time to get up, wash, ownership of a comb, and so on. As well as group therapy, he emphasized the importance of listening and learning from the patients as part of the work to build a new society inside the institution. That one could learn from those who are made to be passive by the institution was innovative, requiring the staff to change their ideas. News about Fanon and the project quickly spread, attracting new staff and interns.

However, Fanon's own critical ethnopsychiatry emerged out of failures of the institutional therapy program. Questioning his own methods, Fanon realized that they had engaged in a program of what he called "masked assimilation." But the failure was not worthless. It helped highlight the issue of an unquestioned ethnocentrism and Fanon began involving all the staff in a reorientation of practical measures such as celebrations of Muslim holidays and meetings with professional storytellers.

### The limits of socio-psychotherapy: Psychiatry must be political

The experience, including self-criticism, was written up by Fanon and his intern Jacques Azoulay (who was writing a dissertation under Fanon's supervision) and published in 1954 as "Sociotherapy on a Muslim Men's Ward." While Fanon took the work earnestly, it assumed a universality where specific situations and experiences were the real testing grounds for the efficacy of treatment. At Blida-Joinville, sociotherapy was considered successful in the European women's ward, but it failed in the Muslim men's ward. Among the reasons for failure, Fanon and Azoulay argued, was that neither of them could speak Arabic. They had to rely on interpreters who, in the mind of the Arab patient, could be associated with the police and the courts and whose presence "fundamentally vitiated the psychotherapeutic doctor–patient relationship" (see 2018: 367). Often, the translation of a patient's detailed speech would become a short interpretation stripped of all content, trivializing complex experiences. When, for example,

Fanon was told the patient hears djinns (spirits), he couldn't tell "if the delusion was real or induced." Additionally, alongside what might be considered problems of interpretation, Fanon noted that a specific aspect of technique in a psychodynamic situation is arrived at through language: "How could a structural analysis be possible if we bracketed off the geographic, historical, cultural, and social contexts?" (2018: 362).

Self-critically, Fanon and Azoulay argued that their "attitude was absolutely not adapted to the Muslim men's ward. In fact, a revolutionary attitude was essential – for we needed to move from a position where the supremacy of Western culture was self-evident to one of cultural relativism" (see Fanon 2018: 362–3). Underlining the importance of language to the psychodynamic process, Fanon quoted Merleau-Ponty – as he had done in *Black Skin, White Masks* – that "to speak a language is to carry the weight of a culture" (2008: 16). Refusing to accept the Algiers school explanations for failure put forward by the staff, Fanon maintained that the problem wasn't with the Muslim men, but with the presuppositions of the experiment itself. As Azoulay put it in his dissertation: "We proposed to implement a Western-based sociotherapy program that disregarded an entire frame of reference and neglected geographic, historical, cultural, and social particularities in a pavilion of mentally ill Muslim men" (quoted by Cherki 2006: 69). In practice, the idea of *Notre Journal* as a space to discuss what was going on in the hospital was limited because most of the Muslim patients were illiterate. Out of the 220 patients in the unit, "only five knew how to read and write in Arabic and two, how to read and write in French" (Fanon 2018: 370). In their conclusion, Fanon and Azoulay wondered: "Are we not guilty of having thoughtlessly embraced a policy of assimilation?" (quoted in Cherki 2006: 69). As they argued:

North Africa is French, and if you are not looking for it, you will not see why approaches should differ from one ward to the next. The psychiatrist *unthinkingly adopts the politics of assimilation*. Algerians do not need to be understood in their cultural originality. They are the ones who must make the effort to adapt and it is in their interest to resemble the kind of person being proposed. (Fanon 2018: 362; my emphasis)

A "politics of assimilation," they continued, "does not propose a reciprocity of perspectives," but rather an insistence that one "culture must disappear for the benefit of the other" (2018: 362). Thus, on reflection, Fanon and Azoulay "orchestrate[d] a major leap and undertook a transmutation of values . . . to move from the natural to the cultural" (2018: 363).

Written before the outbreak of the Algerian war of liberation, Fanon and Azoulay's initial spatial study of pro-letarianization of the population already recognized that the French occupation had brought about "the decline of the old nomadism . . . as inescapable as the rise of its replacement: proletarianization." This seasonal migrant labor, meeting the demands of industries in France and the settler colonial farms of Algeria, was "leading to the dissolution of both sedentary and nomadic groups which also explain the formation of shan-tytowns [*bidonvilles* or *Hay Kazdiri*] on the outskirts of large cities" (Fanon 2018: 366). Before the outbreak of the revolu-tion a few months later, Fanon and Azoulay were seeing that "Muslim society . . . so often seen as fixed in its ways . . . is fermenting at its base from the bottom up" (2018: 367).

Shifting his perspective outside the colonial hospital, Fanon began to learn Arabic and spent time with his team visiting local Kabylian (Berber-speaking) villages, undertaking basic research. In 1956, he co-authored a short, introductory paper with François Sanchez entitled "Maghrebi Muslim Attitudes to Madness" (1956). This and the draft paper titled "Introduction to Sexuality Disorders among North Africans" (with Azoulay and Sanchez, 1955) were not only critiques of Porot's ethnopsychiatric generalizations about the North African, but part of a critical endeavor to begin from an entirely different standpoint, "from the inside" (see Fanon 2018: 421).

It is interesting to read these papers alongside the studies collected in *L'An V de la révolution algérienne*. "Introduction to Sexuality Disorders among North Africans" is made up of fieldnotes. Having come across cases of sexual disorder in their psychotherapeutic practice, the authors embarked on an ethnographic study in Kabylia. Perhaps also influenced by Sándor Ferenczi's concept of the confusion of tongues,[4] the questions concerning language and culture are essential. The draft report's beliefs about sexual impotence – "all the more preoccupying as Muslim society is founded on male authority" (Fanon 2018: 385) – are not dismissed as irrational or unscientific, but rather just recorded. Their report is based on an informant, a learned man with a "good reputation in the region," but "whose explanations left us rather confused" (2018: 386). This "taleb," whose knowledge of the causes of sexual impotence was based on a historic text on medicine and wisdom, is reproduced without comment. Rather than a critique of Porot's ethnopsychiatry, the notes indicate Fanon's desire to begin a critical endeavor from inside the culture their patients lived. As he and Sanchez argued in "Maghrebi Muslim Attitudes to Madness," the Maghrebian view of therapy "possesses a value (on the human level) which cannot be limited solely to its 'effectiveness'" and should be studied for its own sake. Fanon was interested in North African conceptions of mental illness that were quite different from those held in capitalist Europe. While the Western view is that madness alienates (and thus separates the mad from society) and the mentally ill are somehow responsible for their illness, the Maghrebian sees the mentally ill as "absolutely alienated" (see Fanon 2018: 422), and thus not at all responsible for their actions. For them the mentally ill remain human. There is a respect and dignity in the Maghrebian attitude that are lost in the Western view of madness. In the Maghreb, rather than the embarrassment and distrust found in the West, the formerly ill can thus "resume their role in society without fear of arousing suspicion or ambivalence from the group" (see Fanon 2018: 423).

Fanon continued the self-critique he began in "Sociotherapy on a Muslim Men's Ward" in a paper co-authored with his intern Charles Géronimi in 1956, titled "The Thematic Apperception Test (TAT) in Muslim Women." The TAT, developed by Harvard psychologist Henry Murray and lay psychoanalyst Christiana Morgan, is essentially a projective psychological test where scoring and conclusions are based on the viewer's interpretation of ambiguous pictures on cards. Because the images on the cards were culture-bound, the tests became an ordeal for Muslim women; their responses were disconnected and empty and "without any psychoanalytic value" (Fanon 2018: 430). In other words, there was a complete disconnect between the card's "stimuli" and the patient's cultural context. It quickly became clear that the patients were "stumbling over a world [of images] that excluded them" and that a "rich and varied narrative" could only be "animated by cultural dynamics consistent with the psycho-affective structures examined" (2018: 432). Thus a critical and culturally sensitive psychiatry was sharply opposed to the Algiers school linking of the Muslims' so-called inability to imagine to a so-called genetic constitution. After all, given a blank card, the women were able to "unleash their imaginations" (2018: 432). The TAT was a "systematic failure," illuminating the importance of the historical, geographic, and sociocultural specificity to apperception. Importantly, "the patient's refusal and elemental resistance to cultural assimilation was far from hysterical" (Gibson and Beneduce 2017: 157). Rather, it indicated the significance of sociocultural lived experience to psychodynamic situations, and Fanon and his interns shifted their research orientation not simply toward a cultural relativism, but toward what local cultures offered them.

Reporting on the failure of some of the reforms at Blida-Joinville Hospital, Fanon told Charles Géronimi that sociotherapy was not about applying a method, but about owning a process that is implicitly political:

> It was not simply a matter of imposing imported methods ... I also had to demonstrate a number of things in the process: namely, that the values of Algerian culture are different from those of colonial culture; that these structuring values had to be embraced without any complexes by those to whom they pertained – the Algerian medical staff as well as Algerian patients. (Quoted in Cherki 2006: 71–2)

The project and results were all part of sociotherapy. Fanon needed "the support of the Algerian staff in order to incite them to rebel against the prevailing method, to make them realize that their competence was equal to that of the Europeans"; psychiatry, he concluded "has to be political" (quoted in Cherki 2006: 72).

When Géronimi "approached Fanon a year or so after . . . to express his surprise that the author of *Black Skin, White Masks* and 'The "North African Syndrome"' could have been so wide off the mark about the sociotherapy program, Fanon reportedly smiled and said: 'You can only understand things with your gut, you know.'" In other words, Fanon was always learning through practice.

The point is not what he should have known, but how Fanon learnt through the process. One thing that became clear was that, for psychiatry to be political, action had to be

taken. Because the psychiatric hospital creates institutional-
ized patients, alienating them from the community, Fanon
sought to address this by developing day hospitalization programs. The idea of the day hospital, first developed while at
Blida-Joinville Hospital, encouraged building up the social
self, constituted by integrating the patient back into the local
community, and by bolstering the their sense of self through
therapies in an "open" day hospital.

"The Conduct of Confessions in North Africa" (1955),
co-written with a fellow director at Blida-Joinville, Raymond
Lacaton, was concerned with the idea of confession and notions
of reciprocity, social reintegration, assimilation, and elemental
resistance to colonialism. The article follows a similar critique
of medical practices developed in the articles already discussed. Like other psychiatrists in Algeria's colonial hospitals,
Fanon was called on by the colonial justice system to evaluate
the sanity of the accused. As well as the question of "confession," questions about language and culture were also raised.
By definition, confessions, Fanon and Lacaton argue, require
"reciprocal recognition" because, for the court, the confession
signals taking ownership of one's wrongdoing and guilt. This
notion of guilt – and paying one's debt – is connected to reintegration into society. But after Algerians are interviewed by
psychiatrists for the court, 80 percent of the confessions made
earlier were retracted. Something clearly was awry. If one dis-
misses the then hegemonic notion of the North African as a
pathological liar, not only does the idea of the role of the confession itself have to be investigated, but, by extension, so does
the validity of the court. In other words, if both the confession
and the retraction of the confession are true, retraction can
be connected to an implicit refusal to recognize and to refuse
reintegration. Logically, we are back to the lie of the situation: the truth of retraction can be understood as a rational
response to the colonial society and its judicial system.

Fanon and Lacaton suggest that this is possible because the confession was built on pseudo-reciprocity. The pseudo-truth of the initial confession is a result of submission to colonial rule and "not to be confused with acceptance." Retraction in fact represents a real truth expressing "total separation" between the two social groups – the European and the North African. Thus, given "the refusal of the accused Muslim to authenticate the social contract," the confession retraction is an elemental resistance to European colonial rule (Fanon 2018: 412). Similarly, the idea of elemental resistance is found in notes from Fanon's course on social psychopathology at the Institut des hautes études in Tunis (1959–60), where he asks, "Is the colonized a lazy being?" He raises the same question in *Les Damnés de la terre*, seeing laziness as a "remarkable system of auto-protection" (Fanon 1968: 294). Here, he responds:

> The idleness of the colonized is a means of protection, a measure of self-defense above all physiological. Work was conceived as forced labor in the colonies and, even if there is no whip, *the colonial situation itself is a whip*. It is normal that the colonized refuses to do anything since work leads nowhere. (2018: 530; my emphasis)

Already employed by the state to evaluate confessions, psychiatrists actively collaborated with the colonial forces in the most terrible and degrading practices of forced confession. The participation of psychiatrists in the "torture industrial complex," seen in the American Psychological Association's bolstering legal and ethical justification for the torture during the George W. Bush administration's Iraq war (see Gibson and Beneduce 2017: 15–17), is highlighted by what Fanon calls neo-Hippocratism (the degeneration of the ethics of the medical sciences, in particular psychology). Fanon extends his ethical critique in his "Letter to a Frenchman" who was leaving

Algeria for France. "Concerned about Man but strangely not about the Arab," the Frenchman mingles among them but has "never shaken hands with an Arab. Never drunk coffee. Never, exchanged commonplaces about the weather with an Arab." He had "been alarmed at everything, except at the fate to which the Arab is subjected" (1967: 48).

An awareness of not understanding becomes for Fanon not simply the path to understanding but the ground for a new reason and action. After all, in the context of the unfolding war in Algeria, it was becoming clear that psychological decolonization, the recovery of the dignity of the human being crushed by colonial rule, had to become connected to the emerging political and social struggle. The consequence of the idea that psychiatry had to be political at first meant taking account of the colonial situation and becoming aware that all psychiatry and psychotherapy also had to be challenged. The logical consequence was Fanon's joining in the struggle.

## Politics inside the hospital

As news of Fanon's work at Blida-Joinville spread, it attracted more politically engaged nurses and interns. Although none of them had read "The 'North African Syndrome'" or *Black Skin, White Masks*, by "early 1956, intensive psychiatric work was matched by an equally important political activity" (Cherki 2006: 38). With Fanon in charge, there was really no clear division between what could be considered political work and what might be seen as psychiatric work. By the time Alice Cherki arrived in late 1955, the hospital had already become divided between supporters of French Algeria and the "more recent arrivals, who were progressive supporters of psychotherapy and sociotherapy and understood cultural oppression as alienation," and who were willing to support the FLN fighters on a daily basis. "The situation was explosive, and in this, the hospital was no different from the rest of Algeria" (Cherki 2006: 79).

Fanon's boundless energy meant that the psychiatric work continued: "Morning rounds, afternoon meetings . . . evening classes for the nursing staff, and, on a rather regular basis, discussions on assigned readings with the interns" (Geismar 1971: 79). All this, of course, was in the context of war. Close to the hospital was an airforce base, and, as the war escalated, the number of planes taking off and landing made a deafening sound over the wards throughout the day and night. Everyone knew it was disturbing patients' sleep and their recovery, but it was Fanon who complained. According to Geismar:

> [Fanon] went to the Chief-of-Staff of the air force in Algeria, then to the Resident Minister's office, to complain about the noise, explain the situation, and request that the patterns of air flights be altered to preserve the restful atmosphere of the institution. For a year or so, the French air force tried to comply with Fanon's request. (1971: 79)

Soon after the FLN's declaration of a war of independence, the French launched a counterinsurgency targeting nationalists, including those who did not support the FLN. A state of emergency was soon declared, and thousands of people were interned. Torture became systemic. Among those arrested were staff from the hospital, some of whom disappeared. The continued police intrusions into hospital life meant that searches took place at all hours of the day and night, announced by the arrival of black vans. Fanon intervened to convince the authorities that the police should not be allowed to carry guns when they entered the hospital grounds.

In January 1955, Fanon got the shocking news that his sister Gabrielle had died during childbirth. He was heartbroken and immediately wrote to his family, remembering Gabrielle as one of those people who was "truly present." With her, he remarked, "there was no scorn of others, no hatred, no pettiness, only that abundant sap from which flowed a balanced life . . . Gabrielle's death is not just that of a sister. In her I've lost one of the rare women who trusted me, pure and simple. In her I've lost a simple, tender heart, without devices or pettiness" (Fanon 2014: 78–9).

By this time, Josie was pregnant and, in June, Fanon wrote to his mother. They had decided that Josie should go to France to give birth; Fanon would follow. "Josie has been in France and is expected to give birth in the first weeks of July," he wrote to his mother, "I'll leave Algeria on June 28 and travel to France via Spain. You're certainly aware of what's going on in Algeria. Where I am life is tranquil, but there's clearly a risk that this may not last. In any case, nothing has dimmed yet." He was already working with the FLN.

Fanon became known to the FLN through Pierre Chaulet as a "'safe' psychiatrist who could address the mental and emotional problems of its recruits" (Cherki 2006: 79).[5] A few years younger than Fanon, Chaulet was finishing his medical studies with a specialization in tuberculosis. He and his wife, Claudine, were part of the progressive Christian Amitiés algeriénnes that supported families of political detainees. The "organization was in reality run by nationalist militants" with ties to the armed struggle in the Chrea area close to Blida (see Cherki, 2006: 77). By the winter of 1954/55, Fanon had become known as somebody doing "good work" at the hospital and, through Chaulet, had "shown himself to be openly and staunchly anticolonialist, in discussions at the Blida cine-club, for example" (Cherki 2006:78). It was Chaulet who asked Fanon to submit a critical piece on the Algiers school, which was published in the summer of 1955 in *Consciences maghrébines*. Fanon's critique came as Algiers school concepts were informing "counterinsurgency" army programs. The army's Section administrative spécialisée (Special Administrative Section), founded in 1955, fully employed Algiers school terminology and graduates from the school were working in its torture programs.

By February 1955, just three months after the war had been declared, meetings organized by Chaulet were held between the FLN and Fanon. Soon, Fanon was counseling FLN fighters and providing hiding places for local FLN leaders at Blida-Joinville. None of this was done without Josie's involvement; she fully supported the struggle. Through sleep therapy and sedation, the "safe psychiatrist" helped Si Sadek, a local Wilaya commander, recover from nervous exhaustion in Fanon's house in the hospital grounds. Fanon became friends with Colonel Si Sadek (Slimane Dehilès) and Commandant Azzedine (Rabah Zerari); they would continue to meet later in Tunis. Both were self-identified Marxists and part of the military command in the Blida area. Fanon also would become close to the FLN liaison officer Omar Oussedik, who would be part of the early delegation of FLN representatives in West Africa. Later, he and Fanon would travel to Congo to attend Patrice Lumumba's Pan-African Congress.

One of the main intermediaries between the FLN and Fanon was Mustapha Bencherchali, who apparently drove through French roadblocks in his American convertible under the pretext of studying psychotherapy at Blida-Joinville Hospital (Macey 2012: 262–3). But it was through the Chaulets that Fanon first became identified with the FLN. Pierre Chaulet had read *Black Skin, White Masks* and he and his wife Claudine, who was training to become a sociologist, frequently spent evenings with the Fanons. They continued this friendship in Tunis, where Pierre would join the editorial board of the FLN's official publication *El Moudjahid* alongside Fanon. Dedicated to Algerian liberation, the Chaulets gave up their French citizenship when Algeria became independent.

Josie Fanon shared little about her and Frantz's life together. But according to their son Olivier, the revolution "served as a catalyst to bring Fanon and my mother closer." "She was there on the battlefield, on the borders," he adds; Frantz, Josie, and the Algerian revolution became inseparable from each other (see Mezine, 2018).

## Therapy and the war inside the hospital

As time went on, Fanon was being drawn into working with the FLN, becoming actively involved in the anticolonial struggle. It is difficult to imagine Fanon the doctor, spending time with patients, discussing patients with nurses, planning treatments, and presenting psychiatric cases, while also seriously working for and engaging with the FLN. But this was exactly what he did. His critical work as a psychiatrist and his critical work as a political activist were in many ways integrated. As Geismar explains:

> At night he would be removing shrapnel from a nationalist soldier's leg; the next day he would be just as conscientious about organizing the patients' first excursions outside of the hospital . . . In the early morning, the doctor would discharge an FLN recruit who had been resting from shell shock; at noon he would take a tour of the spring gardens and inspect the newest completed fabrics from the female patients' looms. During lunch hour the same day the ambulance would bring in the nationalists' political commissar for the Blida region almost dead from an encounter with the French police; in the afternoon Fanon would be in the office of the hospital's administrative director going over plans for increased religious facilities within the institution. (1971: 89)

Even before the Battle of Algiers, which began in the autumn of 1956, the colonial regime had issued orders to control the distribution of medicines and medical supplies to stifle the flow to the FLN. At Blida-Joinville, some staff surreptitiously appropriated supplies, while others carried information or provided safe houses. Fanon was contacted by the FLN, in part, to help counsel militants about how they might withstand the torture they were likely to face if caught. This kind of practical work was what Fanon alluded to in *Les Damnés de la terre* as the duty of colonized intellectuals "to put at the people's disposal the intellectual and technical capital that was snatched when going through the colonial universities" (1968: 150). In a remarkable passage in Simone de Beauvoir's autobiography, she describes Fanon's service in 1955–6:

> He harbored guerrilla leaders both in his home and at the hospital, gave them drugs, taught the freedom fighters how to care for the wounded, trained teams of Moslem nurses. Eight out of ten bomb attacks failed because the "terrorists," completely terrorized, were either getting discovered straight off or else bungling the actual attack. "This just can't go on," Fanon said. They would have to train the *Fidayines*. With the consent of the leaders, he took the job on; he taught them to control their reactions when they were setting a bomb or throwing a grenade, and also what psychological and physical attitudes would enable them to better resist torture. (1992: 315)

He would then leave these sessions, adds de Beauvoir, "to attend a French police commissioner suffering from nervous exhaustion brought on by many 'interrogations.'"

The critical space that Fanon had hewed out within the hospital since his arrival, however, was quickly diminishing as it all became increasingly caught up in the war. As Fanon explains in one of his cases, both the torturer and the tortured were being treated. Another policeman, whom he had been treating privately, had one day decided to walk around the grounds and became panic-stricken when he met another of Fanon's patients, whom the policeman had questioned and tortured. Neither fared so well. Fanon administered sedatives to the policeman, who later, under Fanon's advisement, resigned and left the country. The tortured patient was found in a toilet trying to commit suicide.

The double track that linked psychiatric and political work continued, "inscribed in our daily lives," remembers Cherki (2006: 82). Fanon played an important part in maintaining the connection between these two spheres. It wasn't simply "a matter of parallel pursuits linked by abstract and tenuous connections," Cherki adds, as the army and police raided the hospital looking for militants on the run, while the increasing repression in Algiers meant more demand for psychiatric care and medical supplies: "Our days revolved around the nexus of politics and psychiatry . . . in a very real sense that was fraught with danger" (2006: 83).

## The Congress of Black Writers and Artists

This was the context of Fanon's trip to France to present at the First Congress of Black Writers and Artists in September 1956, which would also include such figures as Richard Wright, Léopold Senghor, Édouard Glissant, Cheikh Anta Diop, and Aimé Césaire.[6] Beforehand, Fanon met Jean Ayme in Bordeaux at the Congrès des médecins aliénistes et neurologistes de France et des pays de langue française. Ayme was one of François Tosquelles's close colleagues, an "institutional psychiatrist with a long history of anticolonial activism" who had spent his adolescence in Algeria and supported the

revolution (Cherki 2006: 86, 92). With these immediate connections, they drove to Paris together. Fanon stayed in Ayme's
apartment; one night, Ayme (a Trotskyist) introduced Fanon
to his comrade Pierre Broué. The same age as Fanon, Broué
had become a revolutionary socialist in 1944 and co-authored
a definitive work on the Spanish revolution and its "betrayal"
from the inside, a dialectic which would be echoed by Fanon
in *Les Damnés de la terre*. The three of them talked through
the night (Cherki 2006: 86).

The next day Fanon presented "Racism and Culture" at
the Congress. According to his future publisher, Maspero,
Fanon's presentation was quite an experience.[7] He started
out by arguing that racism was "not the whole but the most
visible, the most day-to-day and ... the crudest element of
a given structure" (1967: 32), suggesting that, connected to
modes of production, it changes over time. In the colonies,
ways of life and modes of production have been broken,
destroyed by colonization "because the enslavement ...
of the native population is the prime necessity" (1967: 33).
This process, Fanon argued, is accomplished and maintained through violence: "The destruction of cultural values
and ways of life" and the undermining of systems of cultural
reference are necessary for "a new system of values" to be
"imposed ... by the heavy weight of cannons and sabers"
(1967: 33–4). A once living culture becomes closed down,
"present and mummified."

Referring to the period of slavery and forced labor where
"vulgar racism in its biological form corresponds to the period
of crude exploitation of man's arms and legs," Fanon said
that this gives way to "a more refined argument [of] ... cultural racism" as production techniques and the necessity of a
more collaborative work force "impose a new attitude upon
the occupant": "The complexity of the means of production,
the evolution of economic relations inevitably involving the

evolution of ideologies ... The perfecting of the means of production *inevitably* brings about the camouflage of the techniques ... [of exploitation], hence of the forms of racism" (1967: 33, 3436).

Racism can easily return to its cruder forms. In the US, Fanon continued, it is a "dialectical gangrene," haunting and vitiating American culture. Mocking the commissions on racism at the UN and the hand-wringing about "racial prejudice," Fanon argued that a society is either racist or it is not. There is no such thing as a society being "unconsciously racist." Racism is carried by popular culture and "by the life-stream of psycho-affective and economic relations."

Blistering in its critique, Fanon's presentation was hopeful in its conclusion. Saying little about Algeria, he called for a struggle of "total liberation ... to fight all forms of exploitation and of alienation" by any means necessary. Reflecting on his experience in Algeria, he concluded that in this struggle culture becomes revalorized just as the liberal colonists make new appeals for assimilation and integration (1967: 43).

It was around this time, during Ramadan in April 1956, that Fanon recounted a situation of feeling Algerian. He was sitting in his car smoking a cigarette with "the windows down and his elbow resting on the car door, Italian style," writes Cherki, when "an Algerian, who probably mistook him for a local because of his dark skin, approached him out of the blue and said, 'We disapprove of people smoking during the month of Ramadan.' Fanon demurred, and, without a word, extinguished his cigarette. 'I felt I had been designated as an insider,' he later told Ayme" (Cherki 2006: 94).

## Leaving Algeria

The events in Algeria are the logical consequence of an
abortive attempt to decerebralize a people . . . A society that
drives its members to desperate solutions is a non-viable
society, a society to be replaced.

Fanon, "Letter to the Resident Minister",
*Toward the African Revolution*

The war was increasingly seeping through the hospital. The
number of patients with psychosomatic complaints and situational psychoses triggered by torture increased; the atmosphere
of violence permeated daily life. Many of the cases referred
to in the final chapter of *Les Damnés de la terre* come from
this period. According to the police, the hospital had become
known as a "Fedayin den." While the police knew that some
hospital staff were aiding the FLN and had informants among
the staff, Fanon had somehow remained off their radar. Things
came to a head after his active support for a strike at the hospital on July 5, 1956 (called by the FLN to mark 126 years
of French occupation). A police intelligence report written
after the strike reflected the extent of their knowledge, noting
that the "highest percentage of strikers was recorded at the
Reynauld Pavilion under Dr. Fanon's authority" (see Gibson
and Beneduce 2017: 176). It also stated that Fanon had close
ties to nationalists, including FLN combatants.

One of Fanon's visitors at the hospital was his friend Marcel
Manville; he was staying with the Fanons in October 1956
when the Cazouna massacre took place. Fanon and Manville's
reactions express the reality of the situation. Fanon woke
Manville early in the morning. From a nurse at Blida-Joinville
who had escaped death, he had heard of a massacre of 20 men.
They had been taken from a small village, lined up, and shot

in cold blood by a local settler militia. "Here is what the French habitually do in this country," Fanon said angrily, "and to think that some of my intellectual friends, who pretend to be humanists, reproach me for my total commitment to this struggle, for love, and the dignity of humanity" (Ehlen 2001: 132). Fanon and Manville visited the village where Fanon introduced Manville as a lawyer. None of the villagers wanted to lodge a complaint so Manville decided, against Fanon's advice, to do so himself. Fanon warned Manville that he could easily be taken and disappeared.

Since the strike on July 5, 1956, the hospital was no longer safe; indeed, it had become a dangerous place to be. One of Fanon's interns, François Sanchez, was arrested in January 1957, tortured, and then imprisoned. Another intern, Slimane Asselah, was arrested in March 1957 and disappeared. Pierre Chaulet was arrested. Raymond Lacaton, who had supported the sociotherapy reforms inside the hospital but was absolutely uninvolved in the struggle outside it, was arrested and tortured. When it became clear that he was not at all involved with the FLN, they dumped him in a pigsty. When Lacaton then heard that he was going to be arrested again, this time alongside Fanon, he informed Fanon. A turning point had been reached. It became clear that their work inside the institution was impossible. When the police turned up to arrest Makhlouf Longo, a psychiatric nurse and ward supervisor, in early January 1957, he asked that they give him an hour to get his belongings. He searched for Fanon, whom he greatly admired (see Cherki 2006: 70–1), but couldn't find him. Fanon had already left.

Meanwhile, through Pierre Chaulet, Fanon had met the FLN leader, Ramdane Abane, who would play an essential role in developing a platform for the revolution at the Soummam conference, which took place right under French noses near Akbou in the in August 1956. Up until then, the National Liberation Army (ALN) had been a locally organized, poorly coordinated and armed, heterogeneous group, which had become militarily bogged down and lacked a shared political ideology. At Soummam, a balance sheet was taken, alongside an analysis of revolutionary forces – the peasantry, lumpen-proletariat, and working class – articulated in a politics that would include women and minorities.

Developing a coherent program and an "effective organization" to reflect the new stage was the order of the day, and the "Revolution" was given some structure and political principles. Critical of the autonomy of the military districts, it was declared that the struggle was to be "an organized revolution and not an anarchist revolt," "a step forward in the history of humanity and not a return to feudalism," "a struggle for the birth of an Algerian state in the form of a democratic and secular republic, and not a restoration of a monarchy or dead theocracy." In effect, FLN underwent a restructuring, with military leadership coming under the command of a political leadership and the external leadership coming under the command of the internal.

An Executive Coordinating Committee (CCE) of five members was set up and, immediately afterward, Abane, Benyoucef Benkhedda, and Larbi Ben M'hidi became the leaders of the revolutionary Autonomous Algiers Zone. They met regularly, coordinating a new stage of the struggle to bring the war from the countryside to the heart of French colonial power, Algiers. By doing so, they also anticipated bringing the war onto the global stage. Though collective decision-making was practiced, Abane was considered the "secretary general." It was he (signing his name "Ahmed") who called an eight-day general strike to coincide with the opening of the United Nations session in New York, hoping to underscore mass Algerian support for the FLN. The French response was brutal. They cordoned off the Casbah, rounded up hundreds of people, and began systematic torture of the Algiers population. Over the coming months, information gathered by the torturers would lead to more round-ups and more torture, until Algiers was pacified.

Detractors argue that the battle of Algiers was a campaign run by a small elite of terrorists, but in fact it depended on the organization of thousands and on the support of a huge majority of the population, along with aid from a small number of Europeans. Indeed, those arrested for terrorism came from every sector of Algiers society. While some called the strike a failure and a miscalculation, Abane, Benkhedda, and Saad Dahlab considered it a success because it brought the struggle into international view. Fanon agreed, arguing in *El Moudjahid* that it "reaffirmed the national unanimity of the struggle and the maintenance of the objective." In other words, it was "the first real action of a united people with a national consciousness," and in this sense, it was a turning point.

Ultimately, from an international perspective, the French regime of torture to win the battle of Algiers and criminalize the Algiers population (30–40 percent of the male population of the Casbah were arrested) became as important as the campaign itself. Hence Fanon's proclamation in *L'An V de la révolution algérienne* that French colonialism was finished in Algeria; the only question was, when? Charles de Gaulle and the discovery of oil would strengthen French resolve to stay.

Before leaving Algeria, Fanon met with two of the CCE's political leaders, Abane and Benkhedda, "signaling that the FLN's confidence in Fanon was now total" (Macey 2012: 297).[8] Abane asked Fanon to move to Tunis and become involved in the reorganization of *El Moudjahid*. By February 1957, M'Hidi had been arrested in Algiers. Five days later, the four remaining members of the CCE left Algiers in a car driven by Claudine Chaulet, who was arrested several days later. M'Hidi was later murdered in jail.[9]

Abane and Dahlab traveled to Morocco, then to Tunis through Madrid and Rome. According to Mohamed Harbi,

Fanon grew close to Abane during Abane's eight-month stay in Tunis. They shared a concern about the development of a future society after the revolution. Thus, Fanon's "exile" to Tunis put him right back in the thick of the situation, and his closeness to Abane gave him an inside view of the intrigue and shortfalls of the anticolonial politics and leadership, allowing him to hone his ideas about Algerian liberation. In *Les Damnés de la terre*, several years later, Fanon would go on to fully develop the concern shared by Abane: what was to happen to Algeria after independence?

The Soummam platform created a national political body – the National Council of the Algerian Revolution – divided Algeria into zones (wilayas), including the autonomous zone of Algiers, created a leadership structure wary of a "cult of personality," and considered political decisions to have precedence over military ones. In addition, the platform announced that the revolution was not a religious war and the goal was not an Islamic state but a democratic socialist, secular, and multicultural project. The platform also reflected Abane's skepticism of a negotiated settlement. In fact, only a few months later, the jailing of the external leadership of the movement put an end to the question of their involvement in a negotiated settlement. Perhaps also reflecting the Kabyle tradition of the Djemma (or democratic Berber assembly), Abane's preference for collective leadership was reflected in the Soummam idea of a democratic future that would include agricultural workers, the landless, and the urban poor, as well as the "veritable pariahs" created by the colonial regime (Abane 2011: 38). Rather than a "Kabyle myth," what was at stake were questions of "minorities" in the future Algeria. Often associated with "Berber separatism," some of the most leftwing and secular leaders of the FLN were from Kabylia, which also meant that as the revolution's leadership became more militarist, with conservative and narrow nationalist elements holding sway, these leaders were threatened.

In Blida, it is interesting to note Fanon's close proximity to Kabylia and his interest in the Djemma as a possible local democratic form that (as he argues in *Les Damnés de la terre*) could be reinvigorated through the revolution. Just as Fanon would speak of the importance of "minorities" in the Algerian revolution, such as European and Jewish supporters, one cannot help but think of the Kabyle militants as both the left wing of the revolution and as a question at the heart of Algerian nationalism. It was not coincidental that Soummam criticized both authoritarianism and the regionalism of some of the wilayas.

In 1955, Abane had informed the readers of *The French Observer* that the Algerian struggle was for "honor, justice, and liberty." In the face of death, the struggle was "for the right to live as dignified free" people (Abane 2011: 32). As Fanon began to make more contact with FLN militants, he experienced face-to-face this will to live with dignity or not live at all. The colonized, including some patients at the hospital who had been overwhelmed by colonial reification and oppression, were changing, shaking off the shackles of colonial subjugation and becoming "masters of their fates" (Abane 2011: 30). For Fanon this was something completely new, and it affected him profoundly.

By the fall of 1956, "the Algerian revolution under Abane's leadership had matured" (Abane 2011: 32) and Fanon experienced, and was involved in, this maturation. The primacy of the political over the military would be seen almost immediately in the battle of Algiers, and in the importance of including mass movements, general strikes, and media bringing the struggle to the world's attention.

It would not be an exaggeration to claim that Abane, as well as the Soummam platform, would continue to have a profound influence on Fanon's politics. Indeed, one could argue that the language of the Soummam platform's analysis was also influenced by Fanon, as it describes how the ALN's violent action "provoke[d] a psychological shock which had liberated the people from torpor, fear and skepticism," making Algerians "conscious of their national dignity" (Panaf Editors 1975: 179).

When Fanon left Blida and Algeria (he had in fact received an expulsion order), the plan was to go to Tunis. He first went to Paris. Josie and their son, now a toddler, stayed behind with the Chaulets before meeting Frantz a few days later. They stayed with the Aymes for a couple of weeks, and then with Manville until they left for Tunis on January 20, 1957. Aware of Fanon's dire financial situation, Tosquelles took over the support of Fanon's daughter Mireille, while Ayme, as secretary general of the Psychiatric Hospital Physicians Union, looked at ways that Fanon could retain his salary. This was unsuccessful. Still, Fanon "continued to devour books" including "transcripts . . . of the first four Congresses of the Communist International; these documents had a special fascination for Fanon, and they accompanied him through many long nights" (Cherki 2006: 93). Certainly, the question of creating a new society after the revolution concerned Fanon even then. While the situation in Paris was not safe, the question was how to get to Tunis. Direct air travel was not viable. This had become clear just a few months earlier when the French pulled off a coup arresting the external leaders of the FLN: on October 22, 1956, a plane provided by King Mohammed V, whom they had just met, to carry them from Morocco to Tunis (where they were going to meet with Prime Minister Habib Bourguiba) was re-routed by the French authorities. Fanon described this moment in *L'An V*:

> I remember a woman clerk in Birtouta who, on the day of the interception of the plane transporting the five members of the National Liberation Front, waved their photographs

in front of her shop, shrieking: "They've been caught. They're going to get their what-you-call-'ems cut off!" Every blow dealt the Revolution, every massacre perpetrated by the adversary, intensified the ferocity of the colonialists and hemmed in the Algerian civilian on all sides. Trains loaded with French soldiers, the French Navy on maneuvers and bombarding Algiers and Philippeville, the jet planes, the militiamen who descended on the douars and decimated uncounted Algerians, all this contributed to giving the people the impression that they were not defended, that they were not protected, that nothing had changed, and that the Europeans could do what they wanted. This was the period when one heard Europeans announcing in the streets: "Let's each one of us take ten of them and bump them off and you'll see the problem solved in no time" . . . Any Algerian man or woman in a given city could in fact name the torturers and murderers of the region. (1965: 56).

Traveling through Switzerland and Italy, the Fanons arrived in Tunis on January 28, 1957. In the few weeks since he had left Algeria, the situation there became more desperate as the war took a serious turn. In December 1956, General Salan had been promoted to commander-in-chief of the army in Algeria and on January 7, 1957, the responsibility for order moved from the police to the army's elite forces under the control of Salan and General Massu, commander of the elite tenth parachute division. Salan and his chosen deputies, who were veterans of the counterinsurgency in Vietnam, rigorously applied what they had learnt to Algeria. The science of counterinsurgency was being put in charge.

The FLN called a general strike, marking not only the movement's popularity but also its strategic flexibility. Algiers ground to a halt. "Never before in Algeria had a strike been so successful" (Woodis 1972: 100). But the reaction was brutal.

At gunpoint, workers were forced back to work, shopkeepers forced to open shops, students forced back to school. Mass arrests, widespread torture, imprisonment, and execution continued; networks and safe houses became compromised as the French secret services penetrated the organizational structure in the FLN's "autonomous zone" of Algiers. Politically, this would have an effect on Abane's standing as leader once Fanon reached Tunis.

## Fanon and Jeanson

Fanon's first publication, "The Lived Experience of the Black" was the opening article in a special section, entitled "La Plainte du Noir" (the complaint, or lament, of the Black) of the monthly non-communist Catholic-left journal *Esprit*, published in May 1951. His second article, "The 'North African Syndrome'" was part of special section in *Esprit*, "The North African Proletariat in France," published the following February. *Esprit* shared its offices with the small press, Éditions Seuil. It was through these connections that *Black Skin, White Masks* would be published. Fanon's editor was Francis Jeanson, who was an editor at *Les Temps Modernes* and co-editor of Éditions Seuil. It was Jeanson who suggested Fanon change the title from *An Essay on the Disalienation of the Black* to *Black Skin, White Masks*.

Jeanson had spent some time in Algeria during the war, and had become fervently opposed to French colonialism. This was also expressed at Seuil as it was beginning to emerge as a main publisher of fiction from North Africa. Like his later friendship with Ayme, Fanon seemed to have much in common with Jeanson. They first met at the Seuil office. Jeanson had found *Black Skin, White Masks* exceptionally interesting; he reported in his 1965 foreword: "I made the mistake of telling him so, which made him suspect that I had thought that 'it wasn't too bad for un nègre'; whereupon I had, on showing him the door, formulated my own reaction in the sharpest terms – which he had the good sense to take positively."

When Jeanson met Fanon again in early January 1957, they shared connections to the Algerian revolution; Jeanson and his wife Colette had published *L'Algérie hors la loi* (which argued for independence and reproduced FLN material). For Fanon, the meeting was purely practical: how to get to Tunis, and meeting Jeanson made sense since he had intimate knowledge of underground networks and also coordinated financial support for the FLN. He would later be viewed as the leader of what became known as the Jeanson network. Jeanson, in other words, was completely committed to the Algerian revolution, but Fanon showed little interest in being involved in or discussing Jeanson's work. So, nothing came of it, which Jeanson seemed to take as a slight.

When Fanon had met his brother earlier in Paris, he told Joby that he had resigned from the hospital and would be working for the FLN in Tunis and that Josie and Olivier would accompany him. Joby thought that Frantz was making the same mistake he'd made in 1943: "Frantz, stop! Get a grip on yourself! Stop dreaming . . . Don't make the same mistake again. Your commitment to the cause of Algerian independence is just and I support it. But you're not Algerian. You're not Muslim." And he advised Frantz to support the revolution by writing and activism from France. "Joby, that's not how I see things," Frantz responded. "I don't commit myself to a cause with words. And I'm not a French intellectual. I'm a free man who cannot be satisfied with partial engagement . . . You're not credible if you're not at the heart of the action. There's no going back" (quoted in Fanon 2014: 85). Fanon wanted to be inside the revolution not supporting it from outside. What could he add in France that was not already covered by Sartre and other public intellectuals? "They don't need me here," he said to Joby, "they need me in Tunis" (Ehlen 2001: 140). Manville also tried to convince him to change his mind. Perhaps all this pressure affected the meeting with Jeanson. In his mind, any French support had to be completely subservient to the movement and he wanted a complete break with France and to live "the drama of the people" (1965: 142).[10] According to Leo Zeilig, Fanon had "considered fighting the French directly – abandoning his post at Blida and moving into the *maquis*" in 1955 (2016: 87). Like many of the FLN leaders, he was a war veteran and knew how to fight. The FLN, of course, valued his work elsewhere, but at the end of his life he again lamented: "I'm dying in Washington of leukemia . . . [and] I could have died in battle with the enemy three months ago when I knew I had this disease" (quoted in Geismar 1971: 185). He wanted a "heroic death," Joby remembered – perhaps thinking of earlier conversations and themes in his plays – to take up arms at the front, not die like a sick person in hospital (2014: 101). The FLN leadership had seen things differently, not only in 1956 but also in 1961, when they helped organize the trip to Washington in an attempt to prolong his life.

# 5

## The Algerian Revolution and Beyond: Fanon in Tunis

Arriving in Tunis, Fanon immediately got a position as a psychiatrist at the Razi Hospital in Manouba, in the west of the city. One advantage of the position was that it provided accommodation for the Fanons. Built in 1912, the hospital is situated on extensive grounds with pavilions set off from each other surrounded by lawns, gardens, and trees. Fanon worked there under the name Dr. Farès,[1] treating Tunisian patients and a large number of Algerian refugees, many of whom were suffering from traumas inflicted by the French.

The introduction of sociotherapy programs, informed by his experiences at Blida, were not fully successful for two reasons. First, the hospital had significant numbers of long-term patients; second, the programs were actively resisted by the conservative nationalist director Ben Soltan, a French-educated administrator who considered himself an absolute authority at the hospital. He was the typical national bourgeois characterized by Fanon in *Les Damnés de la terre*, and he remained the hospital's director into the 1970s. He had no interest in any of Fanon's programs (especially if they required any budget) and, as an anti-Semite and racist, he questioned Fanon's professional competence, insisting that Fanon couldn't understand Arabs. The shadow of the Algiers school fell across Razi as it did Blida-Joinville, and although Tunisia was now independent, the idea of structurally decolonizing the hospital was not on the agenda: so Razi essentially remained a colonial hospital. As Fanon argued in *Les Damnés de la terre*, colonialism is in its essence "a fertile purveyor for psychiatric hospitals . . . seeking to 'cure' the colonized properly . . . [and] seeking to make them thoroughly a part of a social background of the colonial type" (1968: 249–50; 2004: 181–2).

In response to Soltan's intransigence, Fanon went over his head, receiving support from Tunisia's minister of health and thereby deepening the tensions between himself and the director. He became responsible for the mental health of the entire émigré Algerian population of Razi Hospital, with the number of fighters and refugees displaying a range of traumatic symptoms growing larger every day (Cherki 2006: 114). Soltan accused Fanon (and his interns) of being involved in a Zionist plot. The fact that Fanon's patients included FLN leaders made that accusation a serious one. It was totally fallacious, of course, and nothing came of it – but it ended Fanon's time at Razi Hospital.

Before he left Razi, Fanon had already started to work at Charles Nicolle Hospital in Tunis. Unlike both Blida-Joinville and Razi, Charles Nicolle was a general hospital and had the advantage of not having a "deeply ingrained prejudices in public opinion [that] transforms the mad into a patient" (Fanon 2018: 496). Joby Fanon (2014: 91) recalled Charles Nicolle as being rundown and "less well ventilated" than Blida-Joinville Hospital, but it was here that his brother developed a psychiatric day center, the first in North Africa, and wrote a two-part article on the subject.[2] Fanon continued to train nurses, assistants, and translators; he remained completely focused on the patients, developing therapy programs based on their needs, situated in their sociocultural environment. A Dutch social worker arrived to work at the hospital, and wanted to create an occupational therapy program for women. Unable to get sewing machines, she had the idea of buying a burnous (a long wool cloak with a pointed hood worn by men in the Maghreb) from the souk and creating tablecloths embroidered with traditional designs. Two women were paid to embroider, and, as others gathered around, they created a new "talking session" involving discussions about colors and patterns between patients, nurses, other staff, and embroiderers as part of the therapy of integration (see Manuellan 2017: 78). Aware that sociotherapy was not a cure-all, Fanon nonetheless considered it indispensable at the Razi and at Charles Nicolle where, with dynamism and innovation, it helped preserve the "patients' socialized dimension" (2018: 499). The day hospitalization program that Fanon instituted at Charles Nicolle underscored how, for him, "the social therapeutic milieu is and remains concrete society itself," with the hospital providing a range of therapies including psychotherapy and insulin therapy "oriented toward awareness, verbalization, explanation and strengthening the ego" (2018: 493).

## El Moudjahid

*El Moudjahid* had first appeared in June 1956 in Algeria and survived for seven or eight irregular issues. It was reconstituted in June 1957 in Tunisia as the official organ of the FLN, with a print run of 10,000 in two editions (Arabic and French); Redha Malek and Ahmed Boumendjel acted as editors-in-chief. On Abane's advice, Pierre Chaulet joined the editorial committee in December and was made head of FLN's documentation center. As well as writing for *El Moudjahid*, Chaulet and Fanon also worked in the FLN refugee camps and nationalist health centers on the Algerian border. While Fanon did write articles at the Charles Nicolle Hospital, most of the editorial work was collaborative, carried out at "the base," the FLN offices at 24–26 rue Sadikia, Tunis. "Fanon's political education progressed rapidly as he wrote for the paper," argues Geismar (1971: 109); between them, Chaulet and Malek were "a gold mine of information on every detail of the history of the nationalist movement." Articles would be refined through these discussions and Malek was a good critic, tempering "Fanon's idealism with . . . more immediate goals" (Geismar 1971: 106). Abane was also involved, critically advising Fanon and others (see Abane 2011: 34–5).

As a collective endeavor, the articles in *El Moudjahid* were not signed. Alongside security reasons, there were also reasons of principle: the paper was the official voice of the FLN, not of individuals, and so authorship was not a private matter. It was only after Fanon's death that the question of authorship became important.

Fanon worked on *El Moudjahid* from 1957 to 1960, but the vast bulk of his writing was done in the first two years.[3] Discussions after Fanon's death between Maspero, Josie, and Malek led, in 1964, to the collection of 20 articles published in *Toward the African Revolution* (the English edition left out the January 1958 piece "In the Caribbean, Birth of a Nation?"). Josie's original list was much longer than Malek's,[4] who emphasized the anonymity of the project and the collective approach to writing. Malek also claimed that Fanon's *Les Damnés de la terre* was "basically a development of topics treated in *El Moudjahid*, and elaborated by the editorial board" (see Fanon 2018: 535). No doubt Fanon was an active member of the team and was certainly not concerned about attaching his name to his articles. While some of the ideas in what became *Les Damnés de la terre* were no doubt discussed at editorial meetings, Malek is too quick to downplay Fanon's originality as a revolutionary theorist. The truth is that if Fanon had not written *Les Damnés de la terre*, no one else would have written anything like it.

## Ramdane Abane

Ramdane Abane had been able to leave Algeria overland and arrived in Tunis by way of Morocco. Fanon frequently met with him in Tunis. A few months before *El Moudjahid* was reconstituted, Abane appointed Fanon to the press office to work on *Résistance algérienne*. But Abane's position in the leadership of the FLN had suffered with the failure of the general strike in January 1957 and the success of the French counterinsurgency in Algiers. These setbacks had had enormous costs. Thousands were killed, imprisoned, and tortured, and much of the FLN infrastructure and its networks was destroyed. As a result, tensions were running high between Abane and the wilaya colonels, who now were the majority on the expanded Executive Coordinating Committee (CCE). Ousting Abane's supporters and marginalizing his influence, they wanted more control, challenging the Soummam decision that the military be subservient to the political leadership.

In Tunis, Abane was "demoted" to news and information outlets; Fanon saw quite a bit of him and began to further understand the internal dynamics of the Algerian revolution. Constantly vying for power, much of the leadership had no vision of a future Algeria. "Ask them what this future Algeria will look like, and they don't have a clue," Cherki reports Fanon saying. "The idea of a secular state or of socialism, the idea of man for that matter, these are things that are entirely alien to them . . . They think that anything that is not a simple truth is dangerous to the revolution" (2006: 105, 112). Safia Biaz, a high school student when she joined the *maquis* (guerrillas) in 1956, remembered:

> Many of our leaders couldn't see beyond independence. Most of the young volunteers couldn't either. Abane and Ben M'Hidi were different. Ben M'Hidi had a very human side. He would talk to us, some of us were still high school students, wanting to know more about our motivations, our ideas about the future of the country. Abane was more radical. One night he told us this is going to be a long struggle; many of you will not live to see the end of it. And independence, when it comes, will be only the beginning.

It became clear to Biaz that the fighters "were not all motivated by the same things: some wished only for independence and didn't concern themselves with political change, some wanted to create a new society, and some simply wanted to defend Islam" (quoted in Cherki 2006: 104–5). Fanon would develop his critique of the military and the nationalist party in *Les Damnés de la terre* where, he argued, after independence the army becomes an "indispensable tool for systematic repression" and "goes into politics" as the national bourgeoisie sells itself to multinational companies (2004: 118, 142).

As the tensions between the colonels and Abane simmered, he and Fanon continued to meet in Tunis. Abane was open and often sharp in his criticism of the colonels and no doubt shared his views with Fanon. Although politically, he still had enormous support in the FLN, tensions persisted and one of the colonels, Abdelhafid Boussouf, took the lead in plotting his assassination in December 1957. His death was not remarked on until an announcement was made on the front page of the May 9, 1958 edition of *El Moudjahid*. It was written by Ahmed

Boumendjel, who had taken over a leading role in the editorial group and would accompany Fanon to Accra later that year:

> In the first fortnight of April a violent encounter between our troops and those of the enemy forced the protecting company of our brother Abane to take part in the engagement. In the course of the fighting which lasted several hours, Abane was wounded ... A grave hemorrhage became fatal. (Quoted in Horne 1977: 227)

If Fanon had known the truth about Abane's assassination five months earlier, he had to keep quiet about it. According to Mohammed Harbi: "Fanon's name was on the list of those who were to be eliminated in the event of a violent reaction to Abane's liquidation" (Macey 2012: 353). Certainly, one could understand why Fanon was considered part of Abane's tendency as he continued to be committed to Abane's politics. They both rejected compromise with the colonial system and they both died before seeing an independent Algeria. As Mohamed El Mili, one of the editors of *El Moudjahid*, put it: "During the whole war of liberation, I did not know any militants as sincere as Frantz Fanon and Abane Ramdane ... I found certain of Abane's ideas in *The Wretched of the Earth*" (quoted in Abane 2011: 28). Fanon would continue to feel a great responsibility for the death of his comrade.

Just days after the news of Abane's death broke in *El Moudjahid*, the Algiers putsch occurred, which resulted in the collapse of the Fourth Republic in France. In what essentially amounted to a coup d'état, the National Assembly granted de Gaulle power to rule by decree for six months before a new constitution, which would confer on the executive branch vastly increased powers, was drafted.

Fanon immediately wrote about this, naming it a fascist experiment (see 2018: 607) and viewing it as a counterrevolution. It reenacted, he argued, "French colonialism's old campaign of Westernizing the Algerian woman," as "servants under the threat of being fired, poor women dragged from their homes, prostitutes, were brought to the public square and symbolically unveiled to the cries of 'Vive l'Algérie française!'" (1965: 62). Although De Gaulle offered Algerians political equality – something that no popular front or socialist government had done – Fanon underscored how little the left – the socialists and communists – as the largest voting bloc in parliament, had done to oppose de Gaulle. While this gave hope to imperial France, Fanon was highlighting in *El Moudjahid* the specificity of the form of struggle of the Algerian revolution and its influence on the continent's liberation.

Also in May 1958, the young author Assia Djebar arrived in Tunis.[5] She met Fanon at "the base" (the FLN offices) and became friendly with Josie, with whom she remained close. At the time, Josie was contributing articles to the Tunisian journal *L'Action*, and appeared on Radio Tunis every Sunday, discussing literature.

As formal editors-in-chief of *El Moudjahid*, Malek and Boumendjel met with M'hamed Yazid,[6] who was named the FLN's minister for information in 1958. These meetings took place in "the base" and it was partly as a result of these relationships and discussions, and of his work in building relationships with African liberation movement radicals in Tunis, that Fanon became integrated in the formal structure that would become the Provisional Government of the Algerian Republic (GPRA). The GPRA was founded in September 1958 and in December, at the First All-African Peoples Congress (AAPC) in Accra, Ghana, Fanon was appointed as a representative. He gave a rousing speech on the importance of violence in the struggle against French settler colonialism in Algeria (which will be considered in the next chapter). In March 1959, he represented the FLN at the Second Congress of Black Writers and Artists in Rome. And in April, he visited India with Ferhat Abbas, and then traveled to Casablanca and Cairo with the GPRA minister of foreign affairs Krim Belkacem.

## The border

While in Tunis, Fanon was directed to set up a psychiatric service on the Algerian border. In 1958 and 1959, he spent a lot of time at the refugee camps on the border between Algeria and Tunisia. He never forgot those in the camps and the experience would continue to haunt him. Every weekend, teams from Charles Nicolle Hospital (including Fanon and his bodyguard Youssef Farès), would visit facilities established by the Tunisian government. They worked under awful conditions made worse by French planes strafing the border. The notion of a cure for the suffering seemed impossible. Fanon's basic treatment for those in the camps, as well as for exhausted militants in the field, was sleep therapy, rest, and time – ideally spent in relative calm that was not available in the camps.

In *L'An V de la révolution algérienne*, Fanon writes of the tragic scattering and fragmentation of family, and the hidden traumas in the "regroupment camps" produced by the bombing of villages, torture, and rape (1965: 50, 119). In *Les Damnés de la terre*, he writes of 300,000 refugees on the Moroccan and Tunisian borders forced there by the French government's scorched earth policy. In extreme poverty and precarious living conditions, he reports on the sense of permanent insecurity:

> It is therefore inevitable that the pregnant women are particularly prone to developing puerperal psychoses. These refugees live in an atmosphere of permanent insecurity, the combined effects of frequent raids by French troops applying the "right to hunt and pursue," aerial bombardments – there

is no end to the bombing of Moroccan and Tunisian territories by the French army . . . machine gun raids as well as the breakup of the family unit as a result of flight. In truth, there are few Algerian women refugees who do not suffer from mental disorders following childbirth. (2004: 207)

As his case notes demonstrate, Fanon treated many people who were traumatized by the war. One was a 37-year-old *fellah* from a village near Constantine who had desperately tried to be unaffected by the war. His village was attacked and, for no military reason, was ordered to be destroyed and its inhabitants shot. The man was wounded and taken by ALN soldiers to the medical center. There, he violently attacked a number of patients and vowed to kill everybody because "all the so-called Algerians are really French." He remained severely suspicious and hostile, but after a month asked to learn a trade. Fanon saw him for six months. Another case was a 22-year-old man who was dedicated to his technical profession and had little interest in the national struggle. But by 1955 he began to become paranoid that his parents considered him a traitor. He tried to avoid his family and friends, but his anxiety increased. He locked himself inside and, after four days of confinement, ventured into the town, making his way to the European section. Taking him for a European, the soldiers left him alone as they arrested others. This increased his paranoia. He went up to a soldier, tried to grab his machine gun, shouting, "I am an Algerian." After days of police interrogation, they sent him to a hospital. Fanon saw him at Blida-Joinville and notes that these sorts of cases were extremely numerous in Algeria in 1955. "Unfortunately, not all of them had the good fortune to be admitted to a hospital" (2004: 204).

Fanon also worked with fighters who had experienced personal loss and the full force of the French military brutality – from air, sea, and ground, including the electrified fences and minefields set up by the French along the borders between Algeria with Morocco and with Tunisia.[7] Attempts to breach the lines often resulted in burnt skin, smashed bones, and extensive trauma. Many of the young Algerian fighters were treated at the Razi Hospital in Manouba and also at Charles Nicolle Hospital, where treatment included art therapy as a means of nonverbal communication (see Fanon 2004: 206).[8]

While in Tunis, Fanon was also involved in the preparation of a short film, *J'ai huit ans*,[9] a "product of a new therapeutic strategy of visualization that Fanon was experimenting with in his clinical work with Algerian refugees" (Mirzoeff 2011: 246–251; see also Mirzoeff 2012). Drawings by children from refugee camps on the borders were part of a therapeutic effort and often reflected the French military's sadistic violence. Fanon had spoken with his friend and Italian editor, Giovanni Pirelli, about publishing a book of drawings and narratives, but he changed his mind, apparently "deeply upset" by some of the children's stories (Cherki 2006: 195). The remarkable book was nevertheless later published in French and translated into Italian, with Pirelli adding other first-hand accounts of the Algerian war (mainly written by prisoners and those in internment camps) alongside the children's accounts and drawings.[10] Both the book and the film make clear not only the importance that Fanon placed on visualization for therapy, but also the depth of trauma and the importance of continuing sociotherapy and analytically oriented psychotherapy after liberation. After all, insofar as the struggle for liberation is successful, it opens up new spaces for treatment, new sensitivities about trauma, and new avenues for therapy. Indeed, Fanon envisioned himself and his colleagues being part in these developments after Algeria became independent.

It was during one of his visits to the overcrowded refugee camps in May 1959 that Fanon's car was blown up. I mention this to underscore the reality of the situation, as well as

Fanon's vigilance. Everyone thought it was a terrorist bomb, though no terrorist organization claimed responsibility and there remains uncertainty about whether it was a bomb or a car crash. Fanon was thrown out of the vehicle and fractured his spinal vertebrae. He was taken to a local hospital and then to Rome. The GPRA representative in Rome, Taïeb Boulharouf, was to have met Fanon and Josie at the airport, but that morning his car was detonated when it was hit by a football from children playing nearby. In hospital, Fanon came across a newspaper article mentioning him and his hospital room number. He immediately insisted on being moved. He wasn't wrong: that night, gunmen gained admission to the hospital and entered the room (see Geismar, 1971: 144; Macey, 2012: 392).[11]

Fanon had been in Rome a few months before representing the FLN at the Second Congress of Black Writers and Artists. The theme was "Unity and responsibility of/for Black African culture." Invited by the Italian government, with financial support from UNESCO, the conference was also supported by the Pope, who gave an address and granted an audience to all the delegates.[12] This theme of political consensus was contradicted by the refusal of many Negritude leaders to support the FLN and by many others to openly support De Gaulle. Fanon's presentation was titled "The reciprocal bases of national culture and the fight for freedom" (and was reprinted as the second part of Chapter 4 in *Les Damnés de la terre*).

Speaking on behalf of the FLN and with Algeria in focus, Fanon begins with the "cultural obliteration" wrought by colonialism, which forces the colonized to "confess the inferiority of their culture." While intellectuals hurl themselves into a "frenzied acquisition of the occupier's culture," there is among the masses a defensive and instinctual holding onto culture that can be understood as "self-preservation" (2004:

171, 170). The net result of colonization, however, is a pet-rification of culture, which becomes an inventory of customs without creativity, without life, without movement (2004: 172). In Fanon's view, cultural renaissance has to be connected to political struggle, and the development of national consciousness should be connected to the increasing clarity of the liberation struggle. He dates this in Algeria to 1952–3 – that is, before November 1, 1954, and during his early period at Blida-Joinville – and can be seen in his use of storytellers in the sociotherapy program. On reflection, he says, the story-tellers, who had "grown stale and dull, radically changed both their methods of narration and the content of their stories." By 1955, storytellers were being systematically arrested (2004: 174). It is in this period that a "combat literature" emerged that was connected with the liberation struggle by invisible threads alongside similar changes in plastic artists like ceram-ics and pottery. Fanon hardly mentions negritude, but he does speak of bebop and other new jazz styles coming out of the US, which were, he says, "one of the definite consequences of the inevitable, though gradual, defeat of the Southern universe in the USA" (2004: 176). His conclusion sums up the dialectic of culture in the liberation struggle: "The liberation strug-gle does not restore to national culture its former values and configurations" because the aim of new social relations means "not only the demise of colonialism, but also the demise of the colonized" (2004: 178).

While Fanon was working at Charles Nicolle Hospital and on the borders, and was actively involved with *El Moudjahid*, Marie-Jeanne Manuellan (who had been a member of PCF and had broken with the party after the Suez crisis) had taken a job at Charles Nicolle and became Fanon's assistant, typing *L'An V de la révolution algérienne* in the spring of 1959. Manuellan was a 30-year-old social worker and had come to Tunis with her husband and two children.[13] She published a valuable perspective about Fanon's life, *Sous la dictée de Fanon* ("Under Fanon's Dictation"), just before she died in 2019. Slowly integrated into the service's daily work, with Fanon as its head, she was given the job of taking notes of conversations with patients and staff on his rounds, with a particular focus on what patients said. This, she says, became part of her psychoanalytic education, with Fanon acting as a "master teacher," encouraging a constant discussion among the staff. Fanon loved to teach, she remembered, to "grow brains," as Fanon would put it, filling them with ideas, and making them human beings (see Fanon 1968: 197). At the hospital, this process involved everyone.

Fanon's constant critical self-reflection meant that he expected high standards of all the staff toward the care of patients and he connected this with his ideas about serving the Tunisian people. He did not waver from the view that psychiatry and the work of mental health care were political. Despite his status as chief, he abhorred bureaucratic hierarchies, encouraging all the staff to be involved in therapeutic discussions.

During this time, Manuellan and Fanon were meeting a child who would only walk on her tiptoes. Manuellan was soon seeing this child twice a week, following Fanon's instruction to record everything in writing. Manuellan would bring dolls and modeling clay to the meetings. The child played with dolls reconstituting her family, but she ignored the modeling clay. After the meetings had been going on for weeks, Manuellan told Fanon that the child had spoken of a bird that whistled in the mother's womb. The Arabic translator and supervisor, Si Aissa, pointed out to Fanon that in Arabic the word bird or whistle can designate a penis. Fanon thought this was an essential breakthrough and questioned the child about it. The child didn't respond to Fanon, but afterward she began to make sexual objects out of the modeling clay. Relaying this to Fanon, he told Manuellan that she had made an important breakthrough. She didn't believe it at first, but she was being educated into a patient-centric practice, and beginning to understand how being part of the unit, listening to Fanon and to the patients and to her colleagues, she was in fact being trained.

It took a while for Manuellan to appreciate Fanon. Shortly after her arrival, Fanon made it very clear to her that he didn't want anything to do with French people. He was driving her part of the way home when the conversation started. Fanon had asked what her husband did. She told him that he was an engineer working for the ministry of agriculture and then added, why don't you and your wife and son come around for lunch or dinner. Like others at the psychiatry unit at Charles Nicolle, she knew that Fanon also worked for the FLN and, indeed, was always shadowed by his bodyguard. Fanon's response to her suggestion was that, given his "responsibilities in the FLN," he doesn't "frequent with the French" (see Manuellan, 2017: 76). This made Manuellan furious. As a political person, she did not associate with the French state or with its colonial regime, and she reacted defensively. But their working relationship continued amicably enough; as Alice Cherki puts it: "Fanon's own efforts to appear austere and hard never came to much, he never could keep up the pose for any length of time. He was much too fond of love and friendship and too sensitive to human suffering" (2006: 146). Some weeks later, as Fanon was driving Manuellan to the bus, he said: "Your husband must be a good person because you are a good person" (2017: 77). And out of the blue, a few weeks after he had returned to Tunis from the meeting with the army of the borders in Morocco, which led to the car "accident," Fanon asked her to come to his apartment, where he was recovering following spinal surgery in Rome. At the time, the Fanons were living in the same building where the FLN representative to the UN, Ferhat Abbas, lived.[14] Josie answered the door and showed Manuellan into Fanon's office where he stood with the plaster-cast up to his shoulder. "I am going to need you," he said, "to type a book." She told him that she didn't know how to type but would learn. It was at that same meeting that she told Fanon that the young girl was no longer walking on her tiptoes. Fanon smiled, the first time she had seen him smile since his injuries from the accident (Manuellan 2017: 85).[15]

To write the book, Fanon met with Manuellan every morning from 7am to 9am. But after a week he told her it wasn't working and he'd have to find a typist. A week later, he came back to her office, which was small closet opposite his own office at the hospital, and said the typist was making too many mistakes. Manuellan immediately suggested that she could write the dictation out by hand and then type it up in the evening, which she did. Mornings in Fanon's office became "ceremonies of the book":

> Fanon never had a piece of paper in his hand, he walked and spoke the book as if by his footsteps, by the rhythm of his body running, his thoughts sprang forth, without jolts, with few interruptions, flashbacks, or resumptions. I was sitting down at his desk and he paced up and down the room, looking concentrated, without haste or hesitation. It was he who set the time and "closed the session." He never spoke to me of any plan, never asked me what I thought of this or that.

Manuellan concentrated on recording every word but also realized the way in which Fanon needed to speak his book to a human ear. She didn't have time to think as she recorded, but "certain words hit me like bullets, beyond, or below my thoughts, in my guts" (2017: 114–15).

Though there were suggestions that Fanon writing a book

was creating tension at the hospital, everyone there knew he was working on it. Overall, Fanon was respected amongst his colleagues, and he asked Charles Géronimi to take over:

"For how long?"
"Three weeks or so?"
"Sure. But could you tell me why?"
"I have to write a book."

(Geismar 1971: 113)

Once the "book ceremony" was over, Fanon's and Manuellan's regular hospital work resumed.

Géronimi didn't quite believe he could write a book in three weeks, but within a month Fanon had finished *L'An V* (which would include an appendix by Géronimi to the concluding chapter "Algeria's European Minority"), and he was ready to submit it to a publisher. Clearly Fanon had already spent a while thinking and composing the book in his head. It was built on his thinking and experiences since arriving at Blida and especially after the war of liberation had begun. It included experiences from his work at Blida-Joinville, at the hospitals in Tunis, and in the refugee camps, as well as his developing ideas from his writings in *El Moudjahid*. The last chapter of the book appeared in *Les Temps Modernes* (May–June 1959), titled "La minorité européenne d'Algérie en l'an cinq de la révolution." Maspero, who had just begun publishing a new anticolonial series, wrote to Fanon after learning about the book offering to "prioritize its publication" (Fanon 2017: 676). Warning Fanon that the book would likely be seized on publication, he wondered about changing the title, and suggested "Birth of a Nation." Fanon was open to the suggestion but preferred "Reality of a Nation" (a concept he had been working with), reflecting the new reality of a new nation that was coming into being and replacing the North

African French colony.[16] In the end, the title *L'An V de la révolution algérienne* was kept. The revolution, Fanon argued, was the new reality and it would only be a matter of time before the Europeans would recognize it.

Dated July 1959, Fanon's powerful preface, which was not included in the first two editions,[17] begins with the paradox of violence framed by the idea of Western civilization. The "Western nation," he argued, is assumed to be naturally humane and the anticolonial revolt is assumed to be naturally barbaric (consider the British references to the then recent Mau Mau revolt). The anticolonial revolt is thus obliged to "practice fair play ... while its adversary [explores] ... new means of terror" (1965: 24). When threatened, settler colonialism, which is built on systemic violence, reaches for unheard levels of brutality, terror, and vengeance on the populace, creating a continuous "apocalyptic atmosphere" that is "the sole message [of] French democracy" (1965: 26). This ferocious and "shameless colonialism," only matched by South Africa (1965: 26), with a million hostages behind barbed wire, is preparing new offensives. It is in this context, in the fifth year of the Algerian revolution that the book seeks to show "in this first study that on the Algerian soil a new society has come to birth. The men and women of Algeria today resemble neither those of 1930 nor those of 1954, nor yet those of 1957." The old Algeria is dead and the Algerian nation "is no longer in future heaven" but at the "very center of the new Algerian ... *a new kind of Algerian* ... a new dimension to [their] existence" (1965: 30). In the new Algeria that is being built, everyone is Algerian and "in the free Algeria of tomorrow, it will be left up to every individual to choose Algerian citizenship or to forgo it in favor of another" because, "we want an Algeria open to all, in which every kind of genius may grow" (1965: 136, 32).

Speaking in part on behalf of the FLN, Fanon tackles the problematic of revolutionary violence head on, arguing that "because we want a democratic and a renovated Algeria, because we believe one cannot rise and liberate oneself in one area and sink in another, we condemn, with pain in our hearts, those brothers who have flung themselves into revolutionary action with the almost physiological brutality that centuries of oppression give rise to and feed" (1965: 25).

*L'An V de la révolution algérienne* was published by Maspero in October 1959. Fanon addresses the European left-liberal readership directly in his concluding chapter, "Algeria's European Minority," writing that "for a long time history is made without" them, and explaining: "They were unable to prevent the sending of contingents to Algeria, unable to prevent Guy Mollet's capitulation. They were passive under Lacoste, powerless before the military coup of the 13th of May [1958]." The left haven't done anything for a long time, Fanon continues, "yet by its action, its denunciations, and its analyses, it has prevented a certain number of things" (1965: 149). Importantly, he adds, it has "forced the neo-fascists of Algeria and France to be on the defensive."

Géronimi's appendix also speaks directly to the French left and of the impossibility of a third position (against the French and against the FLN) in Algeria. He tells the story of his awakening as an Algerian European who was shaken out of his ambivalence after the November 1, 1954 revolt. It took him six months to understand the futility of his left-liberal position, which he calls an attempt to "humanize repression." This "third position" was an illusion based on the triumph of the French left in 1954 (the Pierre Mendès France-led coalition), which disintegrated "in the face of the fascist-Lacoste."[18] The "Third Position," Géronimi argues, "could have had meaning only if it had been supported by the French left," but, he adds, the French left "was playing the game of Algerian fascism" (1965: 174). The situation became unbearable and Géronimi left Algiers for the "psychiatric hospital in Blida . . . as an intern with a doctor known for his anti-colonialist views" (1965: 174), where he stayed until December 1956, joining the FLN before leaving for Tunis.[19] The second appendix is written by Yvon Bresson[20] who joined the Algerian police in 1953 and who, soon after November 1, 1954, was contacted by the FLN; at great risk to himself, he became an important source of information.[21]

Quite soon after publication, Fanon's book was, as expected, banned as being a threat to national security. A second banning and the seizure of the book occurred just a few months later. Maspero wrote a preface denouncing censorship but it became difficult to find distributors. Even the *Présence Africaine* bookstore refused to do so, and Maspero was charged with "inciting the military to insubordination and desertion" (Cherki 2006: 132). Despite these seizures, the book did circulate.

## Lectures at the Institut des hautes études in Tunis (1959/60)

Increasingly connected to the FLN and to the GPRA, working in the hospital, and writing for *El Moudjahid*, Fanon nevertheless "found time" to give a series of lectures in late 1959 and early 1960 on social psychopathology at the Institut des hautes études in Tunis. The series was titled, "The Encounter of Psychiatry and Society." A student's notes from the lectures reveal that Fanon connected a range of issues, including the conditions of workers in colonized societies, the effect of new production methods on mental health, specific kinds of dreams and mental disorders common among certain categories of workers, racism in the US, while also highlighting the controversial role played by psychiatry as the gatekeeper of social order where the psychiatrist is the auxiliary of the police, "the protector of [a] society" seeking "to rid itself of these anarchic elements" (quoted in Gibson and Beneduce 2017: 169). Madness, Fanon argues, "is forbidden in the hospital" and the physician must find a way to "permit" madness.

Fanon spends some time considering racism in the US, where one can observe "behavior characterized by the predominance of nervous tension that quickly leads to exhaustion": "Among Black Americans, a permanent control of the self is required at all levels: emotional, affective ... If Blacks are dominated, one cannot demand human behavior from them" (quoted in Gibson and Beneduce 2017: 19). All relationships in a racist society are permeated by racism: "When a Black American meets a White, stereotypes immediately intervene ... because their systems of value are not the same; at base there is a lie which is the lie of the situation itself" (Fanon 2018: 525). The lie of the situation is a wonderfully Fanonian phrase that he expands in *L'An V de la révolution algérienne* as one challenged by the revolutionary situation, in which "the 'truth' of the oppressor, formerly rejected as an absolute lie, was now countered by another, an acted truth," he argues there, *"because it avowed its own uneasiness, the occupier's lie became a positive aspect of the nation's new truth* (1965: 76; my emphasis).

Judging from these lecture notes, Fanon considered the situation of Black Americans akin to that of the colonized and the disinherited described in *L'An V*:

> The disinherited in all parts of the world, perceive life not as a flowering or a development of an essential productiveness, but as a permanent struggle against an omnipresent death. This ever-menacing death is experienced as endemic famine, unemployment, a high mortality rate, an inferiority complex and the absence of any hope for the future. All this gnawing at the existence of the colonized tends to make of life something resembling an incomplete death. (1965: 128)

The notes also include topics not discussed elsewhere, such as alienation in the workplace, focusing on new technologies such as clocking in and out as machines which introduce "a moral notion of guilt," as well as new behaviors among workers and symptoms directly related to "workers' specific activities (obsessive disorders, nightmares, somatoform disorders)" (Gibson and Beneduce 2017: 171). Forms of control exercised by employers, as well as his references to workplace accidents and "absenteeism," reveal the fine detail of his analysis of alienated labor. Quoting studies conducted by the communist psychiatrist Louis Le Guillant, Fanon discussed the particular difficulties experienced by telephone operators in the 1950s, many of whom were affected by a specific form of neurosis with serious symptoms such as suicide. He also considered the working conditions of employees under constant surveillance in department stores, arguing that technological innovation reduces communication "transform[ing] the human being into an automaton" (quoted in Gibson and Beneduce 2017: 171). Fanon's awareness of surveillance connected with the Manichean politics of space he describes in *Les damnés de la terre* where the colonized breathing as an observed breathing could easily be expanded to our own period of facial-recognition technology.

During the lectures, Fanon also responded to the question of the alleged laziness of the colonized, arguing that it should be understood as a "means of protection, a measure of self-defense" because work in the colonies is forced labor and, "even if there is no whip, the colonial situation itself is a whip" (2018: 530). This is another theme that Fanon returned to and developed in *Les Damnés de la terre*, considering the "so-called indolence of the Black, the Algerian, and the Vietnamese" as a kind of unreflective somatic resistance against an "ever-menacing" death and "a remarkable system of self-preservation" (2004: 220).

Taken together, these lectures not only demonstrate the breadth of Fanon's epistemological struggles against psychiatry, but also indicate the range and depth of his project of humanizing humanity which "was not a liberal humanist one," argues Stefan Kipfer, (2022: 70), but one "transforming the character of humanity by means" of "fecundating relations of generosity," as Fanon puts it in one of his lectures (2018: 530).

# 6

## Writing from Inside the Algerian Revolution: *L'An V de la révolution algérienne*

Fanon, as mentioned in the introduction, took Bertène Juminer and his wife, Michelle, to the Manuellan's 1959 New Year's Eve party. Juminer was a doctor and writer from Guadeloupe, who had been working as a biologist at the Louis Pasteur Institute in Tunis since 1958.[1] Fanon met with Juminer frequently, and gave his friend a copy of *L'An V de la révolution algérienne*, in which he wrote a dedication that perfectly expressed his conception of the book:

> This book illustrates a principle: if action does not transform the individual consciousness then it is nothing more than incoherence and agitation. The intensity of the subjective evidence that has come to light in the Algerian nation's epic struggle against colonial oppression attests to the impossibility of deferring a collective awakening. Have faith in your people and devote your life to their dignity and betterment. For us, there is no other way. Your brother, Frantz. (Quoted in Cherki 2006: 236n.23)

To understand Fanon's thesis of radical mutation in *L'An V*, it is necessary to resituate the book in its historical context and specificity, reflecting a revolutionary moment with all its excitement and possibilities. It also cannot be separated from Fanon's experiences of the Algerian war, which created a continual crisis not only in "French Algeria," but also in the French republic and across the French colonies. The book sheds light on the Algerian revolution, to what Fanon calls its "impatient richness" (1965: 179); while it claims the death of colonialism, it documents an ongoing Algerian struggle that continued to believe in victory. The greatest immediate threat to a negotiated settlement came from the French settlers who, on May 13, 1958, demonstrated against a proposal by Pierre Pfimlin, the French prime minister, to negotiate with Algerian nationalists. Instead, in what became known as the Algiers putsch, they demanded that a Committee of Public Safety be set up, led by General Massu, while French army generals in Algeria begged Charles de Gaulle to take over the government. Across France and its overseas departments and territories a plebiscite was held, calling for ratification of a new French constitution. Sékou Touré's Guinea was the only nation that voted "No." Despite FLN directives, 80 percent of the Algerian electorate (with women allowed to vote for the first time) voted for de Gaulle's vague proposal of a French commonwealth, thus shaking the FLN's external credibility as the representative of the Algerian people. In response, leading French democrats asked themselves how an independent Algerian nation could possibly come into being. The referendum marked am important political divide and a radical break in independence politics.

While De Gaulle's regime is hardly mentioned in *L'An V de la révolution algérienne*, one of the book's purposes was to apply pressure on French liberals and the French left to address, as Fanon put it in an article in *El Moudjahid*, their "doctrinal oversimplification ... mechanization of thinking and ... fetishism of causes taken in the most automatic and least dialectical sense" (1967: 107). For Fanon, it was precisely this lack of dialectical thinking that had prevented both the left and, for that matter, many in the FLN from noticing the fact "that today a new humanism ... is coming into being, which has its root in [the hu]man" (1967: 125) born out of an absolute rejection of colonial dehumanization. In the chapter "Algeria Unveiled," Fanon argues that revolution is a double process that simultaneously dictated both organized action and invention where there is a radical mutation in consciousness, politically and psychologically. As he put it in an April 1958 article in *El Moudjahid*, "Decolonization and Independence": "the Algerian combatant is not only up in arms against torturing parachutists. Most of the time [they have] to face problems of building, of organizing, of inventing the new society that must come into being" (1967: 103). Fanon's idea of this continuous revolution is set in motion by the people's own self-determination:

> That is why colonialism has lost, has irreversibly lost the battle in Algeria ... This contempt for the "stages" that break the revolutionary torrent and cause the people to unlearn the unshakeable will to take everything into their hands at once in order that everything may change, constitutes the fundamental characteristic of the struggle of the Algerian people. (1967: 103)

Critical of colonial intellectuals and those whom Fanon calls "Islam specialists" (1965: 64) who, with their "mechaniz[ed] thinking," view colonized culture as inert and unchanging, he distinguishes three periods of the revolution: before the rebellion of 1954, the initial phase of the rebellion, and the period after the Soummam conference. Additionally, the revolutionary agency of the lumpenproletariat that Fanon insists is an objective phenomenon was being created by not only massive migrations to the urban areas, but also, by way of the war, the more than two million people who had been "piled up in internment centers." A "policy of regroupment" and internment, as well as the effects of the war, had ended "mechta" (small village) ways of life forever (see 1965: 117). The dialectic of "regroupment," its violence and repression, created, alongside the fragmentation of the Algerian family, an elemental solidarity across Algerian society, which, Fanon argues, led to greater and unprecedented participation of women in the war (1965: 116–17).

*L'An V de la révolution algérienne* opens with "Algeria Unveiled," inspired in part by women's actions in the Battle of Algiers. Written just as the battle was entering the second phase, the chapter's appendix was the first article Fanon penned after arriving in Tunis, and considered not only women's actions in the battle and their emergence as political subjects, but also the change of attitudes in the FLN: "[R]evolutionary war is not a war of men," Fanon argued: "The Algerian woman is at the heart of the combat. Arrested, tortured, raped, shot down, she testifies to the violence of the occupier and his inhumanity. As a nurse, a liaison agent, fighter, she bears witness to the depth and the density of the struggle" (1965: 66).

## The Battle of Algiers

Though the "Battle of Algiers" is often dated from September 30, 1956, when three unveiled women, Zohra Drif, Djamila Bouhired and Samia Lakhdari, placed bombs at a milk bar and a café, the preamble had already begun on June 19, 1956, when two members of the FLN were guillotined in

Barberousse Prison in Algiers. Between June 21 and 24, the FLN responded by shooting civilians in Algiers. On August 10, European settlers retaliated by detonating a massive explosion in the Casbah, destroying three buildings and killing 79 people.

Positing women as an integral part of revolutionary war became a measure of Fanon's thesis of revolutionary change. In an important and radical articulation at the time, Fanon was giving an important place to the "creation of new forms of being a woman" (see Ruedy 1992: 174) that put his work at the heart of an anti-imperialist feminism. Privileging cultural creativity, *L'An V* offers a nonessentialist and nuanced framework for understanding the functioning of the veil and women's activity during the Algerian war of liberation that does not succumb to orientalist projections of women as passive objects, but rather posits them as a force that threatens colonial and patriarchal power.

To begin to fully understand *L'An V*, it is first necessary to position Fanon's work in the context of the first five years of the Algerian revolution. In this sense, it may be informative to consider both *L'An V* and *Les Damnés de la terre* as representing the two periods of the revolution, where the first, "November 1954 to September 1958, constitutes a synchronous whole centered upon the primary task of converting and mobilizing the Algerian people and proving 'the authenticity of the revolution,'" while the second, which extends from late 1958 to independence, is "predominantly political" (Ruedy 1992: 189). While it is only in *Les Damnés* that Fanon fully develops the problematics of political independence, it is precisely in *L'An V* that he engages with the issue of revolutionary authenticity, namely the Marxian thesis that men and women change at the same time that they change the world (1965: 30).

After August 1957, the *El Moudjahid* masthead began to note the days of the revolution. On September 6, 1957, the

1041st day of the revolution, Fanon published two articles: "Deceptions and Illusions of French Colonialism," on the opening page, and "Algeria Face to Face with the French Torturers," on the back page. On the 1305th day of the revolution (May 29, 1958), the front page mourned the death of Abane.

As I have already argued, Abane, like Fanon, hoped for a multicultural Algeria where Algerian Jews and Algerians of European descent would all be included. Abane "believed in the possibility of a new form of human interaction, a new society that could be achieved only through a revolutionary dismantling of the colonial state" (Cherki 2006: 104–5). Despite Abane's assassination, the optimism about the revolution expressed in *L'An V* is remarkable. For Fanon, it was precisely the lack of vision of a new society grounded in the actions of the Algerian masses that would pose the greatest threat to its development. Thus, as he argued in *Les Damnés de la terre*, it was important to find different concepts connected with the new ways of a life that the revolution was making possible.

Concentrating on political change from below and emphasizing the dual process of the revolution – destruction of the old colonial society and construction of a new society – *L'An V* is positioned as a revolutionary text *within* the Algerian revolution. Grounded in the revolution, each chapter productively engages with its contemporary contexts. "Algeria Unveiled" and "The Algerian Family" highlight the concurrent changes inside the family, the emergence of new subjectivities, personalities, and social relations, such as between the daughter and the father, that sprang up during the revolution; "Medicine and Colonialism" speaks to the raced, classed practice and epistemologies that still echo in the contemporary medical industrial complex;[2] "This Is the Voice of Algeria" uncovers changing attitudes and revolutionary possibilities of new communication technologies and forms of dialogue that emerge in social struggles; and "Algeria's European Minority" focuses on the question of the commitment not only of Europeans in a revolutionary struggle, but of finding a new concept of Algeria. In addition, a "socioeconomic analysis" of the Algerian Jew affords an explanation of different attitudes among the Jewish community; while the fate of minorities was closely tied with colonial rule, three-quarters of the Jewish population (whom Fanon calls "an Arabized mass") suffered from European racism and considered themselves "natives." Each chapter in the book recognizes an ongoing shift in attitudes that begins with the outbreak of the struggle for liberation and a more active subjectivity when "the Algerian's reaction was no longer one of pained and desperate refusal" (1965: 76). By reclaiming their subjectivity as historical protagonists, there was a shift away from a Manichean reaction.

One site on which this struggle played out was the veil. In the long resistance to colonialism, there was little individuality or agency for women. As a metaphor for the civilizing mission, on the one hand, and anticolonial reaction to it, on the other, the woman became a metaphor for the nation to be fought over. The veil became a site of struggle with the French attempt to "liberate" women by "breaking her resistance" and thus, they believed, breaching the nation. Fanon argues that, "on the level of individuals, the colonial strategy of destructuring Algerian society very quickly came to assign a prominent place to Algerian women" (1965: 46), and "the tenacity of the occupier in his endeavor to unveil the women . . . had the effect of strengthening the traditional patterns of behavior" (1965: 49).

Fanon's analysis also includes a study of colonial sadism, arguing that, from the 1930s onward, colonial "reformers" had insisted on liberating women from oppressive "traditional" society. Unveiling them became a battleground and

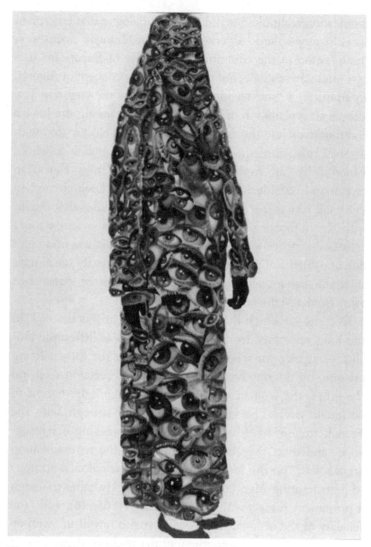

Françoise McAree, "Burqa Silhouette" (2014)

was resisted in an absolute way. The dominant attitude of European men not directly involved in this unveiling reform was one of "romantic exoticism, strongly tinged with sensuality." In the European's eyes, Fanon argues, "the veil hides a beauty," and their dominant desire is to see behind the veil.[3] He explains: "This woman who sees without being seen frustrates the colonizer. There is no reciprocity. She does not yield herself, does not give herself, does not offer herself." The idea is reflected in Françoise McAree's "Burqa Silhouette" (2014).

For the colonizer, Fanon argues, the veiled woman becomes an "overwhelmingly beautiful" object of desire: "A strand of hair, a bit of forehead, a segment of an 'overwhelmingly beautiful' face glimpsed in a streetcar or on a train, may suffice to keep alive and strengthen the European's persistence in his irrational conviction that the Algerian woman is the queen of all women" (1965: 43). Alongside this fantasy is the European man's aggressivity toward the veiled Algerian woman, who must be possessed. He wants to see the Algerian woman and "reacts in an aggressive way before this limitation of his perception."

> Unveiling this woman is revealing her beauty; it is baring her secret, breaking her resistance, making her available for adventure. Hiding the face is also disguising a secret; it is also creating a world of mystery, of the hidden . . . There is in it the will to bring this woman within his reach, to make her a possible object of possession. (1965: 44)

The aggressivity "evolves with his frustration" and comes to light in his dream material (1965 43–6). "Every rejected veil disclosed to the eyes of the colonialists, horizons until then forbidden, and revealed to them, piece by piece, the flesh of Algeria laid bare" (1965: 42). Thus, the colonizer's desire to unveil the Algerian woman stood as a double deflowering, a rape and a possession, both of which Fanon saw as a product of the sadism of the occupier whose history in Algeria literally included the pillaging of the country and the raping of women. The context for all this is, of course, settler colonialism, which makes possible, indeed encourages, a freedom for brutality and sadism. Fanon had spoken similarly in *Black Skin, White Masks* criticizing Mannoni (see Fanon 2008: 29n.5). The history of French conquest in Algeria

> has contributed to the birth and the crystallization of the same dynamic image. At the level of the psychological strata of the occupier, the evocation of this freedom given to the sadism of the conqueror, to his eroticism, creates faults, fertile gaps through which both dreamlike forms of behavior and, on certain occasions, criminal acts can emerge. Thus the rape of the Algerian woman in the dream of a European is always preceded by a rending of the veil. (1965: 45)

After November 1954, women not only joined the revolution but demanded to be part of it as "her activity assumed really gigantic proportions." Able to move more freely in the European quarters, women became absolutely indispensable during the Battle of Algiers. They carried messages, guns, and bombs under the veil, which was then strategically abandoned in their passage through the European sector. For Fanon, this was completely new: "Removed and reassumed again and again, the veil has been manipulated, transformed into a technique of camouflage, into a means of struggle" (1965: 61). The veil was now taken over, reappropriated by women, and used in the struggle, taking the FLN by surprise. The process of taking off and putting on the veil stripped it "once and for all," Fanon enthusiastically claims, "of its exclusively traditional dimension," and enabled it to become an "instrument" of liberation (1965: 63). It would take a while before

the radical implications of women's actions were fully understood, since they clearly exceeded the limited classification of
women's actions as delineated by the Soummam platform. For
Fanon, it was precisely such attitudes and actions of women
that provided the clearest proof that Algerian society had
undergone important modifications.

A further example of this was that, "before 1954, in the
psychological realm, the radio was considered an evil object,
anxiogenic and accursed": "[S]witching on the radio meant
giving asylum to the occupiers . . . [and] having a radio meant
accepting . . . being besieged from within by the colonizer"
(Fanon 1965: 89, 92). Quite simply, the radio was an instrument of occupation, a "violent invasion" (1965: 88). After 1956,
however, rather than being seen as an alien object of conquest,
the radio became a source of information for the struggle as
well as a means through which people could identify with the
revolution. Just as antibiotics and "Western" medicine became
important for the liberation fighters (more on this below), the
radio was transformed into a kind of social glue. The FLN
broadcast, "The Voice of Algeria," not only provided a new
objectivity for those relatively uninvolved in the struggle, but
also brought into being historical protagonists who began to
communicate, live, and breathe with the revolution (1965:
83). Over 15 years before Fanon wrote the chapter in *L'An V*,
"This Is the Voice of Algeria," he experienced the power of the
radio, listening with his brother and friends to the voice of the
Free French on the BBC and then reconstructing battles on
maps. Frantz was "electrified by the broadcasts," remembered
Joby (Fanon 2014: 22). "This Is the Voice of Algeria" takes
that group listening to a more socially active level. Staying
informed about the revolution became a new social action,
part of the changing subjectivity and consciousness among the
Algerian people from the bottom up. For the broadcasts tell
"the story of the Liberation on the march, incorporate[ing] it

into the nation's new life" (1965: 79). He describes groups of Algerians listening to the radio which is being jammed by the French. Listening becomes a group activity, with ears close to the radio, trying to outwit the jammers by finely twisting the dial and reconstructing what was being said. Through intense discussions, the listeners became active participants in the construction of a fighting Algeria while at the same time discussing and spreading the news.

The colonial regime reacted to the changes by not only jamming the airwaves and restricting the sale of radios, but also restricting and monitoring the use of antibiotics and other medical equipment. The whole Algerian population became suspect and put under surveillance. With the two sides locked across the Manichean divide, siege was the order of the day, but this was also the time, Fanon argues, "during which men, women, children, the whole Algerian people, experienced at one and the same time their national vocation and the recasting of the new Algerian society" (1965: 62). Among European Algerians, there were some who experienced an "awakening of consciousness" of belonging to an Algerian nation, and more than a few European Algerian students, who had never spoken with Muslims, began to meet and talk and read about the history of the country. As Charles Géronimi puts it in the appendix to the final chapter of L'An V, "Algeria's European Minority," "it was [now] up to the Algerian people to decide" and make the decision that being "with the people . . . was the only way to transform the national revolution into a social revolution" (1965: 169).

In his presentation to the First Congress of Black Writers and Artists in 1956, Fanon argued: "In order to achieve this [total] liberation, the inferiorized person brings all their resources to play, all the acquisitions, old and new, their own and those of the occupant" (1967: 43). Taking over radio and medicine, as well as including members of the European community, are examples of using the occupants' "acquisitions." But such a takeover was not just strategic. Fanon makes clear that taking over an "alien" technique and using it against the colonist does not merely give the people "a fighting instrument for the people," but also gives technologies like the radio itself "totally new meanings." Describing the collective struggle to find "The Voice" across the bandwidths and hear it through the static, Fanon describes an almost physical and strategic social struggle with colonialism: "By common consent, after an exchange of views . . . a real task of reconstruction would then begin. Everyone would participate, and the real battles of yesterday and the day before would be refought . . . The listener would compensate for the fragmentary nature of the news by an autonomous creation of information" (1965: 86). In other words, when the seemingly ordinary struggle against something as meaningless as static becomes actional, the truth of the radio is created, somehow "out of nothing" (1965: 96), as a national consciousness – indeed, as a national culture – "open[ing] up limitless horizons." It reflects the new openness of the subject's own self-activity born out of the revolution. For it is through such radical openness that the autonomous creation of a social collective, the "nation," becomes real.

In the colonial situation, there is nothing neutral about the technology of a transistor radio or the science of medicine; the "truth" of such technologies is determined by the types and forms of oppression they communicate and impose. It is the liberation struggle that shifts viewpoints, which became clear in people's changing attitudes toward the French language. "The Voice of Algeria," broadcast in Arabic, Kabyle, and French, expressed a new element, uniting the nation in its multilingual transmission. "The same message transmitted in three languages," Fanon argues, "unified the experience and gave it a universal dimension" (1965: 89). And it is this radical openness, manifested in the broadcast's ability to include and integrate these multilingual transmissions and unite the nation's "fragments," that attested to the untidiness of the process through which national culture could be conceived in the new reality of the Algerian nation. Fanon's insistence on language's openness as part of the dialectic of national consciousness – "a new language and a new humanity" (1968: 36) – opens up to the world its liberating potentials. In short, the revolution had created new opportunities for the common people to refashion social relations, and what is at stake in Fanon's dialectic is not simply the realization of the revolution, but also something quite new. The former language of threat and insult "lost its accursed character, revealing itself to be capable also of transmitting, for the benefit of the nation, the messages of truth that the latter awaited" (1965: 89).

Thus, for Fanon, taking over the radio also suggests a fundamental change in values born out of a new identification with the revolution, and it is this that he considers a mutation, "a radical change in valence ... not the emergence of an ambivalence ... but a dialectical progression" (1965: 90n). This mutation was also evident in the fact that even Algerian women who were not actively involved in the struggle had "formed the habit of abandoning the veil" (1965: 61). Fanon argues that a new revolutionary subject is unveiled. Revolutionary women appear without preliminary instruction; history is made, with their entry into the public sphere becoming "an intense dramatization, a continuity between woman and revolutionary" (1965: 50). They reinvent their sense of themselves in space, traveling unaccompanied. They set bombs, they stay with unknown comrades, and give refuge to militants in their own homes. On their own initiative, they take part in discussions and activities.

All this marked a new point of departure for Algerian society as "female cells of the FLN received mass memberships."

The impatience of these new recruits and their "exceptional enthusiasm and radicalism that are always characteristic of any youth engaged in building a new world" (1965: 108)[4] exploded "the tight, hermetic, and hierarchical structure of the family" (Caute 1970: 52). Fanon was writing about the meaning of the actions as they were taking place, and the idea of an authentic birth without any previous instruction resonates with his conception of Black self-consciousness as an "absolute intensity of beginning" discussed in *Black Skin, White Masks*.

By 1955, many women had joined the revolutionary movement. Indeed, their actions forced the male leadership of the FLN to recognize them. Before the revolution, women had been held back by illiteracy, poverty, and custom; domestic life had allowed little innovation. The "girl had no opportunity," Fanon argues, "to develop her personality or take any initiative" (1965: 105–7). The revolution upset these restrictions as women "assumed an increasingly important place in revolutionary action" and discovered "the exalting realm of responsibility. The freedom of the Algerian people from then on became identified with woman's liberation, with her entry into history" (1965: 107). If Fanon describes the phenomenology of colonial life as an "occupied breathing," his phenomenological descriptions of the being-in-the-world of the Algerian woman who undertakes the action of unveiling can be seen as a clandestine "combat breathing." Unveiled in the context of the revolutionary movement, the woman forced herself to relearn her own body, to appear at ease unveiled on the colonizer's streets and to invent new dimensions of sublimation and of muscular control. Where the veil had given a feeling of protection, she had first to address the sense of incompleteness without it. Fanon explains that, in the context of the struggle, the young Algerian woman who takes off the veil and experiences a new sense of body-in-the-world is at first manifested by a sense of dissolution and the breakdown of her body's integrity, expressed spatially. Crossing the street, the absence of the veil "distorts the Algerian women's corporal pattern." She "commits errors of judgment" and has to invent new dimensions for her body-in-the-world.

In a remarkable passage, which expresses the beginnings of Fanon's conception of the birth of a new subjectivity psychologically and phenomenologically, he writes: "[The Algerian woman] experiences a sense of incompleteness with great intensity. She has the anxious feeling that something is unfinished, and along with this a frightful sensation of disintegrating. The absence of the veil distorts the Algerian woman's corporal pattern." Remembering that removing the veil is a social action within a revolutionary movement, Fanon continues: "She quickly has to invent new dimensions for her body, new means of muscular control. She has to create for herself an attitude of unveiled-woman-outside. She must overcome all timidity, all awkwardness (for she must pass for a European), and at the same time be careful not to overdo it, not to attract notice to herself." Speaking of the young woman during the Battle of Algiers, navigating the European city, Fanon adds: "The Algerian woman who walks stark naked into the European city relearns her body, re-establishes it in a totally revolutionary fashion. This new dialectic of the body and of the world is primary in the case of one revolutionary woman" (1965: 59).

Removed and reassumed over and over, the veil begins to lose its sacred character, going from an inert object to a vital link in the revolutionary movement. The women negotiating the European sectors negotiated a new sense of bodily disintegration arising from a fear of being frisked, caught, raped, and tortured.[5] As to how women might overcome this "vicious cycle" of debilitating fear, they had no precedent, no example to work with, though Fanon saw that overcoming such fear would create a "calm that [would] t[ake] hold of us and sharpen our senses" (quoted in Lazreg 1993: 131) Thus, for

Fanon, the drama of negotiating the forbidden spaces of the European quarters is intimately connected to challenging colonial as well as patriarchal attitudes within Algeria.

While there was a tradition of women's resistance to French colonization, joining the revolutionary movement as militants was unprecedented, and women initially found themselves having to learn their revolutionary role "instinctively." Their actions, Fanon argues, were "an authentic birth in a pure state"; without a character to imitate, "there [wa]s an intense dramatization, a continuity between the woman and the revolutionary" where the young, urban women became original characters (1965: 50). After 1956 some of these women became models for other women and "constitute[d] the points of reference around which the imagination of Algerian feminine society was to be stirred to the boiling point" (1965: 108). Changes also occurred inside the family. As Fanon puts it, "women were no longer silent" and "men's words were no longer law" as the woman "*literally forged a new place for herself by her sheer strength*" (1965: 109; my emphasis). During this period, "even the Algerian father, the founder of every value" underwent a radical change. Living side by side with the male militants, women began to break away from the traditional ways of life (1965: 47).

Fanon's hope for the future is nowhere more apparent than in his writing on women in *L'An V*, where he insists that the action of the revolutionary woman had an effect on Algerian society as a whole, liberating women from a double dependency of "feudal traditions" on the one hand and colonialism on the other, and mobilizing others to become part of the struggle.

In each chapter of *L'An V de la révolution algérienne*, Fanon moves beyond anti-colonial Manicheanism, emphasizing the changes in life and attitude caused by the revolution. "Medicine and Colonialism," focuses on the radical change in attitudes toward "modern" medicine during the war of liberation, problematizing the division between "tradition" and "modern" associated with sociological approaches, and challenging the idea that the colonizer is the harbinger of progress. Fanon presents "Western" medicine as a tragic feature of the colonial situation whereby the establishment of the colonial medical system goes hand in hand with military conquest and the doctor as part of the settler class. In the name of science, Western medicine is utterly opposed to the persistence of "traditional" medicine. And the reaction of the colonized was similarly absolute; colonial medicine had to be rejected because it meant a choice against the local community and the local healer. This led to a refusal to use colonial medicine even when it was "objectively worth choosing" (1965: 63). The reactions of the colonized are understandable, Fanon argues, because doctors, schoolteachers, and engineers are literally not very different from the police and military. All had to be dismissed. And the doctor's office, the hospital, and the clinic were enemy spaces where the colonized have to go. Like the North African patient in France whom Fanon had written about, "the colonized person who goes to see the doctor is always diffident, answering in monosyllables, giv[ing] little in the way of explanation" (1965: 126)

But the colonized rejection of all colonial medicine sometimes has tragic consequences that also need to be understood. Fanon describes a scenario: "My son has meningitis and it really has to be treated as a meningitis ought to be treated. But the colonial constellation is such that what should be the brotherly and tender insistence of one who wants only to help me is interpreted as a manifestation of the conqueror's arrogance and desire to humiliate" (1965: 125–6). Therefore the antibiotics that would address the meningitis would have to be rejected. Reflecting on this, Fanon tells his readers: "Every time we do not understand [the reactions of the colonized], we must tell ourselves that we are at the heart of the drama – that of the impossibility of finding a meeting ground in any colonial situation" (1965: 125). I think this is significant and I will get back to it. Here, because Fanon believes that colonialism is not a simple occupation of a territory, but an occupation of body and mind, he argues that the struggle against it follows "one of the laws of the psychology of colonization," where, "in its initial phase the action . . . of the occupier . . . determine[s] the resistance around which a people's will to survive becomes organized" (1965: 47). In this situation, "it is not possible for the colonized society and the colonizing society to agree to pay tribute to a single value," because "every qualification is perceived by the occupier as a confession of congenital impotence" and as an invitation to perpetuate the oppression. Thus all colonial values are rejected, "even if these values objectively be worth choosing" (1965: 126, 122, 62–3). Thus, colonial schoolteachers, doctors, and engineers are dismissed in "one lump" alongside the police and military (1965: 123) – and rightly so, since they are considered part of the whole "system" and are sometimes coextensive (doctors became part of the legal use of torture in a system that denies it).[6] Any compromise with colonialism is viewed as an evil, a threat to psychic and bodily integrity. Indeed, in such a Manichean reality, truth itself is absolutely split; what is true for the colonizer is a lie for the colonized so that, in reaction to "the enemy's congenital lie . . . the people's own lie . . . suddenly acquire[s] a dimension of truth" (1965: 87). This becomes viciously clear, for example, when the "objective truth" of an antibiotic treatment for an infection becomes "constantly vitiated by the lie of the colonial situation" (1965: 128). A whole series of cultural resistances to "Western" medicine are enacted to reject the occupier's presence (1965: 93). As Fanon writes of the phenomenology of colonialism in the appendix to "Algeria Unveiled":

There is not occupation of the territory, on the one hand, and independence of person on the other. It is the country as a whole, its history, its daily pulsation that are contested, disfigured, in the hope of final destruction. Under these conditions, the individual's breathing is an observed, an occupied breathing. It is a combat breathing. From this point on, the real values of the occupied quickly tend to acquire a clandestine form of existence. (1965: 65)

*L'An V de la révolution algérienne* is a sociodiagnosis employing social, political, and psychoanalytic perspectives. Years before publication of Edward Said's *Orientalism*, Fanon was already taking aim at sociologists, ethnologists, medical professionals, and French liberals. But the focus of his book is not the Orientalists. Taking off from his presentation at the Second Congress of Black Writers and Artists in Rome, the focus is on the radical social and cultural changes, and the thinking occurring in Algerian daily life as a result of the liberation struggle. *L'An V* is the product of that context, and Fanon makes it clear he can only speak of actions "known to the enemy" and can "say nothing about the new forms of action adopted by women in the Revolution" (1965: 50n.10). One essential difference between *Black Skin, White Masks* and *L'An V* is the revolutionary context. While the focus in the former is on the quest for disalienation provided by Fanon's analysis of alienation in a racist and anti-Black society, *L'An V* begins with action expressed in the thesis that people "change at the same time they change the world," which "has never been so manifest as it is now in Algeria" (1965: 30). In *Black Skin, White Masks*, Fanon concludes that "bourgeois society" is rotten and its people putrefying, and anyone "who takes a stand against this living death is in a way a revolutionary" (2008: 199). In *L'An V* the stand is already taking place and people's revolutionary action is blowing apart the putrefying ways of thinking and doing as well as the internalizations of colonialism's daily dehumanization, humiliations, and violence, which are brought "into the homes and minds of the colonized subject" (2004: 3). The changed attitudes toward Western medicines are a product of the liberation struggle because it became important to treat injured anticolonial fighters. Using all their resources, both their own and those of the occupier (1967: 43) stripped the antibiotic of its negative associations and (like the radio) was assimilated "at an extraordinary rate" (1965: 145).

Fanon wrote and collected the essays in *L'An V de la révolution algérienne* while breathing in "the oxygen of the revolution" as he worked at his characteristically breathtaking pace. As noted, the title gestured to a new French revolutionary calendar beginning on July 14, 1789. The Paris Commune of 1871 also re-established the revolutionary calendar. What is often forgotten is the connection between the Paris Commune and the national liberation uprising in Algeria[7] with the Commune de l'Algérie sending delegates to Paris to discuss solidarity.[8] The French destroyed both communes, but the idea of radical changes in social consciousness and in social relations, a people no longer in fear in the face of brutal violence, was a valuable lesson that echoes across Fanon's chapters proclaiming a liberated Algeria "no longer in future heaven." Fanon concludes the book with this claim: "The essence of the revolution, the true revolution which changes [hu]mankind and renews a society is . . . this oxygen which brings about and sustains a new kind of human being – that too is the Algerian revolution" (1965: 80–1). In other words, convinced of the truth of his revolutionary concept, Fanon saw *L'An V* as a challenge both to the half-million-strong French colonial military machine in Algeria, recently defeated in Vietnam at Dien Bien Phu, and to the French liberal left attitude that saw the armed struggle as one that would only end violently. For

Fanon, the problem was that the colonialists (and, he would add, the narrow nationalists) had shut their eyes to the real facts of the problem; they had imagined "that our power is measured by the number of our heavy machine guns. This was true in the first months of 1955. It is no longer true today ... The power of the Algerian Revolution *henceforth resides* in the radical mutation that the Algerian has undergone" (1965: 31–2; my emphasis). Following the spirit of Soummam and anticipating political negotiations with France, it was clear to Fanon that neither the military nor external leadership, but only the revolutionary struggle and the radical mutations in popular consciousness, could truly liberate the nation. What was at stake, therefore, was articulating the *new humanism* that had to be born, self-reflexively, out of the revolutionary process itself, and in a revolutionary program. Fanon's critique of the "barbarism" of the cycle of violence and counterviolence is also an implicit critique of the elitism, substitutionism, and adventurism of a purely military model of revolution. Going behind the reciprocity of violence (exponentially increased by the colonialists), Fanon challenges the idea of a military solution divorced from politics, asking: "Was freedom worth the consequences of penetrating that enormous circuit of terrorism and counter-terrorism?" His concern, in other words, is with the oxygen of the revolution, the new human relations and freedom, "which creates and shapes" the new reality of the nation coming into being (1965: 181).

Including himself, "we Algerians" is radically multicultural, multilingual, and multifaith, a political principle that being Algerian includes all who are willing to fight for new social relations and is grounded in their emergent possibility. Ultimately, for Fanon, the reconfiguration of Algeria has to be based on the reconstruction of the self, what he calls "an inner mutation" (1965: 179) stripped of the "mental sedimentation of the emotional and intellectual handicaps which resulted from 130 years of oppression" (1965: 179). The revolution opened up the possibility of a new society, no longer as a dream but based on the radical changes in consciousness that revolutionary action had engendered. Because of this revolutionary presence, Fanon's book has a remarkable contemporaneity.

The book's first chapter, "Algeria Unveiled" (or, more literally and actively, "Algeria unveils itself") has been much discussed.[9] And today one can see its immediate relevance to the "Woman. Life. Freedom" revolt in Iran[10] which became a daily occurrence (at the time of writing in October 2022[11]), resonating across the region. The daily mobilizations taking place throughout the nation threaten the regime, not only by challenging the strict rules of the "morality police" but also by expressing new figures of resistance of unveiled women in urban spaces.

Asking the question, "Is the uprising in Iran a feminist revolution?" an Iranian feminist (L 2022) writes of her own experience of being drawn into the protests, the ordinariness of burning headscarves, police attacks, and new experiences of her body in space where "the body moves ahead of cognition," becoming newly social and "unconsciously execut[ing] what I had watched other protesters do." This an element of what Fanon meant by a "new dialectic of the body" as women unlearn, relearn, and "invent new dimensions" for their body on the streets (1965: 59). L explains that, "released from our bodies," women become "figures of resistance" stimulating "the desires of other women," making it a "feminist revolution" distinguished by a "collective desire and consciousness." A radical mutation is occurring personally, politically, and imaginatively so that women "go to the street not with the bodies that they are, but with the bodies that they can and want to be ... When every organ of the body goes beyond its self-awareness and the ways it has learned to be." These figures of resistance, she adds, "were already present in the unconscious of the protestors without ever having been practiced, as though they had been practicing them for years." What could be considered "unconscious," or perhaps spontaneous acts of resistance, have become self-organized as collective and political bodies where new subjectivities who have "only now discovered the possibility, the beauty, of its own resistance" are "maturing anew" (L: 2022).[12]

After November 1, 1954, the European sector of Algiers (which was unknown to all women except domestic cleaning women, the faceless "Fatmas") became the space for a new persona to emerge from behind the veil. In the chapter "The Algerian Family," Fanon focuses on how commitment to revolution has radically changed social relations in the family. As Ato Sekyi-Otu puts it: "To hear Fanon tell it . . . 'to speak and tell a story about itself' derives its legitimacy from the degree to which women win their rights to speak, hear, and shape the 'nation's words,' the degree to which they win their fundamental human rights as citizens" (1996: 217–18). But after independence women's political power was fleeting. The new Algerian constitution guaranteed equality and women's right to vote. Women were elected deputies and, veiled and unveiled, they voted in the National Assembly. But the memory and language of women's actions were soon muted. A conservative reaction against "cosmopolitanism" began, manifested by attacks on women who walked down the street hand in hand with a man and who were then ordered to be married immediately. One example of the retrogression and the retreat from the radical changes that Fanon had described just three years earlier was seen with the formation of the Union Nationale des Femmes Algériennes, which in its original constitution spoke of equality and rights while at the same time emphasizing woman's role as mother, wife, and guarantor of Arab-Islamic values.

Women's institutional equality in Algeria turned out to be only temporary, as women were soon forced back from public life. But this new reality does not undermine Fanon's claim that radical changes in consciousness and in social relations had taken place. Rather, it indicates the power of conservative forces within the nationalist movement and the importance of a clear liberatory ideology of "founding another humanity." The fact that the idea of woman's liberation remained crucial for Algeria underlines the unfinished nature of decolonization, which became a paramount concern in Fanon's last year of life.

Was Fanon too uncritical of these internal realities, a political conservativism in the name of Islam? In an undated response to a letter he received from the Iranian activist scholar Ali Shariati,[13] who underscored the importance of a revival of Shi'ism to the struggle, Fanon made his position clear. He hoped that what Shariati called "authentic intellectuals" "may make good use of the immense cultural and social resources harbored in Muslim societies and minds, with the aim of emancipation and the founding of *another humanity*" (2018: 668; my emphasis). But he notes that Shariati's "interpretation of the rebirth of religious spirit and [his] efforts to mobilize this great power [is] . . . now prey to *internal conflicts* or impaired with paralysis [and] . . . *appears as a withdrawal into itself*" (2018: 669; my emphasis). This withdrawal into itself is the critical philosophical concern that Fanon discusses in *Les Damnés de la terre*, and which Steve Biko quoted as a philosophic principle of Black consciousness in South Africa: "The consciousness of self is not the closing of a door to communication. Philosophic thought teaches us, on the contrary, that it is its guarantee. National consciousness, *which is not nationalism*, is the only thing that will give us an international dimension" (1968: 245; my emphasis). This dialectic is what was at stake in Fanon's critique of Shariati, who was instrumental in making Fanon's writings available in Iran before the 1979 revolution. In the letter, Fanon continues, "my path diverges from, and is even opposed to yours" (2018: 669). Fanon's criticism is embedded in what he called the "misadventures" of national consciousness that he sees taking place across the continent, in the name of tradition, custom, religion, and the nation. He critically remarks that Shariati's path is similar to "Senghor, Jomo Kenyatta, Nyerere and Kateb Yacine all of whom undertook to revive African nationalism" (2018: 669). Instead, in *Les Damnés de la terre* he advises that the anticolonial struggle "must guard against the danger of perpetuating . . . tradition which holds sacred the superiority of the masculine element over the feminine. Women will have exactly the same place as men, *not just in the clauses of the constitution but in the life of every day: in the factory, at school, and in assemblies*" (1968: 202; see also 2004: 142; my emphasis).

# 7

# Fanon, a Revolutionary Pan-Africanist Ambassador and His Last Days

For nearly three years I have been trying to bring the misty idea
of African Unity out of the subjectivist bogs of the majority of its
supporters. African Unity is a principle on the basis of which it is
proposed to achieve the United States of Africa without passing
through the middle-class chauvinistic national phase with its procession
of wars and death-tolls.

Fanon, "This Africa To Come", *Toward the African Revolution*

With Josie and Olivier, Fanon left for Accra in February 1960
to become an ambassador for the GPRA, but after catching
malaria, Josie returned to Tunis with Olivier about six months
later. Jeanne-Marie Manuellan reports that Josie told her she
did not want to stay in Accra because she had become the continued object of rumor and innuendo for being married to a
Black man. After leaving Accra, Josie started working at *Jeune
Afrique* and a decision was made that Frantz would shuttle
between Accra and Tunis.

Fanon was first in Accra in December 1958, just after the
GPRA was formed, and he spoke as its representative at the

First All-African Peoples Congress. By then, he had already begun to meet militants and leaders from African liberation movements who were arriving in Tunis, including the anti-colonialist Cameroonian leader Félix-Roland Moumié. Fanon recognized the importance of developing pan-African solidarity work with the Algerian revolution. He "became the key intermediary for the African community," notes Cherki (2005: 124) and was supported by the FLN in building up these relations with African independence movements.[1]

After a ten year "transition," Ghana was one of the first colonized African nations to become independent, in March 1957. Kwame Nkrumah had been imprisoned by the British during this transition but he never swayed from his pursuance of the nonviolent "positive action" campaign of protests, strikes, and non-cooperation. In 1951, while still in prison, he was elected to Parliament; he was released shortly afterwards. Nkrumah's pan-Africanism became articulated through his notion of a united African Personality. He promoted the first Conference of Independent African States in April 1958, which was limited to the leaders of eight sovereign states: Ethiopia, Ghana, Liberia, Libya, Morocco, Sudan, Tunisia, and the United Arab Republic. The FLN was not invited, but sent delegates; the "'Algeria Question' would come to haunt the transcontinental link Nkrumah hoped to forge" (Ahlman 2010:70). In Ghana, a vigorous debate about violence had already started before the conference began, highlighting "the structural and political violence that colonialism had brought colonized people" (Ahlman 2010: 72). Along with Moumié, the FLN demanded to be given the opportunity to address the conference. After being allowed to speak, they succeeded in getting the Algeria question onto the agenda; it was reported that "Algeria has set the temper of the Conference." This led to a much more militant and inclusive conference in the following December.

The All-African Peoples Congress "was attended by over three hundred delegates from twenty-eight countries ... representing sixty-two radical, often illegal political and labor organizations," including representatives from Algeria, Angola, Cameroon, Congo, and South Africa (Young 2005: 35). Fanon gave a memorable speech that would mark "a new direction in Pan-Africanism" (Turner and Kelley 2021: 324). Its call for the recognition of anticolonial violence as legitimate led to the conference's resolution to support "all fighters for freedom in Africa." Fanon had already said as much, if not much more, in April 1958, in his *El Moudjahid* article "Decolonization and Independence": "the form given to the struggle of the Algerian people is such, in its violence and in its total character, that it will have a decisive influence on the future struggles of the other colonies." And, he added, "the Algerian revolution introduces a new style into the struggles for national liberation" where the "liberated individual who undertakes to build the new society" is quite in contrast to "that pseudo-independence in which ministers, having a limited responsibility, hobnob with an economy dominated by the colonial pact." Liberation, he continued, requires "the total destruction of the colonial system, from the pre-eminence of the language of the oppressor and 'departmentalization,' to the customs union that in reality maintains the former colonized in the meshes of the culture, of the fashion, and of the images of the colonialist" (1967: 104–5).

In Accra, Fanon met other radical nationalist leaders, including Patrice Lumumba from Congo. In Fanon's last article in *El Moudjahid*, "Africa Accuses the West," he writes about Lumumba's assassination, which had occurred two weeks earlier, remembering that Lumumba had become "definitely aware of the solidarity of Africa's people" at the All-African Peoples Congress (2018: 646).

In his conference speech in Accra, Fanon declared that "Africa is at war" in a struggle to "liberate the continent." A report in *The Times* of London (December 10, 1958, which included on its back page a picture of the conference under the title "Hands Off Africa") described the event:

> Dr F. Omar [Fanon was traveling with a Tunisian passport, under the name F. Omar], leader of the Algerian National Liberation Front delegation, called for the formation of a strong force of African freedom fighters. He said nationalist leaders in dependent territories must adopt all forms of struggle to achieve their objective, and not depend only on peaceful negotiations.[2]

The effect of Fanon's speech on the conference was reflected in another report by the pan-Africanist publisher Stan Grant:[3]

> Another speaker, Dr. Omar of Algeria, told the Conference that in the fight for freedom, the African now had to resort to any available devise [sic], including "force and violence." He said that they had gathered in Accra in unity "to prevent the dangers of the future." "In our fight against colonialism and imperialism, we must constitute ourselves into a national front, against inhumanity and poverty." "The colonial structural resemblance [sic] could be seen at its worst in Algeria. The enemy is powerful and there is the possibility of continuing its maneuvers to cripple our plans for freedom." He said that colonialists and imperialists had devised ways and means of remaining on African soil. "The colonialists – English and French – had accused themselves by their policies and doctrines of the domination of Africa," he added. Dr. Omar was wildly cheered as he concluded by saying: "And in our fight for freedom, we should embark on plans effective enough to touch the pulse of the imperialists

– by force of action and, indeed, violence." (Grant 1973: 288)

Writing about the conference in *El Moudjahid*, Fanon said that there was "unanimity" about the settler colonies, where "only armed struggle will bring defeat of the occupying nation" (1967: 156).[4] Critical of the nonviolence and negotiation approaches favored by African leaders (including Nkrumah), the speech was "wildly applauded" (Macey, 2012: 365). More than 30 years later, the Tanzanian revolutionary A.M. Babu still remembered Fanon's "dramatic intervention" as an "historic action that introduced an important new outlook on the conduct of liberation struggles in Africa" (1989: vi) validating the struggle that was already going on.

Whether the British academic Peter Worsley was referring to the December 1958 conference or the 1960 "Positive Action" conference held in Accra,[5] he gives an excellent description of first hearing and witnessing Fanon as fully present in his analytical power and emotional intensity:

The proceedings consisted mainly of speeches by leaders of African nationalism from all over the continent, few of whom said anything notable. When, therefore, the representative of the Algerian Revolutionary Provisional Government, their Ambassador to Ghana, stood up to speak I prepared myself for an address by a diplomat – not usually an experience to set the pulses racing. I found myself electrified by a contribution that was remarkable not only for its analytical power, but delivered, too, with a passion and brilliance that is all too rare. I discovered that the Ambassador was a man named Frantz Fanon. At one point during his talk he appeared almost to break down. I asked him afterwards what had happened. He replied that he had suddenly felt emotionally overcome at the thought that he had to stand there, before the assembled representatives of African nationalist movements, at a time when men were dying and being tortured in his country for a cause whose justice ought to command automatic support from rational and progressive human beings. (Quoted in Hansen 1977: 51)

Fanon's speech had the immediate effect of making the "Algerian question" and the question of armed struggle central to the conference. While the conference remained officially nonviolent, armed struggle had become legitimate. Nkrumah "pledged the support and the active solidarity of the people of Ghana and of its government to the fighting people of Algeria" (Fanon 1967: 152). The reality of settler colonialism's resistance to any reform had moved Nkrumah beyond his own position. The conference chairman, Tom Mboya, expressed Nkrumah's shift in perspective as he responded to questions from the international press: "Africans were not pacifists. If you hit them, they might hit back."

Fanon was considered the leader of the FLN delegation and was received by Nkrumah at the end of the conference. Nkrumah's first act was to announce that the government would "recognize the Provisional Government of the Algerian Republic" (1967: 152) and, after just over a year, Fanon would become its representative in Accra.[6] Out of the conference came a number of proposals to create an All-African Peoples' Revolutionary Army, or African Legion, conceived as a multinational fighting force that could be sent to help any anticolonial struggle. Fanon's report on the conference in *El Moudjahid* (1967: 153–7) concluded that this decision was an important commitment to a radical pan-Africanism. While Nkrumah's internationalism made it clear that national liberation could not be established in one country without being linked to the liberation of the whole continent,[7] his position that, for settler colonies, "only armed struggle would bring about the defeat of the occupying nation" (1967: 156–7) was a remarkable shift. From Fanon's perspective, the African Legion and armed struggle had direct relevance not only to Algeria but also to settler colonies, as well as Angola, where anticolonial actions faced brutal repression. Later, the idea of an African Legion played a part in Fanon's critique of Lumumba's call to the United Nations to intervene in the Congo in 1960; it also played an important role in Fanon's 1960 mission through Cameroon and Mali to create a new front for the liberation war. This perspective can be seen in the introduction to the notebook he wrote on the mission in preparation for a report to the high command of the FLN. Fanon's concept of an African Legion was concretely linked with his idea of "inter-African solidarity [as] a solidarity of fact, a solidarity of action, a solidarity concrete in men, in equipment, in money" (1967: 173). He writes of pan-Africanism as a continent alive, moving, and in motion – proving "by concrete demonstrations that this continent was one":

> Our mission: to open the southern front. To transport arms and munitions from Bamako. Stir up the Saharan population, infiltrate to the Algerian high plateaus. After carrying Algeria to the four corners of Africa, move up with all Africa toward African Algeria, toward the North, toward Algiers, the continental city. What I should like: great lines, great navigation channels[8] through the desert. Subdue the desert, deny it, assemble Africa, create the continent. That Malians, Senegalese, Guineans, Ghanaians should descend from Mali onto our territory. And those of the Ivory Coast, of Nigeria, of Togoland. That they should all climb the slopes of the desert and pour over the colonialist bastion. To turn the absurd and the impossible inside out and hurl a continent against the last ramparts of colonial power (1967: 180–1)

This was all part of his deepening critique of what he would call the "subjectivist bog," hollow calls for African unity instead of developing a "United States of Africa without passing through the middle-class chauvinistic national phase with its procession of wars and death-tolls." While he was already developing such a critique of the "middle-class chauvinistic national stage" in Tunis (see, for example, the paper presented at the Second Congress of Black Writers and Artists in 1959), the short year in Africa would profoundly deepen his critique.

## Fanon and Africa, 1960

The FLN in Africa was basically Fanon.

Mohammed Harbi[9]

Fanon was based in Accra for 10 months, from February to December 1960. In this short time, he was incredibly active. It was his "year of Africa," connecting with African liberation movements and its leaders and becoming fully part of the continent on the move. It was this continental liberation that Fanon wanted to project in a book proposed to his publisher, in July 1960, titled *Alger–Le Cap* (*Algiers to Cape Town*). The title was not only a subversion of Cecil Rhodes's imperialist claims, Cape to Cairo, but also indicated Fanon's Soummamian focus on the struggle inside Algeria. In other words, rather than Cairo, where the external leaders of the FLN were located, it was Algiers, continuing the revolutionary focus of *L'An V* as the ground for liberation of the continent, recognizing how "there was no region or country which was not affected by anti-colonial struggles ... The entire continent was in motion" (Turner and Kelley 2021: 323).

In April 1960, Fanon gave talks at two international conferences. The first was at the Positive Action Conference for Peace and Security in Africa in Accra on April 7–10 and right after, at the Conference of Afro Asian Peoples' Solidarity in Conakry (Guinea), April 11–15. In June, he represented the FLN at the Conference of Independent African States in Addis.

At the Accra Positive Action Conference (which was opened by Kwame Nkrumah), Fanon's paper, "Why We Use Violence," provided a strategic analysis of the necessity of violence in response to colonial regimes that were not only instituted by violence, but also reproduced by daily violence. Listing some of the themes that he would develop in *Les Damnés de la terre*, Fanon argued that violence against the colonized is a daily reality known by "apartheid in South Africa, forced labor in Angola, [and] racism in Algeria" (2018: 654). He called this violence "three-dimensional," expressed in the daily violence of the present, the violence against the past, and the violence against the future. Here the history of colonized peoples is "emptied of all substance" and they are presented "as a people arrested in their evolution, impervious to reason" and thus "incapable of directing their own affairs, requiring the permanent presence of an external ruling power" (2018: 654). This "meeting point of multiple, diverse, repeated, cumulative violences," can only be "logically confronted," he concluded, "by ending the colonial regime by any means necessary" (2018: 654). In Algeria, he continued, the revolution has radically changed everything, including the colonized's defensive mechanisms as the political organization channels (a term he uses in *Les Damnés de la terre*), survival instincts, and reactions toward the source of the violence: the colonial regime.

In the second part of the speech, he shifted the focus to racism and settler colonialism in Angola, Algeria, Rhodesia, and South Africa and to the European settler's obstinate hostility to "any attack on his supremacy" (2018: 657). Referring back to Nkrumah's speech in the face of such obstinacy, Fanon added that "violence must first be fought with the language of truth and of reason" (2018: 655), agreeing with Nkrumah that the idea of "Africa for the Africans does not mean that other races are excluded." To the colonist in Algeria who says that Algeria belongs to them, Fanon responded with a number of radical humanist statements: "We, Algerians, say: 'We agree, Algeria belongs to all of us, let us build it on democratic bases and together build an Algeria that is commensurate with our ambition and our love'" (2018: 656). And to the colonial settlers:

> We do not say . . . "You are a stranger, go away." We do not say . . . "We will take over the leadership of the country and make you pay for your crimes and those of your ancestors." We do not tell him that "to the past hatred of the Black we will oppose the present and future hatred of the White" . . . We say . . . "We are Algerians, banish all racism from our land, all forms of oppression and let us work for the flourishing and enrichment of humanity."

In fact, Fanon added, the revolution in Algeria welcomed the support of Europeans and through their connections with the revolution they "have discovered their love of the Algerian homeland" (2018: 658; translation altered).

In June, Fanon was in Addis Adaba for the Conference of Independent African States. Though he did not give a speech, he did write to his publisher under the name Nadia Farès, and included a rough outline of *Alger–Le Cap*. The book would be "based on the armed revolution in the Maghreb, the development of consciousness, and national struggle in the rest of Africa."

Writing again in early September in the third person, Farès tells Maspero that Fanon had completed the first chapter and wanted it published in *Les Temps Modernes*.

## A new African front of the Algerian revolution

In October 1960, Fanon took part in a reconnaissance mission to consider creating a new southern front. With the eastern and western borders of Algeria almost completely cut off by the electric-fenced and mined Morice line, Fanon considered the possibility of a southern front as a mode of supply for the FLN and discussed options with Mali's president, Modibo Keïta. The idea was supported by the GPRA. It soon became an overland mission after a group of eight (two political commissars, two signal specialists, two medics, and two soldiers) were told their plane from Accra to Conakry via Monrovia was full and that they would have to take an Air France flight. Ever vigilant and suspecting a trap, the group decided to drive to Bamako. During the often grueling six-week trip of more than 2,000 kilometers, Fanon wrote a remarkable notebook (1967: 177–90) expressing his thinking about "This Africa to Come." Though only one of the notebooks survives, it reveals Fanon's mind in motion as he experiences and listens to descriptions of Africa's decolonization as "the untidy affirmation of an original idea propounded as an absolute" (1968: 41). Reading these notes, one can get the sense of Fanon's acute attunement with the continent on the move and his connection to its rhythms and sensibilities: "In every corner arms make signs to us, voices answer us, hands grasp ours . . . Things are on the move" (1967: 179). He writes of one of his traveling companions, the ALN Commandant Chawki: "One can say anything to them but they need to feel and touch the Revolution in the words uttered."[10] Chawki and Fanon were the mission's two political commissars.

The demanding trip is described with the optimism of the African revolution:

To put Africa in motion, to cooperate in its organization, in its regrouping, behind revolutionary principles. To participate in the ordered movement of a continent – this was really the work I had chosen. The first point of departure, the first base was represented by Guinea. Then Mali, ready for anything, fervent and brutal, coherent and singularly keen, extended the bridgehead and opened valuable prospects. To the East, Lumumba was marking time. The Congo which constituted the second landing beach for revolutionary ideas was caught in an inextricable network of sterile contradictions. The colonialist citadels of Angola, Mozambique, Kenya, the Union of South Africa were not ripe to be effectively blockaded.

Yet everything was set. And here the colonialist system of defense, while discordant, was reviving old particularisms and breaking up the liberating lava. For the moment it was therefore necessary to hang on in the Congo and advance in the West. For us Algerians the situation was clear. But the terrain remained difficult, very difficult. Taking the West as a starting point, we had to prove, by concrete demonstrations, that this continent was one. (1967: 177–8)

"Leave it to Fanon," Cherki writes, who, "in the middle of a dangerous mission," finds "time to lose himself in books" (2006: 151). He read histories, reliving "the old Empires" and understanding how the region had been "worked over by so many influences." Mentioning that "Islam and race . . . require extra caution," he warns that the revolution "will require a great deal of rigor and cool thinking" (1967: 186).[11]

Macey describes Fanon's narrative as being "rapid and breathless" (and, I would add, poetic):

He had traveled from tropical forest to savannah and then desert [but] he never describes the landscapes he had seen even though their physical geography would have been of strategic importance to any expeditionary force. He mentions only the sunsets that turned the Saharan sky purple and dark red. (2012: 438)

Fanon's concerns are otherwise deeply embedded in the movement for freedom and the possibilities of building a new society. His notes, not written for publication, resonate critically with the speech he gave at the Second Congress of Black Writers and Artists a year earlier:

But the sun is still very high in the heavens and if one listens with one ear glued to the red earth one very distinctly hears the sound of rusty chains, groans of distress, and the bruised flesh is so constantly present in this stifling noonday that one's shoulders droop with the weight of it.

He then makes it clear that his vision is not a poet's Africa, but an Africa rooted in everyday:

For the people is impatient to do, to play, to say. The people that says: I want to build myself as a people, I want to build, to love, to respect, to create. This people that weeps when you say: I come from a country where the women have no children and the children no mothers and that sings: Algeria, brother country, country that calls, country that hopes. That is the real Africa, the Africa that we had to let loose in the continental furrow, in the continental direction. The Africa that we had to guide, mobilize, launch on the offensive. (1967: 179)

He ends the first section of the notes with a most profound critique that would be developed further in *Les Damnés de la terre*. First, he argues:

Colonialism and its derivatives do not, as a matter of fact, constitute the present enemies of Africa. In a short time this continent will be liberated. For my part, the deeper I enter into the cultures and the political circles the surer I am that the great danger that threatens Africa is the absence of ideology. (1967: 185)

These sentences should be reread carefully. Colonialism is not the present enemy, he says, though he knows intimately of the constant maneuvers and manipulations that are playing a central role in the crisis in Congo, and which would lead to Lumumba's murder and the destruction of Congolese independence. A year earlier, he had argued in *L'An V de la révolution algérienne* that French colonialism in Algeria was finished and that a new Algeria was "no longer in future heaven" (1965: 30). Here he adds an important qualification: the danger to the realization of a new society is not only colonialism, with its maneuvering and its dirty tricks, but the absence of a unifying liberatory ideology. The problem is how to develop a liberatory ideology inside the practice of the popular struggle as well as how to analyze the counterrevolution within the revolution. In the front of his mind would be the systematic execution of the radical leaders of the African revolutions: Abane, Lumumba, and Moumié.

The 1960 notebooks begin with Moumié's murder. Fanon explains that he had met the young leader of the UPC (Union des populations du Cameroun) on the Accra airfield on September 30 after returning from some important meetings in Geneva: "In three months, he told us, we would witness a mass ebbing of colonialism in Cameroon." Fanon continues in short staccato sentences:

In Rome, two weeks later, we were to have met again. He was absent. His father standing at the arrival in Accra saw me coming, alone, and a great sadness settled on his face.

Two days later a message told us that Félix was hospitalized. Then that poisoning was suspected ... A few days later the news reached us: Félix Moumié was dead. We hardly felt this death. A murder, but a bloodless one. There were neither volleys nor machine guns nor bombs. Thallium poisoning. It made no sense. Thallium! How was one to grasp such a cause? An abstract death striking the most concrete, the most alive, the most impetuous man. Félix's tone was constantly high. Aggressive, violent, full of anger, in love with his country, hating cowards and maneuverers. Austere, hard, incorruptible. A bundle of revolutionary spirit packed into 60 kilos of muscle and bone. (1967: 179–80)

Now, just weeks later, Fanon was witnessing Lumumba's murder and seeing the counterrevolution unfold first hand. The two men had been together just a few months earlier at a conference in Leopoldville in the midst of US and Belgian plots, just two weeks before Mobutu's military coup in Congo (see Fanon 2018: 645–52).

In June 1960, Congo gained independence and Moïse Tshombe immediately declared Katanga's "independence," becoming its president with the full support of Belgium and the Belgian mining company Union Minière du Haut-Katanga, backed by US interests, especially in uranium. While the arrival of UN troops meant that African states did not need to offer direct military aid, this did very little to upset Tshombe's secessionist regime. The unfolding counterrevolutionary reality was of course on both Lumumba's and Fanon's minds when they met in September; Lumumba opened the Pan-African Congress in Léopoldville speaking of how far they had come in the continent's liberation since the 1958 Accra conference, where they had first met. But, Lumumba continued, "we can truly attain this goal only if we remain united and stand shoulder to shoulder. Our solidarity has meaning only because it has no limits, and because we are finally aware that the fate of Africa is one and indivisible." Lumumba related this unity directly to what was happening in the Congo at that very moment: "You are aware of the causes underlying what is currently being called the Congo crisis, which in reality is only the continuation of a struggle between forces of oppression and forces of liberation." He mentioned his decision to go to New York and the fact that the UN had answered his plea for help against Belgian aggression; he then returned to the ongoing situation in Congo and the challenges that it faced:

> The classic consequences of colonialism, which we have all experienced or are still experiencing in part, are particularly tenacious here: continuing military occupation, tribal divisions that have long been fostered and encouraged, destructive political opposition that has been deliberately planned, carefully coordinated, and bought for money . . . Our internal difficulties, tribal quarrels, the focal points of political opposition, seem to be centered, by some strange chance, in regions where our mining resources and our power resources are richest. We know how they were deliberately fostered, and how even today they are being furthered within our borders . . . The goal of these plots is the economic reconquest of our country . . . By shattering the colonial framework, our countries, which only yesterday everyone tried to ignore, have upset the old world.

"This is our year," he declared: "You are witnesses to this, and actors in the drama. This year is that of our unconditional victory. It is the year of heroic Algeria, bathed in blood, Algeria the martyr, whose exemplary struggle reminds us that there can be no compromise with the enemy." And then he warned:

> As militants for African unity, all these leaders have said "no" to the attempt to strangle Africa. All of them immedi-

ately realized that the colonialists, in their efforts to regain their former hold, have endangered not only the genuine independence of the Congo, but also the very existence of all the independent countries of Africa. They have all realized that if the Congo dies, all Africa will be plunged into the darkness of defeat and slavery. (Lumumba 1972: 343–7)

The oppressor will not miss an opportunity to mobilize those whom it has marginalized and pauperized, argues Fanon, who gives us examples in *Les Damnés de la terre*, including, importantly, from Congo:

If this readily available human reserve is not immediately organized by the insurrection, it will join the colonialist troops as mercenaries. In Algeria it was the Harkis and the Messalists who were drawn from the lumpenproletariat; in Angola, it supplied the road gangs who opened the way for the Portuguese troops; in the Congo, it can be found in the regionalist demonstrations in the provinces of Kasai and Katanga, while in Leopoldville it was used by the enemies of the Congo to organize "spontaneous" meetings against Lumumba. (2004: 87)

Just months after Lumumba's speech, he was murdered. Fanon's last article asked pan-African leaders: "Lumumba's Death: Could We Do Otherwise?" Published in *Afrique Action* in February 1961, the article predicted that, with Lumumba's death, "Africa is about to experience its first great crisis over the Congo."

For Fanon, the concreteness of an Africa Legion that could be called upon in the struggle against colonialism became a central issue during the Congo crisis. The focus of his last article published in *El Moudjahid* is not "dying colonialism" and its desperation to hang on, but the compromises of "Africans themselves." He spends little time with the "chiefs of puppet governments" who felt endangered by Congo's independence (1967: 194), and views the African heads of state, who are frightened whenever "the question of disengaging Africa from the West comes up," as "consciously . . . contribut[ing] to the deterioration of the situation in the Congo." Moreover, their support of Lumumba's decision to ask for UN intervention had legitimized involvement by an organization "used by the imperialists' interests when the card of brute force has failed." Viewing the UN much like Lenin viewed the League of Nations (that is, as a thieves' kitchen) Fanon argues that Lumumba's mistake was to believe in the impartiality of the UN when he should have called on his revolutionary friends for aid: "They alone can really and totally help us achieve our objectives because, precisely, the friendship that links us is a *friendship of combat*" (1967: 196; my emphasis). The mistake the African nations committed, Fanon continues, was to send troops under the UN banner rather than sending them directly to Lumumba. It is this that has led to "a historic moral defeat." He continued: "The mistake we Africans made was to have forgotten that the enemy never withdraws sincerely. He never understands. He capitulates, but he does not become converted" (1967: 196).

Lumumba's death was a source of personal and political grief, expressing the powerlessness of African leaders. "Our mistake," Fanon continued, "is to have believed that the enemy had lost his combativeness and his harmfulness. If Lumumba is in the way, Lumumba disappears. Hesitation in murder has never characterized imperialism." Yes, traitors exist in Africa, and they should be fought; this is especially hard after "the magnificent dream" of a United States of Africa based on "true independence." But this "does not alter facts". He concludes with the harrowing words: "The stake of all of us is at stake in the Congo" (1967: 196).

## Leukemia

Fanon was exhausted by the overland mission to Mali and didn't seem to be recovering when he got back to Accra. He arranged for a blood test, which revealed that he had an abnormally high white cell count. Josie insisted that he return to Tunis for more tests, which he did. Cherki relates that Fanon shared the news that he had leukemia in Tunis:

> He stepped outside the lab and was still holding the results in his hand when he ran into his friends – Charles Géronimi and the Chaulets – to whom he immediately broke the news. That same evening, he invited himself and Olivier to dinner at the Manuellan's, insisting that they cook him a good meal. When the children went off to play, he turned to his hosts and announced, "Have I got one for you!" and then proceeded to tell them about his illness. (2006: 155)

When Marie-Jeanne Manuellan asked him what he would do, he said: "I will defend myself." She asked: "'With what?' He slapped his forehead with his forefinger and said, firmly, as if it went without saying and that it would be the winner: 'With the cortex'" (Manuellan 2017: 164). And he quickly challenged all his friends: "I don't want to see those faces. You're going to have to help Josie." Later, when his eye fell on an unappealing apple sitting in a fruit bowl, he joked that the "apple . . . probably has leukemia" (Cherki 2006: 155–6).

Diagnosed with myeloid leukemia, discussions began about the best possible treatments that could prolong his life. Nobody thought he would be dead by the end of the year – least of all Fanon. He looked forward to Algerian independence and spoke about returning to his medical interests, undergoing psychoanalysis, and possibly being posted to Havana, Cuba as the

GPRA ambassador. In early 1961, he did not want to go to the US for treatment. France was out of the question, and so it was decided that the Soviet Union (specifically, Moscow) would be the best place for a curative program.[12] The GPRA arranged it. When he returned from Moscow, Fanon immediately contacted Manuellan, who thought she was collecting pages to type up. She should have known better: "Pages! What pages? The book is all here!" he said, pointing to his head (Cherki 2006:160). Though it is unclear exactly when he went to Moscow and for how long he stayed,[13] it does seem that, despite Lanzmann's (2012: 346) opinion that his health worsened, that the therapy did allow him a reprieve long enough to write *Les Damnés de la terre*. Thinking back on that time, Manuellan can't remember Fanon saying he needed to rest. She doesn't remember any medication or transfusions. It was the same as it had been when he had been dictating *L'An V*, pacing the room day after day. She knew the leukemia was there, but in that room "the cortex dominated him" (see Manuellan 2017: 166).

The three murders – Abane at 37, Moumié at 36, and Lumumba at 35 – continued to be on Fanon's mind as he was writing *Les Damnés de la terre*.[14] In early April, Fanon wrote to Maspero saying that his health had slightly improved and that he had "decided to write at least something." He also asked him to contact Sartre about writing a preface (2018: 689), saying: "I think of him each time I sit down at my desk." In May, a version of what would be the first chapter of *Les Damnés de la terre*, "On Violence," was published in *Les Temps Modernes*. Slightly improved, but still quite sick, Fanon mostly completed the book in a 10-week period between April and July 1961. In May 1961, Fanon sent Maspero the chapter "Misadventures of National Consciousness" and indicated that he was working on the fourth chapter (2018: 691).

*Les Damnés de la terre* was a work deeply embedded in its moment and was completed in a race against time. Fanon had wanted to do much more, but the book also reflects his original *Algiers to Cape Town* plan, "based on the armed revolution in the Maghreb [and] the development of consciousness and national struggle in the rest of Africa." Soon after he started work on the book, he became Alice Cherki's neighbor in the El Menzah, a new housing development where many FLN-aligned Algerians were living. Cherki spent a lot of time with Fanon; she remembers him reading the chapter on violence, as it was composed, "to the group of friends who had gathered around him" (2006:161):

> Fanon knew that he had to use his time wisely if he was to finish the book. He did not have time for details, draft revisions, philosophical and literary flourishes, or to engage in debates. He wanted to pass the sum of his experience on to others. He worked at a furious pace but never referred to his own race against death in his correspondence with his publisher. (2006:161)

It was in the apartment in El Menzah that Claude Lanzmann first met Fanon. In his memoir, he describes the meeting as an "encounter that really shook me, unsettled me, captivated me and that was to have a profound effect on my own life." The Fanons had just moved there and Lanzmann remembered "the absolute emptiness of the place – nothing on the walls, not a stick of furniture, no bed, nothing. Fanon was lying on a sort of pallet, a mattress on the floor. I was immediately struck by his fiery dark eyes, black with fever. He was already suffering from leukemia, which he knew would prove fatal, and was in terrible pain." Lanzmann and Marcel Péju, editor-in-chief of *Les Temps Modernes*,

> sat on the floor next to the mattress where Fanon lay and listened to him talk about the Algerian revolution for hours,

stopping several times when the pain became unbearable. I put my hand on his forehead, which was bathed in sweat, and awkwardly tried to dry it, or I held his shoulder gently as though by mere touch I might ease his pain. But all the while Fanon spoke with a lyricism I had never before encountered, he was already so suffused with death that it gave his every word the power both of prophecy and of the last words of a dying man. (Lanzmann 2012: 336–7)

Lanzmann and Fanon met a number of times, not always at El Menzah. Fanon would read parts of *Les Damnés de la terre* to him, talking with such "persuasive power" and "conviction" about the African continent that "one could not but be carried away by his words" (Lanzmann 2012: 339).

During the last year of his life, Fanon spent some time with the Frontier army and its leader, Houari Boumedienne. He had already met some of Boumedienne's subordinates in 1960 and was drawn to their militancy. Boumedienne's restructuring of the army was impressive, but it would be mistaken to think that Fanon had become an uncritical supporter of the colonel. He expressed discomfort, writes Cherki, "with the harsh discipline and lack of freedom of speech" (2006: 159). Certainly, the situation in Congo and the murder of Lumumba informed his critique of the national and military leadership in *Les Damnés de la terre*, but they were also inspired by his observations within the FLN. This was one of the reasons that he gave a series of lectures at the school of the political commissars of the borders at Ghardimaou during his remission. Though the lectures have never been found, Macey and Jean Khalfa (by way of Claude Lanzmann) suggest that they focused, "at least in part on Sartre's *Critique de la raison dialectique*" (see Fanon 2018: 539; Macey 2012: 449);[15] others have argued that they included what would become his chapter about the pitfalls of national consciousness (see Zeilig 2016: 2–3).

Fanon had acquired a copy of Sartre's *Critique of Dialectical Reason* in Accra. When Lanzmann returned to Paris "still completely carried away by this man," he relayed his experience of Fanon to Sartre "in such terms that he felt he too had to meet Fanon, something unusual for him" (Lanzmann 2012: 339). A meeting was arranged for July. Lanzmann and de Beauvoir picked Fanon up at the airport for what would be a physically and emotionally exhausting three days of intense conversation. Sartre, who never compromised his work schedule, stopped writing "to listen to Fanon. De Beauvoir did likewise." "[H]is words burned like flames, [and] he was also a gentle man whose delicacy and warmth were contagious" (Lanzmann 2012: 347).

In her autobiography, de Beauvoir recounts the meeting with a keen eye. Though an advocate of violence, she says, he was horrified by it, describing the "mutilations inflicted on the Congolese by the Belgians or the Portuguese on the Angolans" with an "expression that would betray his anguish" (1994: 316). There were moments when Fanon refused to recognize his illness, and even then, less than five months before his death, his energy was remarkable. Talking without stopping, "with razor sharp intelligence, intensely alive, endowed with a grim sense of humor ... [Fanon] explained things, made jokes, questioned us, gave imitations, told stories; everything he talked about seemed to live again before our eyes" (1994: 314). When at 2 a.m., de Beauvoir said that Sartre needed sleep, Fanon reacted negatively: "I don't like people who hide their resources" (1994: 314). Lanzmann stayed up with Fanon until 8 a.m.

After this meeting with Sartre and de Beauvoir, Fanon wrote to Maspero focusing on the importance of his book as "an attempt to situate the Third World doctrinally in relation to the West" (2018: 690). By August, he had decided to call it *Les Damnés de la terre*, telling Maspero that "Third World political circles are feverishly awaiting the book" (2018: 691). At times he worried that the book was "too vehement" but, he added, "things had come down to the wire. Who knows. It may even be too late" (Cherki 2006:162). In short, he was worried about the direction of Africa's liberation, including Algeria's. And the conclusion, addressed to "comrades," expresses who he was writing for and who he thought his readers would be. He desperately wanted the book, based on his experiences and reflections inside the African liberation struggle, to be readily available in "Third World political circles."

The book title resonates with the opening lines of Eugéne Pottier's song "The Internationale," written after the defeat of the Paris Commune in 1871: "Debout! Les damnés de la terre" (Arise, the damned/wretched of the earth). The title also connects with Jacques Roumain, who writes of the rising of "les damnés de la terre" in the conclusion to his poem "Sale nègre." Fanon had already quoted Roumain in *Black Skin, White Masks*, and his first reference to the poem comes at the end of a 1958 article for *El Moudjahid*, "The Caribbean, Birth of a Nation" (in 2018, 583–90). At the end of the poem, Roumain invokes the rising of "les damnés de la terre," resonating with Fanon's concept:

> For even the tom-toms would have learned the language
> of the Internationale
> for we will have chosen our day
> . . .
> And here we are arisen
> All the damned of the earth
> all the upholders of justice
> marching to attack your barracks
> your banks
> like a forest of funeral torches
> to be done

once

and

for

all

with this world

The damned of the earth in Roumain's poem are the majority of the world's population: working people struggling to
survive, hemmed in by seemingly normalized structures,
discourses of domination, and everyday colonial, racial, and
class violence. The objects of this cascading violence are those
who are constantly pathologized, dehumanized, and incarcerated, and still refuse and resist learning "the language of the
Internationale."

In October, Maspero informed Fanon that he had received
Sartre's preface and the book would come out that month.
David Macey argues that much of the material in Les Damnés de
la terre was produced before 1961, and is based on "emotion"
and rarely justified with "hard facts";[16] I, on the other hand,
view the work as a powerful critical and analytical synthesis
from inside the revolution. To complete Les Damnés in 10
weeks was remarkable, even given Macey's criticism. Certainly,
his presentation at the Second Congress of Black Writers
and Artists and the pages on Carothers and Porot included
in the chapter "Colonial Wars and Mental Disorders" were
written earlier. But his case notes in that chapter had to be
edited and conceptualized and the book as a whole was written
and essentially put together in that short period, representing a significant theorization of the anticolonial revolutions
based on Fanon's experiences and discussions. It also represents Fanon's ability to conceptualize those experiences and
discussions.

One nodal point is his working on the notes from the reconnaissance mission the year before. In the notes he argues that,

to consider the problem of the lack of ideology, "we must once again come back to the Marxist formula"; "the triumphant bourgeoisie are the most impetuous, the most enterprising, the most annexationist in the world" (1967: 187). And he forewarns about two major concerns connected with the problem of the lack of ideology developed in *Les Damnés de la terre*. First, the critique of the hollowness of the idea of African unity highlighted by narrow nationalism expressed in regional tensions is summed up as a retrogressive movement from the promise of national liberation and African unity, "to ultranationalism, chauvinism, and racism" (2004: 103). The emerging neocolonialism recasts the critique of alienation from *Black Skin, White Masks* and is politically expanded and contextualized in the mimicry of the emergent nationalist leadership, which he calls the national bourgeoisie. When Fanon refers back to "the Marxist formula" and puts it in terms of "the theoretical question, which has been posed for the last fifty years," he is referring to the discussion and debates about the failure of the bourgeoisie to carry out its own revolution in the 1905 Russia revolution, which were grounded in Marx's analysis of the failure of the 1848 revolutions.[17] The possibility of "skipping the bourgeois phase" was connected with Marx calling for "revolution in permanence."[18] Fanon has a contempt for the "'stages' that break the revolutionary torrent" (1967: 103).

Second, Fanon's critique of the national bourgeoisie in the colonial countries is damning. It is "incapable of great ideas or of inventiveness." It is a "little greedy caste, avid and voracious, with the mind of a hucksterer, only too glad to accept the dividends that the former colonial power hands out to it" (1968: 175). It should be remembered that when Fanon argues that the national bourgeoisie is useless and merely mimics the European bourgeoisie, he is not suggesting that the European bourgeoisie is useful. Indeed, when he argues the national bourgeoisie is cynical, it is a reflection of the agedness, cynicism, and sterility of bourgeois Europe. The European bourgeoisie is senile, and the national bourgeoisie is its caricature, senile before its time. Like the European bourgeoisie, but without any connection to producing anything, its interest is accumulating finance capital in get-rich quick schemes. Fanon, in other words, is not hoping for the emergence of an authentic bourgeoisie, but rather that the bourgeois "stage" should be avoided at all costs and Europe must not be followed. Europe is stagnant and has nothing to offer. Instead, "let us reexamine the question of cerebral reality, the brain mass of humanity in its entirety whose affinities must be increased, whose connections must be diversified and whose communications must be humanized again" (2004: 238–9).

## Last days

As Fanon's condition deteriorated, treatment in the US became his final hope. He reluctantly agreed to go there in October 1961. En route, he met Sartre in Rome. This time, Fanon was so ill he was unable to speak and remained "embedded" in the hotel. On arrival in Washington, he had to suffer another week in a hotel room alone until Josie and Olivier joined him. On October 10, he was admitted to the Clinical Centre at the National Institute of Health in Bethesda, Maryland, as Dr. Ibrahim Fanon, under the care of a hematologist named David Heywood. Fanon's attitude toward the US, which he called a nation of lynchers, was borne out. In Maryland, segregation still ruled (as it did in nearby Washington, DC). As late as 1957, a State Code made it a crime for a White woman to bear a Black man's child.

Fanon was immediately subjected to intense treatments and full blood transfusions, which resulted in a brief remission.

Before he died, he had a chance to look over *Les Damnés de la terre*, which had just been published. In a letter to Joby (which he received after his brother's death), Frantz wrote that it was lucky he left when he did because "eight days after my arrival, a cycle of cataclysmic hemorrhages began, putting me on the balance between life and death for several days. The Americans admitted to me later that they had never succeeded in attaining such a high transfusion rate to keep someone alive" (Fanon 2014: 100). Now, he wrote, the doctors were optimistic. He said the same in a letter to his friend Roger Taïeb: "If I had left Tunis four days later, I would have been quite dead by now." And added: "I am dying of acute leukemia in Washington DC, when I could have died three months ago facing the enemy on the battlefield, when I already knew I had this disease." Summing up his philosophic point and principle, he wrote: "We are nothing on this earth if we do not first and foremost serve a cause, the cause of the people, the cause of freedom and justice." He concluded that even if the doctors say there is no hope, if he did hold on it would be for "the Algerian people, the people of the Third World" (quoted in Cherki 2006: 165).

There has been speculation about the CIA's involvement in Fanon's last days in the US as well as his wait for a hospital bed. Obviously, the CIA already knew who Fanon was (the agency's case file remains classified).[19] In fact, M'hamed Yazid, the FLN's minister of information and representative in New York City, contacted the CIA's head of the North Africa desk, Oliver Iselin, to help coordinate Fanon's trip. After Morocco's independence in 1956, Iselin spent time cultivating FLN contacts and was even given "a tour of an Algerian Liberation Army camp in Morocco" (quoted in Meany 2019: 986). According to Iselin, arrangements had been made for Fanon to come in the summer, but Fanon put that off. When Josie and Olivier arrived, Iselin arranged a hotel for them. He says of Josie that she "was further to the left" than Frantz (Meany 2019: 990). Olivier was six at the time and Iselin arranged his enrolment in a kindergarten at Howard University.

Fanon certainly knew who Iselin was and shared nothing with him. The CIA monitored his visitors – for example Holden Roberto, the leader of the National Liberation Front of Angola, whom Fanon had first met at the All-African Peoples Congress in 1958. Iselin met Roberto in Fanon's room; he would become a "prized contact" for the CIA's African activities (Meany 2019: 990).[20] Iselin claimed to have "developed a rapport" with Fanon (see Meany 2019: 990). In an interview on Radio Alger on the second anniversary of Fanon's death, Josie reported that Fanon warned Iselin "that the government of the United States would soon have to face the rebellion of [B]lack America and South American guerrilla armies" (Cherki 2006: 166).

Josie was with Frantz every day and many nights, sitting with him during periods of delirium and reprieve and another case of pneumonia. He went into comas and became delirious. In the delirium, he thought the frequent blood transfusions were part of a plot to Whiten him along the lines of lactification. The fact that he was in the US made his statement in *Black Skin, White Masks* about the search for a "'denegrification' serum" all the more real: "In all seriousness they have been rinsing out their test tubes and adjusting their scales and have begun research on how the wretched Black man could [W]hiten himself and thus rid himself of the burden of this bodily curse" (2008: 91). In the end, he caught double pneumonia. On his last morning, he woke up and said to Josie: "Last night they put me in the washing machine" (de Beauvoir 1994: 329).

Constantly monitoring his blood cell count, Fanon lived every moment of his impending death, refusing to accept it. There were days with some improvement when he still believed that he would be able to return to Algeria, and he continued to plan book projects, including a psychological analysis of death that was to be called *Le Leucemique et son double*. He still hoped to march in the Algerian victory. Fanon had been angry with Césaire after he welcomed the former communist novelist (by then the Gaullist torture-denying minister of culture) André Malraux to Martinique to support the French union after the referendum. But he did not forget Césaire's importance and, in the first chapter of *Les Damnés de la terre*, he added a long quotation from Césaire's *And the Dogs Were Silent* that was not included in the version that appeared in *Les Temps Modernes* in May 1961. Where Fanon speaks of how violence shows the militant "the means and the end" of colonial rule, he adds, "Césaire's poetry takes on prophetic significance in this very prospect of violence" (2004: 44). With negotiations for Algerian independence ongoing, the threats that he described in *Les Damnés de la terre* loomed large. Fanon was wary of negotiations and believed that agreements signed by the Europeans for African independence were worthless. He was also aware that while revolutions were not a magic formula, they had to be ongoing to confront the reality of counterrevolution.

Fanon died on December 6, 1961. A day later, French police seized copies of *Les Damnés de la terre*, but this did not stop the book from being discussed and reviews from appearing. Sartre's preface soon became a focal point, though the book did not immediately make it, as Fanon hoped, into the "Third World political circles." "Up to the end, I hoped," Josie said to her friend Assia Djebar years later. She had hoped that

"his friends, those who liked Frantz and admired him ... would understand: that you couldn't send him such a long way to be treated alone." She stiffened, then added, hardly bitter: "I understood his point of view; he thought that all the expenses he was incurring were already quite enough for the Algerian Revolution!" She remained silent, then: "He died alone, in New York, two months later. Alone!" she repeated harshly. (2000: 91–92).

Josie had spent the last decade with him, from Lyon to Blida to Tunis to Accra and back to Tunis, committed to the Algerian revolution and living an increasingly itinerant life. After Fanon's death, she returned to Tunis with her son, supporting her husband's wish that he be buried in Algeria. His body was flown back to Tunis and from there transported to Ghardimaou where he was given a state funeral and "buried in a plot of 'liberated' Algerian soil" (Cherki 2006: 166–8). Josie was the wife of a fallen leader of the revolution, but she remarked to Manuellan in Tunis: "'What is to become of us?' Worried about Olivier she asked, 'What will become of this Black child? He had a wonderful father, and voila! You will see, the brothers will want to remarry me off.' But she never expressed the wish, the idea, of not returning to Algeria" (Manuellan 2017: 171).[21]

# 8

## *Les Damnés de la terre*:
## The Handbook of Revolution

> The colonized's challenge to the colonial world is not a rational confrontation of points of view. It is not a treatise on the universal, but the untidy affirmation of an original idea propounded as an absolute.
>
> Fanon, *Les Damnés de la terre*[1]

As already noted, Fanon's *Les Damnés de la terre* has had a remarkable afterlife. This final chapter will focus on Fanon's argument chapter by chapter.

### "On Violence"

The first chapter declares immediately: at every level, national liberation is always a violent phenomenon, whether it concerns naming sports clubs or relations between people, because it amounts to total change – replacing the colonizer by the colonized. Without a period of transition, there is an "absolute substitution" provided by changing the "whole structure . . . from the bottom." It is willed by the consciousness and lives of the colonized and also experienced as terror in the consciousness of the colonizers. A terror of "replacement" is often expressed by White supremacists.

A few pages on, Fanon argues that "the singularity of the colonial context lies in the fact that economic reality, inequality, and enormous disparities in lifestyles never manage to mask the human reality." And he explains that, considering this immediacy, "it is clear that what divides this world is first and foremost what species, what race one belongs to. In the colonies the economic infrastructure is also a superstructure" (2004: 5).[2]

Fanon argues that while in the capitalist countries "a multitude of sermonizers, counselors, and 'confusion-mongers' intervene between the exploited and the authorities," in the colonies there is no such intervention, the language of pure force is realized everyday as violence is brought "into the homes and minds of the colonized subject" (2004: 2). In the colonies, "[t]he cause is effect: You are rich because you are [W]hite, you are [W]hite because you are rich. This is why a Marxist analysis should always be slightly stretched when it comes to addressing the colonial issue" (2004: 4–5). This reexamination will include a slight stretching of class concepts from Marx's The Eighteenth Brumaire.[3] Essential to both is an evaluation of the colonial world as Manichean. The two different species: the colonizer and the colonized. Manicheanism is expressed spatially in Fanon's description of the compartmentalized urban areas where the colonial civilization is put on display. The wealth of the European sectors is in inverse proportion to the poverty of the ghettoes. Reorganizing this political-economic geography is essential to decolonization.

But what is the original idea propounded as an absolute? For Fanon, it is about the freedom and self-determination of those considered depraved and impervious to ethics and values, the damned of the earth: "When the colonist speaks of the colonized, he uses zoological terms," Fanon argues; "allusion is made to the slithery movements . . . the odors of the 'native' quarters, the stink, the swarming, the seething . . . the bestial" (2004: 7). Systematically dehumanized on a daily basis, they have no value apart from being surplus labor and, as such, they are "congenitally indigent" (2004: 220).

Colonialism is totalitarian; the colonized's body is physically hemmed in by an apparatus of control and unmasked violence whose methods are crude. Brute forces "ensure the colonized are kept under close scrutiny, and contained by rifle butts and napalm" (2004: 4). As we have seen, colonialism pathologizes resistance, but even though the colonized are "treated as an inferior," they are "not convinced of their inferiority" (1968: 54; 2004: 16). So where does the colonized psychic energy go? Fanon points out that they achieve freedom while asleep through muscular dreams of action and aggression. But there is also a dreamlike "magical superstructure that permeates the indigenous society" (2004: 18). The political problem is how to channel this aggression toward its source. "Traditional" superstructures, co-opted by colonialism as part of customary rule, often become spaces where magic and myth become "surprisingly ego boosting" (2004: 19) as they both shrink the colonist's reality and also exhaust the colonized's aggressivity. This can change in the period preceding decolonization when the direction of aggression begins to shift. Soon after the end of World War II, anticolonial armed struggles in Indonesia and Indochina fundamentally shook up colonial rule and introduced the possibility of a new history. It is this contemporary period that Fanon captures in *Les Damnés de la terre* and it marks a radical shift away from elite-based politics toward a mass politics. Fanon will engage these contradictions throughout *Les Damnés*; here, he simply notes that the colonized masses view the colonized elites' demand "to fill senior positions as administrators, technicians, and experts" for what it is: nepotism. And soon after independence has been won, the masses commonly ask: "What was the point of fighting?" and "being independent?" (2004: 35, 10).[4]

"On Violence" extends Fanon's argument from the All-Africa Peoples Conference in December 1958 – namely, that there is an "extraordinary reciprocity" in the settler colonies (such as Algeria, Kenya, and South Africa[5]), where the greater the number of settlers meant "the more terrible the violence" (2004: 86). The "atmosphere of violence" permeates everything as the enemy's congenital lie is confronted by the people's own lie, which acquires a dimension of truth (1965: 87). News and ideas cross borders as colonized people hear of armed resistance and realize they are not alone. Even where there existed a strategy or indeed philosophy of nonviolence, such as with Nkrumah in Ghana, the willingness of colonial regimes to negotiate was created by the effects of counterviolence elsewhere. In response, colonial regimes often became desperate to find African elites who had been educated in colonial schools as the "leaders" they could quickly negotiate with.

Expanded and developed ideas from the Soummam platform, which had stated that armed struggle produces a psychological shock that liberates people from their torpor, Fanon references the struggles in Kenya and Algeria, striking a blow against settler colonialism's absolute power as psychologically liberating: "For the colonized, violence" becomes an "absolute praxis." Returning to his discussion of Hegel, he argues the militant "is the one who works" (2004: 44).

There is a rehabilitative element about taking a stand against colonialism and in seeing how guns in the hands of the colonized creates an ontological dread in the colonizer. Such resistance creates a new sense of solidarity and opportunity for others to become liberated from their passivity. It helps liberate the colonized from their fatalism, bringing to the fore the idea that the colonial power can be beaten, just as the Mau Mau revolt was able to shock the settler regime and the British empire with homemade guns. In addition, armed struggle highlights the "extraordinary reciprocal homogeneity" (2004: 47) of the two opposed and unequal forces. The violence of the colonial army, police, and paramilitary forces, with their planes, bombs, torture, and mass incarceration is pitted against the counterviolence of the poorly armed and poorly resourced anticolonial forces. To survive, Fanon argues, requires involving everyone. And through this struggle, a struggle for survival, the people, as Fanon argues in *L'An V*, become enlightened and unified, and the nation becomes real. And that new reality includes the reawakening of democratic forms that had become dormant during colonial rule, while also undermining the "tribal" structures, chiefs, and *kaids* nurtured by colonialism.

Telling us that decolonization is *always* a violent phenomenon, Fanon includes examples that might not be considered violent, such as changing the names of institutions, buildings, roads, and so on. But once we think about the power and daily psychological violence of these colonial names, we can see that changing them expresses counterpower and counterviolence and is a symbol of victory.

From the colonizer's standpoint, colonialism is the source of goodness bringing enlightenment, and the colonized a source of evil and retrogression. The history of colonization repeats its metropolitan story, especially racism as justification. The colonized are not fully human, but the best, it was argued, could evolve (*évoluer*, as the French argued) through Christian education and training. This small group of intellectuals who try to accommodate themselves to colonialism form a threat to liberation. Educated in colonial schools, they learn from their masters the importance of capitalist individualism and "the cogency of . . . the Greco-Roman pedestal" (2004: 11). But once the colonized intellectual has had the opportunity to return to the people during the liberation struggle, "all the Mediterranean values, the triumph of the individual, of enlightenment and Beauty turn into pale, lifeless trinkets. All those discourses . . . have nothing in common with the real-life struggle in which the people are engaged" (2004: 11). Henceforth, Fanon adds: "That godless form of salvation 'look out for yourself' [in French: "*le 'démerdage', cette forme athée du salut*" (2011: 460)],[6] is in this context forbidden . . . And it is true that already at that level we can say that the community triumphs, and that it secretes its own light, its own reason (1968: 47–8; 2004: 11–12).

The popular struggle "infuses a new rhythm, specific to a new generation . . . with a new language and a new humanity." Decolonization, in short, has to be the creation of a new humanity. "But," he adds, "such a creation cannot be attributed to a supernatural power: The 'thing' colonized becomes [human] through the very process of liberation" (2004: 2). During the liberation, words such as "'brother,' 'sister,' 'comrade'" that had been "outlawed by the colonialist bourgeoisie because in their thinking my brother is my wallet and my comrade, my scheming" take on new meaning. The colonized intellectual who had fully embraced colonial culture and the primacy of possessive individualism now witnesses the destruction of all their individualistic idols and "discover[s] the strength of the village assemblies, the power of the people's commissions and the extraordinary productiveness of neighborhood and section committee meetings" (2004: 11).

Fanon's concern, however, is that many colonized intellectuals continue like "affranchised slaves," playing an ideologically conservative role. Since the social composition of the urban-focused national parties are based on the colonized urban elites, they employ the same political discourse in which they have been educated, which can be reduced to "give us more power." Like the subjects of *Black Skin, White Masks*, these colonized intellectuals wish for a place at the colonizer's table. They have become "a kind of class of individually liberated slaves" and, in stark contrast to the peasantry, have much to lose if colonialism ends (2004: 22).

Thus, divorced from the struggle, these urban colonized elites then try to play a mediating role, declaring that they have nothing to do with the "savagery" of the revolt. They view violence not only as counterproductive to their interests; they have also imbibed the idea that the popular revolt is irrational. Their perspective is framed by the armed might of the colonists and they are catapulted by the colonists "to the forefront of negotiations and compromise" (2004: 24).

Fanon's *El Moudjahid* colleague, Redha Malek, had given him a copy of Engels's *Anti-Dühring*, which includes the famous argument that "triumph of force is based on the production of arms" (quoted in Fanon 2004: 25). Fanon was unimpressed, noting that the colonized elite speak the same language as Engels: "What do you expect to fight the colonists with? With your knives? With your shotguns" (2004: 26). In response Fanon refers to the Peninsular War[7] as "an authentic colonial war" where "the Spanish, buoyed by an unshakeable national fervor, discover guerrilla warfare" (2004: 26) forcing Napoleon and his 400,000-strong army to retreat.

Even as the world's powers decried anticolonial violence, and the US, the "barons of international capitalism," promoted peaceful "self-determination" (Fanon 2004: 36) with "dollars in the vanguard" and "[Louis] Armstrong as the herald of the American Black" (Fanon 1967: 178), they colluded by stirring up violence, for example in the Congo, and were also responsible for the global atmosphere of violence created by the Cold War as well as the nuclear arms race, which included

French nuclear tests in Algeria (see 2004: 36).[8] "Astronomical sums," Fanon writes, were being invested in arms research, which could provide basic necessities, like clean water, for the majority of the world (2004: 41). But at the same time, the days when the imperialists could send in gunboats to put down an uprising were over, as the anticolonial struggle was creating a new moment in world history. While only a few years earlier massacres at Sétif and Madagascar went almost unnoticed, the news of repression spread rapidly, having the effect of intensifying solidarity and building "national consciousness" (2004: 32).

"On violence in the international context" concludes the chapter. Demanding reparations, Fanon argues that Europe, including its "deluxe socialism" (such as the welfare state and unemployment benefit), is "literally the creation of the Third World" (2004: 58). He warns of the "spirit of self-sacrifice" in the newly independent nations, which can amount to forced labor. Instead everything, especially working conditions should be rethought, and Europe must pay up (2004: 57). The success of "reintroducing" humanity in their "totality . . . into the world . . . will be achieved with the crucial help of the European masses (2004: 62). They must wake up.

## "Spontaneity: Its Strengths and Weaknesses"

Focusing on the revolutionary subjects of the anticolonial struggle, the second chapter shifts the discussion to rural revolts and the importance of the peasantry as *the* revolutionary class. It is, echoing *The Communist Manifesto*, the "immense majority" who "have nothing to lose" and a world to gain through the destruction of colonialism. "Stretching Marxism" includes focusing on the revolutionary potential of another class, the lumpenproletariat, whom Fanon views as an important link in spreading the rural revolt into the urban areas. Both classes had been dismissed by the urban nationalist groups whose main goal was political rights within the colonial system. While some nationalist groups might see the need to spread their ideas into rural areas, they have no direct relations with the peasantry and often view them as the colonists do: backward. Fanon points out that in Kenya not a single well-known nationalist declared their affiliation with the Land and Freedom movement (known as the Mau Mau), or even tried to defend those involved in it. And even if the majority of nationalist parties didn't oppose continuing the rebellion, they remained distant from it.

In Chapter 1, "On Violence," Fanon asks: what is the event that creates the turning point? "How do we get from the atmosphere of violence to setting violence in motion?" (2004: 31). Taking Algeria as an example, it was a demonstration called by the Algerian People's Party on May 8, 1945 that led to the massacre at Sétif because it was the first time that the rural masses had linked up with the nationalist movement. The organization's call represented a growing radicalization within it, especially among younger members, and the French reaction to the Sétif rebellion resulted not only in the massacre of 45,000 Algerians but also in the arrest and imprisonment of nationalist militants and a division in the organization between the legal and illegal wings. The latter included "intellectual elements" who would "criticize the ideological vacuum of the national party" (2004: 76). Soon isolated and removed from the party, they became the subject of police actions, and leaders as well as militants – laborers, seasonal workers, and the unemployed – used their time in prison as a school of struggle. In Algeria an underground and secret organization, *Organisation spéciale*, was founded in 1947 to plan the armed struggle. On the run, radicals who escape imprisonment are forced out of the urban areas into "the interior [and] the mountains" and, in seeking refuge, they find "the peasant's cloak will wrap" around them with unexpected "gentleness and firmness"(2004: 78–9). As they make contact with the peasantry, the abstract political discussions in the cafés are quickly forgotten. They discover the "infinite misery of the people" who have never given up the fight for liberation in terms of a "national struggle and armed revolt" (2004: 79). Sharing political and military training and guided by the people, the armed struggle begins.

## The lumpenproletariat

Fanon considers the dispossessed rural people and urban lumpenproletariat as those who truly have nothing to lose and everything to win in an armed anticolonial struggle. The rural people have been systematically expropriated for more than 100 years, forced off the land into itinerant labor (including in France) and toward the urban areas. This new lumpenproletariat retains links to the land and, Fanon argues, deserves significant attention by any national liberation movement.

In contrast to the small number of the privileged working class, the lumpenproletariat is massive and provides an essential link to the rural revolt; it can be considered an extension of the landless peasantry. Recent history is again important for Fanon's analysis. After the end of World War II, a flood of people, without much prospect of employment, ceaselessly moved toward the urban areas, crowding into the Algiers Casbah and creating new settlements on banks and ravines and marginal spaces in urban areas. "The landless peasants, now a lumpenproletariat, are driven into the towns, crammed into shanty towns and endeavor to infiltrate the ports and cities, the creations of colonial domination" (2004: 61). In urban areas they live in the *bidonvilles* (literally, towns of tin [cans]) and are viewed by the colonizers as a threat, lazy and criminal, whose duty it is "to have the slightest effort literally dragged out of them" (1968: 220). They might work as domestics and gardeners for Europeans, but in these spaces they remain unseen. The primacy of racist dehumanization and bourgeois phobia is essential to Fanon's conception because, as well as constituting a serious threat to the security of civil society, they signify "the irreversible rot and the gangrene eating into the heart of colonial domination" (2004: 81).

Fanon's description of the lumpenproletariat as revolutionary and unreliable echoes Marx's concern expressed in *The Communist Manifesto*: "the lumpenproletariat may ... be swept into the movement," but "its conditions of life, however, prepare it ... [to be] the part of a bribed tool of reactionary intrigue" (Marx and Engels: 1848). Fanon underscores the latter, arguing that "it will always respond to the call to revolt, but if the insurrection thinks it can afford to ignore it, then this famished underclass will pitch itself into the armed struggle and take part in the conflict, this time on the side of the oppressor" (2004: 87). In other words, the colonial system and its interests will not miss an opportunity to mobilize those whom it has systematically marginalized and pauperized against popular uprisings; thus, Fanon argues, political engagement with the lumpenproletariat is essential. With the coup against Lumumba on his mind, Fanon gives recent examples, arguing for the importance of insurrectionary organization that would address "the lack of political consciousness" among the lumpenproletariat (2004: 87). He also warns that "if this readily available human reserve is *not immediately organized by the insurrection*, it will join the colonialist troops as mercenaries," as he had seen in Algeria, Angola, and, most recently, in the Congo, as they became the basis for so called "'spontaneous' meetings against Lumumba" (2004: 87; my emphasis).

It is worth remembering both the speed and immediacy of events in Algeria from 1954 to 1956, which Fanon speaks of in terms of periods. During the first period, when the colonists are shocked by the seemingly unorganized character of the anticolonial violence, "spontaneity rules" and victory seem close. The "initiative rests with local areas" and "on every hilltop a government in miniature is formed and assumes power" (2004: 84). This is a period of "spectacular voluntarism" when everything seemed possible. But the idea that the nation could be created in "one fell swoop" proved "to be a great weakness" (2004: 88). Bolstered by orientalist and ethno-psychiatric experts, colonial counterinsurgency focuses on winning hearts and minds (first used by the British in Malaya in 1952) to disarm the colonized; with a few "paltry measures . . . trivial handouts . . . [and] a few coins . . . the colonized subject is at the risk of being disarmed by any sort of concession" (2004: 90). These new measures and tactical changes (détente, divisive maneuvers, and psychological warfare) "throws the euphoria and idyll of the first phase into question" as it becomes clear that spontaneity cannot take the place of organizational and programmatic clarity. Recognizing that the release of pent-up energy and resentment was incredibly powerful in the first days, it comes as a shock to realize that "the mirage of their muscles' own immediacy" (see 1968: 138; 2004: 88) is not enough to win a war. The defeat of a powerful opponent cannot be achieved without raising the consciousness of those in combat (see 2004: 86). Strategically, a guerrilla war is not about holding a village or hilltop; politically, "the leaders of the insurrection realize their units need enlightening, instruction, and indoctrination . . . an army needs to be created" and the "objectives of the struggle" carefully defined (2004: 86, 91). One can very much read the Soummam platform in these terms. And a serious problem for Fanon is the lack of revolutionary theory and analysis. "Antiracist racism" (a term that Sartre had used in *Orphée noir*) and self-defense against colonial oppression might be good reasons to join the struggle, but, argues Fanon, "one does not sustain a war, one does not endure massive repression or witness the disappearance of one's entire family in order for hatred or racism to triumph. Racism, hatred, resentment, and 'the legitimate desire for revenge' alone cannot nurture a war of liberation" (2004: 89).

The nationalist militants had to take responsibility for ideological clarification, which means a critical engagement with the Manichean sloganeering that had been a powerful organizing tool. They had to explain why not all the colonized support the struggle. They had to explain why there were war profiteers and how the treason they saw was social, not national (2004: 94). The necessary clarification was bewildering, complicating "the unreal clarity of the early days" (2004: 94). But the militants and leaders understood the necessity of the experience, realizing that, while they are "demolishing colonial oppression," they are "indirectly building another system of exploitation" (2004: 94). By taking up these issues directly with the people, Fanon argues, "the insurrection proves to itself its rationality" (2004: 95). And while some in the movement "are inclined to think that any nuance constitutes a danger and threatens popular solidarity," the leadership has to understand that a politics based in hatred, resentment, and brutality is "counterrevolutionary, adventurist, and anarchist" and "if this pure, total brutality is not immediately contained it will, without fail, bring down the movement within a few weeks" (2004: 95). Moving away from the Manichean simplicity of the early days means adding depth and analysis to the political discussion. There are colonists who support the liberation struggle and "native sons" who support colonialism. "Not every Black or Muslim is automatically given a vote of confidence" (2004: 95). Then, rather like a credo, the "power of ideology is elaborated and strengthened" and the struggle grows "by exposing mistakes and through experience" (2004: 95). Through this praxis, the militants discover a new politics that "in no way resembles the old." Because it is the struggle that "explodes the old colonial truths and reveals unexpected facets, which brings out new meanings and pinpoints the contradictions camouflaged by these facts. The people engaged in the struggle who because of it command and know these facts, go forward, freed from colonialism and forewarned of all attempts at mystification, inoculated against all national anthems" (1968: 147; see also 2004: 96).

Spontaneity needs organization and thought, and thought needs the praxis of the struggle. Ending Chapter 2, Fanon seems optimistic: ideological clarification is achieved only "if the people are organized and guided" (2004: 92).

## "The Misadventures (or Pitfalls) of National Consciousness"

The upheaval reached Blacks from the outside . . . Values that were not engendered by their actions . . . They went from one way of life to another, but not from one life to another.

Fanon, *Black Skin, White Masks*

One must analyze the accommodation not merely to expose it, but in order to discover the inadequacy of the principle which compelled the accommodation.

Dunayevskaya, *Rosa Luxemburg, Women's Liberation, and Marx's Philosophy of Revolution*

It turns out that the problem of creating a decolonized society is not solved by the end of "Spontaneity: Its Strengths and Weaknesses," but, rather, leads to a further consideration of the problem: how liberation can be betrayed and how the radical nationalist party can be transformed into an agency of a new neocolonial elite. What actions are needed to avoid this? Chapter 2 ended in the confident belief that the colonized get to know the new facts and the contradictions that the struggle had unearthed and are "forewarned of all attempts at mystification" (1968: 147; 2004: 96) as the national becomes real. But working out these contradictions inside the struggle and detailing the mystifications now becomes essential.

This chapter, "Misadventures (or Pitfalls) of National Consciousness," begins in contradictory terms: "History teaches us that the anticolonial struggle *is not* automatically written from a nationalist perspective." Based in the urban areas and excluding the majority of the population in its perspectives, nationalist party work and its ideology is concentrated on reforming colonialism rather than on getting rid of it. Its politics are phrased in the discourses of Europe's liberal bourgeoisie against "forced labor, corporal punishment, unequal wages, and the restriction of political rights." Moreover, as well as a lack of connection to the rural masses, it is characterized by "apathy and . . . cowardice at the crucial moment in the struggle," which "are the cause of tragic trials and tribulations" (2004: 97).

Rather than gaining knowledge through the struggle, the national bourgeoisie remains mystified by colonist logic and incapable of understanding the rationality of the revolt. Fanon sums up the problem on the opening pages of the chapter: "Such shortcomings and dangers derive historically from the incapacity of the national bourgeoisie in underdeveloped countries to rationalize popular praxis, in other words their incapacity to attribute . . . any reason" to the revolutionary striving and action of the masses (2004: 97–8). This epistemic failure is reflected in the national party's social composition and its organizational form. Often aided by leftist parties from the colonial metropole, the nationalist organization mimics them, viewing the peasantry as backward and lacking in any progressive social value. This lack of connection with the dispossessed masses will lead, Fanon argues, to its idea of national consciousness becoming empty and easily open to colonial manipulation.

As I argued earlier, Fanon makes it very clear that the so-called "bourgeois stage" must be avoided at all costs. Here, Fanon is being critical of both pro-capitalist political leaders and self-appointed reformists and Communist Party members for whom the nationalist bourgeoisie was essential to decolonization. In contrast to the latter, Fanon's stretching of Marxism rejects the idea of stages, with the nationalist bourgeoisie playing a progressive role. Why is this?

In the colonial context, Fanon insists, the nationalist bourgeoisie is a pseudo-bourgeoisie. It is really a petite bourgeoisie who have among their number artisans, shop owners, tradespeople, salespeople, professionals, intellectuals, and minor administrators, all of whom are concentrated in the capital. As a bourgeoisie, they are not "geared to production, invention, creation, or work" but, rather, their "energy is channeled into intermediary activities. Networking and scheming seem to be its underlying vocation" (2004: 98). In other words, this is not the creative and productive bourgeoisie described by Marx in the *Communist Manifesto*; rather, this bourgeoisie is not at all productive. It is a caricature of a bourgeoisie, accumulating capital through schemes and deals.

In the age of financial capital, it is the local fixers who become elected to its boards and who become the face of the multinational corporations in the neocolony. They are simply part of the management of these interests, the Black faces on the board that tick the diversity box. In our day, Fanon might have been describing the President of South Africa, Cyril Ramaphosa, as one of its richest men, and a nonexecutive director on the boards of Macsteel Holdings, SABMiller, Anglo-American, Lonmin, and Standard Bank. This is, in other words, not an innovative bourgeoisie but, in Fanon's mind, a bourgeoisie that is corrupt and "good for nothing" (1968: 178; 2004: 120). It mimics the lifestyles of the international financial bourgeoisie but without the financial capital. The national bourgeoisie doesn't even produce fictitious capital; it takes no risk, it doesn't accumulate capital, but prefers lavish consumption, which has been "described by economists as typical of an underdeveloped bourgeoisie" (2004: 103). With the national bourgeoisie as intermediaries in the national economy, independence brings no change in its structure.

Through nationalization and insider deals, the national bourgeoisie also become new landowners, often through party connections. Production for export mirrors what it had been during the colonial period and rather than improving conditions for the farmworkers the exploitation is intensified and justified by "two or three slogans . . . in the name of the national interest, of course" (2004: 102).

Fanon calls the national bourgeoisie "a caste" consisting of a number of factions. The party is the vehicle for its reproduction divided by regional and ethnic factions (2004: 73). After independence, there might be statements about supporting artisanship and local production, but the same extractive industries and the same mono-crops dominate, and the national bourgeoisie demands for nationalization and "Africanization" for their own interests are echoed by small traders and artisans, who pick fights with "Africans of other nationalities" seen as competitors. We quickly move, Fanon argues, from nationalism to "chauvinism, and racism." (2004: 103). Tradition and "tribalism" are invoked as the slogan of the national bourgeoisie – "replace the foreigners" – informs every sector of the economy and "the petty traders such as taxi drivers, cake sellers, and shoe-shiners follow suit and call for the expulsion" of foreigners (2004: 105). A "racism of fear," xenophobia, and claims of authenticity fill the empty shell of national consciousness. And as we have seen over the past 60 years: "The most despicable aspects of the colonial mentality" encourage "the growth and development of racism that was typical of the colonial period" representing the "intellectual and spiritual poverty" (2004: 108, 126) of Africa's national bourgeoisie.[9]

"True liberation," Fanon wrote in *El Moudjahid* in 1958, has absolutely nothing to do with a "pseudo-independence in which ministers, having a limited responsibility hobnob with an economy dominated by the colonial pact" (see 1967: 104). And yet this is what happened. And thus there is only one option. The national bourgeoisie must "repudiate its status as bourgeois and an instrument of capital and to become entirely subservient to the revolutionary capital which the people represent" (2004: 99). Of course, this will prove to be easier said than done.

The same critical logic can be applied to the nationalist parties. As parties of independence, they are "cynically bourgeois" (2004: 110–11). "Achieving power in the name of a narrow-minded nationalism, in the name of the race," argues Fanon, their "magnificently worded declarations" are devoid of content. Full of "Europe's treatises on ethics and political philosophy," they are "incapable of implementing a program with even a minimum humanist content" (2004: 109). Their elitism is often expressed in one-party rule, which "takes priority over a rational study of colonial society" (2004: 64). When a study of reality is undertaken, it is framed by categories (such as development and security) developed in the European metropole, ignoring the real life of the majority of the population. By 1961, pan-Africanists like Nkrumah and Touré were also calling for a single party, and Fanon was withering in his criticism, considering such a concept as nothing other than "the modern form of the bourgeois dictatorship – stripped of mask, makeup, and scruples, cynical in every aspect" (2004:

111). It was a remarkably proscriptive judgment. Whether the party was an elite formation, as with Nkrumah, or mass-based, as with Touré, each saw decision-making coming down from the top and being carried out by the ranks. Fanon, on the other hand, wanted decisions to be decided and administered by the people from the bottom up, understanding that freedom was impossible without a liberated society and thus had to be expressed in the program and practice of the organization. The now dominant nationalist party, in contrast, instead becomes "an intelligence service [and] the militant becomes an informer" looking to control the masses and reminding them "to be obedient and disciplined" (2004: 125).

But the wait for houses, jobs, water, electricity, and sanitation never ends. The local party's work is to stall the people and then criminalize and destroy any organization among the pauperized masses.[10] Increasingly authoritarian, the party is run by "a big boss" or leader (the word, Fanon says, comes from the English, to drive, like a herd). In contrast, the masses humanized by the anticolonial struggle "are no longer a herd and do not need to be driven" (2004: 127). Since colonial cities, the offices of colonial government, and the colonial economy are objects of desire for the nationalist bourgeoisie, their dream of the colonial metropole means that the political administration swells "out of all proportion." Consequently, rural populations also "turn their backs on an unrewarding soil and set off for the urban periphery, swelling the lumpenproletariat out of all proportion" (2004: 129). The struggle continues.

While Fanon ends the previous chapter arguing that the revolutionary party unifies and leads the struggle, the perspective here focuses on how decolonization means breaking with the bourgeois notion that the "masses are incapable of governing themselves" (2004: 130). Thus, the first task of decolonial intellectuals is to take a stand by appropriating all the resources they have "culled from colonial universities" (2004: 99) and putting them into the service of the people. Fanon had seen this during the Algerian revolution, which put Algerian intellectuals in touch with the masses, allowing them to see their "unspeakable poverty" and "the awakening of their intelligence and the development of their consciousness." While an isolated individual may obstinately refuse to understand a problem, it is the struggle itself that helps create new social individuals who "fully understand the most complex issues (2004: 130).

So rather than an elite organization, the party must become the guide in the struggle to build a new society in which everyone is involved in the administration and decision-making. Involving everyone is behind Fanon's insistence that the liberation organization should be decentralized in the extreme and concentrated in rural areas where, at the time, nearly 80 percent of the continent's population lived. But rather than being merged with local authorities, party militants should have no administrative rank. Fanon puts forward a philosophical conception of how the revolutionary party should operate in practice: "For the people the party is not the authority but the organization whereby they, the people, exert their authority and will." The revolutionary party's role is to "stimulate, revive, and accelerate the citizens' consciousness" (2004: 128). In contrast to this idea, the national party-state reflected an epistemological, theoretical, and practical attitude that was cynically bourgeois. After independence, it quickly demobilizes the people, Fanon argues, acting like "common sergeants major and constantly remind[ing] the people of the need to keep 'silence in the ranks,'" dispatching them "back to their caves . . . as soon as the colonial authorities hand over the country" (2004: 126).

Those on the left who remain within the nationalist party, or who are part of an alliance with it, are not immune to its logic. Fanon had witnessed this dimension during the Algerian revolution, explaining the need to critically and openly address what he calls a "voluntarist shortcut," which is still often experienced in social movements' meetings: "It sometimes occurs during a meeting that a militant's answer to a difficult problem is: 'All we need do is . . .' This voluntary shortcut, which dangerously combines spontaneity, simplistic syncretism, and little intellectual elaboration, frequently wins the day (2004: 139).

The militant feels a responsibility to lay out the nation-building line. For Fanon, in contrast, the new society is constructed through a working democracy where encouraging questions, discussion, and intellectual collaboration among people who have too frequently been told they don't understand, is paramount. In this situation, it is not enough for the militants to admit they are wrong. Rather, they must begin to understand the reason for the shortsightedness of their own thinking (which Fanon calls atrocious and inhuman) and are "encouraged to follow through their chain of reasoning to its conclusion." Thereby, they are "taught to grasp the often atrocious, inhuman, and finally sterile nature of this 'All you need do is . . .'" (2004: 139).

But rather than openly engaging in a full discussion and encouraging different opinions and questions, populations are suppressed for the sake of "national unity." And so "after independence the party sinks into a profound lethargy," with the militants called upon to support the party at events at which a leader gives a speech recalling life during the struggle in order to convey "to the masses they should continue to place their trust in him" (2004: 112).

"Nobody has a monopoly on truth," Fanon continues. There is no *deus ex machina*, no god, no leader, who will bring liberty and dignity. Rather, truth is the responsibility of the community. So where the militant or revolutionary intellectual might be quick to think through a problem, Fanon warns against "overshadowing the people." On the other hand, the revolutionary intellectual must not become a "vulgar opportunist" who simply nods in agreement with everything the people say. Instead, the intellectual should use their thinking and training to help clarify the struggle. To be disciplined by the meeting is to understand how those at the meeting appreciate clarification and want to "understand the reasoning behind an argument, and . . . see where they are going" (2004: 13).[11] The point is that "the successful outcome of any decision depends on the conscious, coordinated commitment of the people as a whole," understanding "we are all in the same boat" (2004: 140). The discussion and reasoning about where, why, and how we are going – namely, Fanon's concern about the nationalist party's lack of an ideology – is spelled out as the fundamental flaw:

> [When] militants asked the leading organizations to elaborate a doctrine, to clarify objectives and draw up a program . . . the leaders categorically refused to address such a task. The doctrine, they retorted, was national unity versus colonialism. And on they forged, armed with only a fiery slogan for a doctrine, reducing any ideological activity to a series of variants on the right of peoples to self-determination and the wind of history that would inevitably sweep away colonialism. (2004: 115)

Fanon argues for a different perspective spoken in the language of every day, in the language of the people, rather than in the technical (and often colonial) language of the specialists whose desire is to rid themselves of any connections with the people (1968: 189; 2004: 131): "Everything can be explained to the people," he insists "on the single condition that you really want them to understand" and "then you will realize that the masses are quick to seize every shade of meaning" (1968: 189; 2004: 131).

Fanon's philosophy of liberation is expressed in its organization and praxis. Mistakes will be made, he argues, but "everyone has to be involved in the struggle for the sake of common salvation": "There are no clean hands, no innocent bystanders. We are all in the process of dirtying our hands in the quagmire of our soil and the terrifying void of our minds. Any bystander is a coward or a traitor" (2004: 140–1). Fanon's idea of "development" is directly related to this. Giving an example of building a bridge, he argues that if it "does not enrich the consciousness of those working on it, then don't build the bridge, and let the citizens continue to swim across the river or use a ferry." Again, the idea of development comes out of discussions and considerations with the people for whom it is intended. While recognizing that architects and engineers might be needed, he insists that the "citizen must appropriate the bridge" and be involved in every detail, so that it "can be integrated, redesigned, and reappropriated" (2004: 141).

This is Fanon's revolutionary humanism in practice. As he concludes, national consciousness needs "to be explained, enriched, and deepened." It cannot be allowed to become a "sterile formalism" which quickly degenerates into chauvinism and racism. If national consciousness "does not very quickly turn into a social and political consciousness, into humanism, it leads to a dead end." In contrast, "only the massive commitment by men and women to judicious and productive tasks gives form and substance to this consciousness" (2004: 144). The nation exists and becomes a living expression, with "the collective consciousness in motion of the entire people ... the enlightened and coherent praxis of the men and women" (2004: 144).

Aware of the growing threat from military leaders to assume political power through coups, Fanon insists that "we should avoid transforming the army into an autonomous body that sooner or later ... will 'go into politics.' (2004: 142). Again, with the Congo crisis in mind (and being wary of the military's continued involvement in politics on the continent), Fanon has practical ideas about how this can be done. First, the army should be "a school for civics, a school for politics ... never a school for war." Second, "there should be no professional soldiers, and the number of career officers should be kept to a minimum" (2004: 142). And finally, politicizing the army means raising "national consciousness, to detribalize and unify" it (2004: 141).

Politics, in short, is the practice of the impoverished masses becoming political subjects. And national consciousness must therefore "humaniz[e]" the people, and "elevat[e] their minds." This new humanism is educational, primarily concerned with restoring the dignity to citizens, to "furnish their minds, fill their eyes with human things and develop a human landscape for the sake of its enlightened and sovereign inhabitants" (2004: 144). Political education means connecting practical work of administration with "opening minds" so that all can becoming responsible for creating a new society. Thus the "bourgeois phase" can be skipped and "resolved through revolutionary action" (2004: 119).

Embedded in addressing the material and psychical reality of the mass of the people, Fanon's successful decolonization does not depend only on a liberated sense of space and a different notion of time that is connected with popular enlightenment:

> Experience proves that the important point is not that three hundred people understand and decide but that all understand and decide, even it if takes twice or three times as long. In fact the time taken to explain, the time "lost" humanizing the worker, will be made up in the execution. People must know where they are going and why. (2004: 134–5).

The new time is in fact the birthtime of history, a new history of the damned of the earth, the time to think and work out new ways of being. That is to say, a time for everyone to be involved in the practical task of rethinking everything – including the land and the rivers, the soil and the sun – that had been robbed by colonialist capitalist expropriation, and to begin doing so at the local level by asking the most practical questions in which everyone can take a part. Thus politicizing the masses is not about making a political speech, but about "driving home . . . that everything depends on them" (2004: 138) and them alone, that they are the new reality of the nation and that self-determination lies in their hands only.

For Fanon, the same political education, directed at raising national consciousness and uniting the nation, is required in the military and civil services. He is critically aware that the demand to nationalize the land can become a "dictatorship of civil servants" (2004: 123) or be controlled from above by the party. Rather, cooperatives for buying and selling have to be organized democratically and decentralized again "by involving the masses in the management of public affairs" (2004: 123–4). Fanon's idea about Africa's "development" is therefore not about stages of growth; rather, it is epistemologically decolonial. Those who work the land have the knowledge and experience, and they need to be encouraged to be part of the rethinking. Of course, Fanon understands this will take time given that colonialism has taken a psychological toll, and he insists that there must be a program that includes a "concept about the future of [hu]mankind. Which means that no sermon, no complicity with the former occupier can replace a program." He remained optimistic that "the people, at first unenlightened and then increasingly lucid, will vehemently demand such a program" (2004: 143). Rather than just telling people what to do, the learning process must be about people and militant intellectuals working together . One source for such thinking was how the struggle itself had played an important part in raising consciousness. Fanon gives an example that again conveyed praxis as central to his idea of "growing brains" and to his critique of nationalist elites:

> In the regions where we were able to conduct these enlightening experiments, where we witnessed the edification of the human being through revolutionary teachings, the peasant clearly grasped the principle whereby the clearer the commitment, the better one works. We were able to convey to the masses that work is not a physical exercise or the working of certain muscles, but that one works more with one's brain and one's heart than with muscles and sweat . . . We did not have technicians or experts from the leading universities of the West [telling us.] . . . the people were not content merely to celebrate their victory. They asked theoretical questions.

The result of this "revolutionary teaching," he concludes, was that "today the people have a very clear notion of what belongs to them" (2004: 133–4).

Rather than worrying about either the withdrawal or the accumulation of capital, Fanon's primary concern is the withdrawal of the human being and the very concrete question of not "dragging [people] towards mutilation, of not imposing upon the brain rhythms which very quickly obliterate and wreck it" (1968: 315; see also 2004: 238). Repeatedly condemning forced labor in the name of the nation, Fanon promotes the importance of humanizing work to the goal of humanizing the world (2004: 57), and he concludes: "It is only when men and women are included on a vast scale in enlightened and fruitful work that form and body are given to that consciousness" (1968: 204; see also 2004: 144).

The beginnings of this involvement, both practically and theoretically, are found in the local political meeting and assemblies, where all are encouraged to participate and everyone's voice counts. In *Les Damnés*, Fanon spoke of these meetings as the practical and ethical foundation of the new society; they represent the revival of suppressed democratic forms that are given a new vitality and meaning through the revolution as well as the new forms of organization that spontaneously arise within the social struggle. Fanon views the meeting as "a liturgical act. It is a privileged opportunity for the individual to listen and speak. At every meeting the brain multiplies the association of ideas and the eye discovers a wider human panorama" (2004: 136).

For the outsider, these meetings might seem tedious. Everyone is sitting around talking about what to do. There is little action, much deliberation, and perhaps some formality. But this is a living politics and the birth of a democratic and communal political form that includes everyone. It is through the meeting that new contradictions are brought to light and new concepts emerge. At first, the form of the meeting seems more important than the political content of the discussion, because the form itself prefigures a nonstate form of popular democracy. This is exactly what the struggle is about: working things out collectively and discovering "a wider human panorama." It is in the simplicity of the democratic and inclusive meeting – which is political in the sense that it is also against "politics" associated with state power – that represents a decolonized space that not only takes thinking seriously, but, in doing so, aims to develop fundamentally different relations between human beings. At the local level, Fanon gives a seemingly banal example of lentil production during the liberation struggle. He writes of a situation where liberated zones were cordoned off from the towns so that peasants couldn't buy goods. Black markets and local grocers flourished, and peas-

ants became indebted to them at high rates of interest. The
FLN intervened and established production/consumption
committees among the peasants. The experience generated
concrete theoretical questions about the accumulation of
capital. The rich were no longer respectable as people began
to understand that wealth was "not the fruit of labor but the
spoils from an organized protection racket" (2004: 133).

## "On National Culture"

Chapter 4 is divided into two sections. It begins with a discussion about intellectuals and ends with the presentation Fanon
gave at the 1959 Congress of Black Writers and Artists in
Rome, discussed earlier. In the first section, Fanon returns to
the problem of the alienated colonized intellectual who has
imbibed colonial culture and considers how disalienation can
occur through their connection with the anticolonial struggle.
"Everything he had written against the intellectuals," opined
de Beauvoir, he had "written against himself as well" (1994:
316).

As we have seen, the small national bourgeoisie played an
outsized role in the anticolonial struggle and the colonized
intellectual was part of this faction. Fanon maps the development of the colonized intellectual in three phases. In the first,
as discussed in *Black Skin, White Masks*, intellectuals throw
themselves into Western culture and assimilate what they have
been taught in the elite colonial schools, including, of course,
its language and epistemology, "the savagery" of African
people, and the civilization and morality of the West (2004:
157). Their cultural inspirations are utterly Western, making
"European culture their own" (2004: 156). At the level of the
unconscious colonialism wants to be perceived as a mother
"protecting the child from itself," a self that it is physiologi-

cally, biologically, and ontologically damned (2004: 149). By internalizing this, colonized intellectuals become like colonial liberals, arguing that "barbarism, degradation and bestiality" will return if the colonists leave (2004: 149). Left in this situation, Fanon concludes, colonized intellectuals become a "colorless, stateless, rootless . . . body of angels . . . faced with extremely serious psychoaffective mutilations" (2004: 155).

In the second phase, of which negritude is an expression, colonized intellectuals have their "convictions shaken"; they reclaim a past that is not specifically national but, rather, a negation of colonialism's distortion, disfigurement, and destruction. Since colonialism's claims are universal and speak of the continent as a "den of savages . . . of cannibals, of nègres," negritude is an "affective if not logical antithesis to that insult" and common ties are made across the Black world (2004: 150). Later, American Blacks realized "that their existential problems differed from those faced by the Africans." "The principle and purpose of the [1961] freedom rides whereby [B]lack and [W]hite Americans endeavor to combat racial discrimination," Fanon argues, "have little in common with the heroic struggle of the Angolan people against the iniquity of Portuguese colonialism" (2004: 153–4). As the anticolonial struggle becomes organized, the colonized intellectuals begin to realize that the nation is realized through a popular struggle and a third stage is ushered in – a "combat stage," when a new revolutionary, national, combat literature emerges. Fanon quotes a poem by Keïta Fodéba telling the story of a hero on the battlefields of Italy and Germany. He finally makes it back to Senegal and is shot dead in a "major dispute between us and our [W]hite chiefs in Dakar" (2004: 166). It is a story, Fanon says, in which "all the 'nègres' and all 'filthy Arabs' who fought to defend French liberty and British civilization will recognize themselves" (2004: 167).

Fanon understood the psychological and historical necessity of colonized intellectuals "to racialize their claims" and to speak in generalities about decolonization but insisted that, if it does not evolve into a national and combat culture, it leads to "a dead end" (2004: 152). Disconnected with the popular struggle, the intellectual is preoccupied with culture as "an inventory of particularisms" in which superficial connections are "merely a reflection of a dense, subterranean life in perpetual renewal" (2004: 160). Fanon is thus angry at those negritude poets-turned-politicians, like Césaire and Senghor, who continue to support France politically, focusing on the actions of negritude poet Jacques Rabemananjara. One of the founders of Mouvement démocratique de la rénovation malgache in Madagascar and imprisoned during the 1947 revolt, Rabemananjara, by then a government minister, voted against the Algerian people at the UN General Assembly.

Negritude can become an abstraction, focusing on "a past where [the people] no longer exist." In contrast, by connecting with people in motion, a combat culture becomes an expression of where the people are. The national culture being created is one in which everything is called into question. Long forgotten songs and stories change and take on new cultural value. In artisanship, "petrified forms loosen up" and an "avalanche of amateurs . . . encourage the traditional schools to innovate" (2004: 175). Recognizing these changes, Fanon concluded his speech to the 1959 Congress of Black Writers and Artists by arguing that the new humanity emerging from the struggle defines a new humanism:

> The liberation struggle does not restore to national culture its former values and configurations. This struggle, which aims at a fundamental redistribution of relations between [people], cannot leave intact either the form or substance of the people's culture. After the struggle is over, there is not only the demise of colonialism, but also the demise of

the colonized. This new humanity, for itself and for others, inevitably defines a new humanism. This new humanism is written into the objectives and methods of the struggle. A struggle, which mobilizes every level of society ... We believe that the future of culture and the richness of a national culture are also based on the values that inspired the struggle for freedom. (2004: 178–9).

## "Colonial Wars and Mental Disorders"

The more that Fanon the political revolutionary saw the possibility of a decolonized society, the more that Fanon the psychiatrist could not forget the wounded reality on which the new nation would have to be built. "Our actions never cease to haunt us," he writes in an opening footnote about a militant suffering from insomnia, anxiety, and suicidal ideation, which occurred around the anniversary of the time he had bombed a café that was "known to be a haunt of notorious racists." After independence, the man had become friends with people from the former colonizing nation and was "overcome by a kind of vertigo," haunted by an anxiety that he might have killed people like his friends (2004: 184n.23).

Can we escape vertigo? Fanon asks, adding a definitive "no": "Who dares claim that vertigo does not prey on every life?" (2004: 185n.23). The militant's individual suffering is social and, faced with this vertiginous situation, "such borderline cases pose the question of *responsibility in the context of the revolution*" (2004: 185; my emphasis). What is this responsibility? No one has clean hands, he reminds us, and decolonization is not a magic formula but has to be an ongoing, constant, and self-critical process of action and thinking, while bandaging "sometimes indelible wounds" (2004: 181). It is the necessity of this rethinking that Fanon feels he needs to justify, writing that "these notes on psychiatry" might seem "out of place or untimely in a book like this," and adding "there is absolutely nothing we can do about that" (2004: 181). In a note, he writes of the human legacy of French colonialism in Algeria with remarkable perception to ongoing realities, arguing that "an entire generation of Algerians, steeped in collective, gratuitous homicide with all the psycho-affective consequences this entails, would be France's human legacy in Algeria" (2004: 183 n.22).

Though less read than other chapters in the book, "Colonial Wars and Mental Disorders" is essential to understanding the depth of Fanon's idea of liberation, leading us back to totalitarian structures of colonialism (including being a purveyor of psychiatric hospitals) that systematically negated and denied the colonized "any attribute of humanity," forcing them to constantly ask: "Who am I in reality?" (2004: 182). It was in that context that the seven-year war of liberation had "become a breeding ground of mental disorders." (2004: 182–3).

The first section of the chapter is a series of studies, each one of which is divided into five groups, but Fanon avoids "semiological, nosological [and] therapeutic discussion" (2004: 183). While the patient's individual history is mentioned, the triggering factor is "principally the bloody, pitiless atmosphere" of inhuman practices that give them the impression of a "veritable apocalypse" (2004: 183). Aware of the "classic" studies of shell shock and war trauma after World War I and the studies of urban warfare on civilian and refugee mental health after World War II, Fanon argues that the "colonial war is a new phenomenon even in the pathology it produces" (2004: 184).

Following the case of a 19-year-old ALN fighter diagnosed with a "major depressive disorder with mood-congruent psychotic features following the murder of a woman while briefly psychotic," Fanon argues that, "as unscientific as it may seem, we believe only time may heal the dislocated personality of this young man" (2004: 194). Fanon was not simply saying that time heals; he was optimistic that time spent in relative calm, in therapy, individual and group, would promote deeper reflection and would aid healing not only of this young man but of society as a whole.

Series A looks at Algerians and Europeans with "severe reactive disorders" (see Burman 2019: 125–40). The trigger for the Series B "is first and foremost the atmosphere of outright war" (2004: 199; see also Gibson and Beneduce 2017: 236–9). Series C is titled "Affective and Mental Changes and Emotional Disturbances after Torture" and considers different methods of torture as they correspond with "their characteristic symptoms of morbidity" (2004: 208; see also Turner 2011: 126–7). The psychiatric consequences of the last group in the series, "After brainwashing," is divided into two sections, for intellectuals and for nonintellectuals. Fanon's conceptualization is innovative and its symptomology is pathbreaking in scope and organization. The logic of torture is not forgetting: Fanon invokes the words of a French torturer after he raped an Algerian woman: "If you ever see that bastard your husband again, don't you forget to tell him what we did to you" (2004: 186). The final case in Series A is about a torturer who admitted himself to the hospital to address his desire to torture his wife and children. He wanted Fanon to help him torture "with a total peace of mind" (2004: 199).

The second section of Chapter 5 is called "From the North African's Criminal Impulsiveness to the War of National Liberation" and includes a critique of Antoine Porot and the Algiers School of Psychiatry, which created a theory for why Algerians were "born idlers, born liars, born thieves, and born criminals," and habitual, savage, and senseless killers (2004: 221–2).

Porot had first developed his theory in 1918 and in 1935 he defined its "scientific basis," arguing that the Algerian's cortex was poorly developed and life was "governed" by the dien-cephalon (2004: 225). Fanon explains that what distinguishes the human "from other vertebrates is the cortex," saying that the "North African is governed by the diencephalon" is basi-cally saying that they "have no cortex" (2004: 226) and this is the reason for violence and criminality. This "scientific theory" became dominant and had been taught for more than 20 years, with graduate doctors learning that the Algerian is born criminal and violent (2004: 223). It was given further credence when in 1954 the World Health Organization published J.C. Carothers's *The African Mind in Health and Disease: A Study in Ethnopsychiatry*.[12] Carothers took a continental view, arguing that the "normal African is a lobotomized European" (2004: 227) and thus colonial disciplining, subduing, and pacifying could be justified. Both Porot and Carothers would describe the emergent anticolonial struggles (the Mau Mau revolt in Kenya and the FLN in Algeria) in similar ways (on Carothers and Porot, see Gibson and Beneduce 2017: 99–113).

Fanon argues that so-called criminality, laziness, and vio-lence are responses to colonial domination whereby "to live simply means not to die" and every date or olive grown "is a victory" (2004: 232). The "daily incitement to murder" results from famine, eviction, joblessness, and poverty, where the colonized see their fellows as enemies. They hardly ever see a European and tend to use each other as a screen, with each preventing the other from seeing the national enemy. When they owe the local Algerian shopkeeper, when they beg for semolina, when they owe taxes to the Algerian *kaid*, they see them rather than the Europeans as the enemy. And thus "once you have seen men and women in Kabylia struggling down into the valley for weeks on end to bring up soil in little bas-kets you can understand that theft is attempted murder and not a peccadillo" (2004: 232). Going beyond predictable clini-cal approaches that reject an encounter with history, Fanon

290 THE HANDBOOK OF REVOLUTION

catalogues the phobias, obsessions, and psychoses of those forced to live in perpetual insecurity.

The war of liberation brings in its wake massive changes, highlighting how Algerian criminality and murderousness are not a "consequence of the nervous system or specific character traits, but a result of the colonial situation," and the fight against colonial domination means the elimination of "all the untruths planted within by the oppressor" (2004: 233). "Total liberation," Fanon concludes, must "involve every facet of the personality" in which "men and women . . . master all the material resources necessary for a radical transformation of society" (2004: 233). But the dialectical prerequisite requires that a "major theoretical problem" be addressed. Here Fanon returns to the important consideration of mental liberation, self-criticism, and self-liberation: "the insult to humanity . . . *in ourselves*" must be "demystified and hunted down at all times and in all places." Expressing the objectivity of subjectivity, he continues: "We must not expect the nation to produce new men [and women]. We must not expect men [and women] to change imperceptibly as the revolution constantly innovates." While it is true that "both processes are important," it is consciousness, he concludes, "that needs help." (2004: 229).


## Fanon's conclusion

Fanon's four-and-a-half-page conclusion is a powerful revolutionary humanist statement written to the "comrades" and, like his three-page letter the Resident Minister on resigning from Blida-Joinville Psychiatric Hospital, wonderfully expresses his philosophy. Fanon demands that we leave Europe, where there is a lot of talk about human rights but where, in the name of humanism, it continues to massacre and enslave humanity. Instead, there is a "very concrete question of not dragging humans toward mutilation, of not imposing upon the brain rhythms which very quickly obliterate it and wreck it." After stating that Europe has become petrified and the dialectic has become motionless, Fanon concludes: "For Europe, for ourselves and for humanity, comrades, we must make a new start, develop a new way of thinking, and endeavor to create a new humanism" (2004: 239). Fanon began *Les Damnés* by arguing that the liberation struggle of the damned of the earth is "an original idea propounded as an absolute"; he ends the book with the absolute as a "new humanism" being developed at the nodal point of the African revolution and threatened by the counterrevolution.

Thinking about a "new humanism," Fanon was not a romantic. Rather, he understood the necessity to keep fighting for human freedom against all odds; engaging with the trials and tribulations of national consciousness at that moment therefore amounted to an analysis of the tragedy of the African revolutions – and also the tragedy of Fanon himself, consumed by the very struggle for a new life for the damned of the earth that he worked tirelessly to bring about.

# Conclusion[1]

## The immediacy of Fanon

There is an immediacy in Fanon's analysis of racial objectification and dehumanization in *Black Skin, White Masks* as well as in the security lines of the "global city" and its postcolonial ghettos described in *Les Damnés de la terre*. Across the world, from Africa and the Middle East to the Caribbean and Latin America, from the US to Europe, spontaneous resistance continues because it is quite literally impossible to breathe under the boot of the militarized police. The #EndSARS movement in Nigeria did lead to the successful ending of the brutal Special Anti-Robbery Squad; and the mass actions that followed the brutal police beating and murder of Tyre Nichols in Memphis did lead to the closing of a special police unit. But . . .

I write this conclusion in the face of a massive revolt sparked by the police murder of 17-year-old Nahel Merzouk in Nanterre, France. The revolt continued for a week, underscoring Fanon's description of such a reaction against the

brutal French police tactics as rational, even as old racist tropes
re-emerged – just as they had in the three-week revolt of the
banlieues in 2005. As that revolt put French civilization and its
claim to be a nonracial society on trial, the same can be said
of the Black Lives Matter mass actions of 2020. Characterized
from its birth, the US Declaration of Independence was meant
only for Whites,[2] and the US became a monster, argued
Fanon in 1961, where "the inhumanity of Europe has grown
to appalling dimensions" (1968: 313), and Black rebellions
against it continuous.

   The velocity and scale of revolt is impossible to predict, but
then an event becomes a nodal point that calls for action as
well as rethinking and self-clarification. Thinking about our
moment with Fanon, we need to be aware of continuities and
discontinuities – or, as he puts it, opacities – between the ages.
Fanon is always speaking to us, but often in ways we cannot
hear. It is said by many who knew him that Fanon had an
acute ability to listen intensely. We have to work to listen
to him and to understand the new contexts and meanings in
"relative opacity" in order to help illuminate the present and
enable an ongoing fidelity to his call in the conclusion of *Les
Damnés de la terre* to work out new concepts, "for ourselves
and for humanity."

## The rationality of revolt

The practice of engaging with the rationality of revolt defines
a uniquely Fanonian dialectic. In the clinic he connects hearing
symptoms to hearing resistances in daily life. "It is necessary,"
he says, and this is essential to Fanon's clinical and political
practice, "to analyze, patiently and lucidly, each one of *the reactions* of the colonized, and *every time we do not understand*, we
must tell ourselves that we are at the heart of the drama" (1965:

125) In other words, understanding requires both careful and critical listening to voices and to actions, while maintaining an awareness of the lie of the situation. Clinically and politically, then, self-critical reflection enables listening as a first step toward working with those who are considered outside history and rationality. For Fanon, understanding the reason in revolt also requires the development of new ways of thinking and new ways of understanding as the people's own lie as a dimension of truth. But nothing is automatic and Fanon is utterly critical of what he calls the common opportunism of intellectuals who simply record without engaging with what they hear.

The rationality of revolt is a concept that becomes a new way of opening up both action and thought. And to this end, Fanon immediately questions the old leadership and old politics – and here he is also speaking of the anticolonists and leftists who want to close down thinking and narrow discussion into a series of reformist or even faux-revolutionary demands constructed by colonial values, or in reaction to those values. "In defiance of those inside the movement who tend to think that [nuance and] shades of meaning constitute dangers and drive wedges into the solid block of popular opinion," Fanon argues (1968: 147) thinking becomes alive and principles can be "worked out" and lived inside the struggles for freedom.

In a context in which time speeds up, Fanon's criticism of bourgeois time and of the idea that we don't have time to think is absolutely necessary. As history becomes alive with those who have been excluded from it, it is they who must be encouraged to "take the lead with their brains and their muscles in the fight for freedom." Fanon's idea of developing brains is essential. This does not happen automatically and Fanon is painfully aware of the weight of oppression. Thus the challenge for revolutionary humanists is to help work out the movement's own self-clarification, including "contradictions camouflaged by these facts" (1968: 147).

## Breath

Settler neocolonialism, like that in the walled-in ghetto that is Gaza, is the denial of movement and space. Daily life is a challenge to survive, a living death, in Fanon's terms, where every moment of life is contested, including breath itself. Under such conditions, revolt is necessary to life; every breath is a challenge, and "a clandestine form of existence" (1965: 65). Revolt sanctions – "at whatever cost," Fanon adds in *Les Damnés* – the invasion of "the enemy's fortress . . . endangering [its] 'security'" and breeding fear into the colonial forces (1968: 130). Combat breathing then becomes another history – a history in the making.

The concreteness of Black lives mattering resonated across the US in a Fanonian way where the militarized police, the schools, the courts, and indeed mental health professionals, are understood as all being part of the same system. It showed a skepticism of the old categories and the reformist promises which understood that the fight has to be "for the birth of a human world . . . a world of reciprocal recognitions" – as Fanon puts it in *Black Skin, White Masks* (2008: 193). This is why life can emerge only from the destruction of colonialism.

But when history is being made, if only for a moment, what is the rationality of revolt? New meanings are brought out and old tropes are countered by participant narratives that quickly become shared through social media. Fanon warns that reactions against colonial Manicheanism must also undergo a dialectical change or be doomed to repetition. The struggle must become a new way of life and new sociality.

## Time

The suffering body described by Fanon in *Black Skin, White Masks* as being locked into thinghood is powerfully redescribed in *Les Damnés*: immobilized, hemmed in and crushed, denied food and clean water, the colonial world as a motionless world of statues. While space is absolutely essential to his analysis, so too is time. Fanon refuses to consider the present as definitive, and searches for glimpses of the future in the present. He phrases it wonderfully when he describes the Algerian revolution as being "no longer in future heaven," in the radical actions and consciousness of the people. The idea of the future time in the present is, as Marx put it, "time as the space for human development."

In *Les Damnés*, Fanon also asks about the timing of revolt. "In this atmosphere of violence . . . which is just under the skin . . . what makes the lid blow off?" It is impossible to predict, but as we look back at the concatenation of events, it seems so obvious. In a Fanonian sense, Black Lives Matter was an opening into historical time – a time in which the racialized again become historical actors, and the future suddenly becomes a matter of contestation where "things no longer repeat themselves as they did before" (1965: 78). What also becomes apparent is that the spontaneity of popular action is not simply unplanned, but the result of ongoing thinking and organizing. For example, when demonstrators in Bristol, England pulled down the statue of slave trader Edward Colston and dumped it in the same harbor where his ships had once docked, there was thinking behind it – a rationality of revolt intimating a different world. When demonstrators defaced the statues of such "national heroes" as George Washington in the US, or Winston Churchill in Britain, or Cecil John Rhodes in Cape Town, they expressed a moment of decolonization reminiscent of Fanon's opening pages in *Les Damnés*. There, Fanon talks about another notion of time and dignity – one that is fully integrated with a conception of human life and one that humanizes and socializes the individual.

Critical of the betrayal of anticolonial leaders, Fanon offers us a different vision: "The yardstick of time must no longer be that of the moment or up till the next harvest, but must become that of the rest of the world." He immediately links this to "humanizing work." Today, his idea of the "rest of the world" takes on a significance that is urgent in this moment of capitalist climate extinction. It is a notion of time that is liberated from the colonial foreclosure of possibility and also from capitalist time. Time, instead, is connected with life, self-determination, and the development of human subjectivities. Nothing, however, is automatic. Fanon's notion of time is also extremely sensitive to the psychological situation that people find themselves in, including the weight of individual and collective trauma and prospects for future health that only time, he says, will fully reveal. He is unsure, in other words; there are no guarantees of recovery, but time, of course, has to become consciously human time. It has to become the time for health and the recovery of those knowingly and unknowingly broken down by racism, colonialism, and capitalism. Fanon is aware that the process of creating liberated people might take time, insisting that there is no magical process, no leader, no other who will do it for us. For Fanon, the absolute negativity of colonialism is a continuous revolution necessitating the humanization of all social relations. The struggle itself must become the basis for a new way of life that begins to question every social relationship. His analysis turns not only on struggle, but on the values of the struggle. This is a new collective breathing, a thinking combat breath.

## Rethinking everything

Fanon theorizes this as new humanism, a new world human-ism, against all forms of physical and mental alienation. As we have seen, Fanon concludes *Les Damnés* by arguing that, despite Europeans' apparent support for humanism, they "murder human beings everywhere they find them," while the "new humanity cannot do otherwise than define a new humanism both for itself and for others. It is prefigured in the objectives and methods of the conflict." There is an implicit radical humanism to the Black Lives Matter move-ment as new subjectivities and voices emerge that want to discuss and understand and plan for the future. Outside negotiations in elite spaces, Fanon believes a new world can come about when the marginalized and so-called worthless become involved in decision-making. This is the intellectual challenge left to us by Fanon, who warns: "If conditions of work are not modified centuries will be needed to humanize this world which has been forced down to animal level by imperial powers" (2004: 57). He's talking about all the forms of forced labor – sometimes called free labor – that consume lives.

Throughout his work, Fanon sustains a fundamental sense of movement and opening to the future in the form of a critical, questioning mode of praxis. He concludes *Black Skin White Masks* with a prayer: "O my body, make of me always a man who questions!" In *Les Damnés de la terre* there is a radical questioning from within the revolutionary move-ment – "Perhaps we need to rethink everything again all over" (1968: 100; see also 2004: 56–7) – suggesting that his notion of the future as a "limitless humanity" seeking new ways of life and work is connected to a re-examination of the soil, minerals, rivers, and "the sun's productivity". There's an ecohumanist dimension connected with human life and dignity that is based on uprooting all the alienated social relations of a racist and colonized capitalist world. The time is now.

# Notes

## Preface

1 https://www.haaretz.com/opinion/2023-10-09/ty-article-opinion/
.premium/israel-cant-imprison-2-million-gazans-without-paying-a-
cruel-price/0000018b-1476-d465-abbb-14f6262a0000.
2 https://www.nytimes.com/2023/11/18/world/middleeast/gaza-child
ren-israel.html?searchResultPosition=1

## Introduction

1 In my edited *Fanon Today*, movement intellectuals write about Fanonian practices not only in the United States, Brazil, and South Africa, but
also in Portugal, Kenya, Trinidad, Palestine, Syria, England, Pakistan,
Ghana, Mexico, the North of Ireland, Algeria, and the Amazon.
2 "Three Words. 70 Cases. The Tragic History of 'I Can't Breathe'."
https://www.nytimes.com/interactive/2020/06/28/us/i-cant-breathe-
police-arrest.html.
3 "Black August, from 1971 to 2011–13." https://sfbayview.com/2019/
09/black-august-from-1971-to-2011-13/.
4 This was Fanon's original title, giving a nod to the French revolutionary calendar of 1789 being year one (changed to 1792 to
commemorate the Republic not the revolution); 1959 was the fifth
year of the Algerian revolution. While Fanon definitely agrees that
French colonialism is dying in Algeria, he writes more of the new
reality of the nation and radical changes in consciousness and social
relations born of the revolution. I thus prefer to use his original title
rather than the English, *A Dying Colonialism*.
5 While the English translation of *Les Damnés de la terre*, *The Wretched
of the Earth*, follows the translation of Eugène Pottier's song, I prefer
the more literal translation, and to emphasize that will use the French
title from now on.

6 On the Manichean anti-imperialist, left-supporting, capitalist "South-South" cooperation, see Robinson 2023.

7 See my discussion with Abahlali baseMjondolo members in *Fanon Today* (2021), which includes an important array of engagements with Fanon by activist intellectuals from around the world.

8 Martin Luther King, who always considered thought and debate to be important in a social movement, lamented in his last book, *Where Do We Go from Here: Chaos or Community?*, that young Black Americans were reading Fanon not Gandhi.

9 It is a point of view that still dominates, as reflected in the title of Adam Shatz's 2001 review of David Macey's biography of Fanon, published in the *New York Times*: "The Doctor Prescribed Violence." https://www.nytimes.com/2001/09/02/books/the-doctor-prescribed -violence.html.

10 A fusion of Bélé (with roots in West African dances) and nineteenth-century French ballroom steps was popular in Martinique and Paris from the 1930s to the 1950s.

11 https://en.wikipedia.org/wiki/Year_of_Africa.

12 Guattari would later co-author with Gilles Deleuze, *Anti-Oedipus: Capitalism and Schizophrenia* (1972).

13 There are a number of connections between Fanon and militant antipsychiatry movements, such as the Socialist Patients' Collective in Heidelberg, whose manifesto *Turn Illness into a Weapon*, prefaced by Sartre, articulated a social-symptomatic model of illness that was explicitly anticapitalist (see Adler-Bolton and Vierkant 2022: 147).

14 See, e.g., Happyfeed, "4 Brain Chemicals that Make Yo You Happy" (2019). https://www.happyfeed.co/research/4-brain-chemi cals-make-you-happy.

15 There has been constant radical resistance to the hegemony of *DSM*. For a psychodynamic approach, see Lingiardi and McWilliams (2017).

16 This of course has been resisted and fundamentally questioned. See, for example, "Depression is probably not caused by a chemical imbalance in the brain – new study." https://www.ucl.ac.uk/ne ws/2022/jul/analysis-depression-probably-not-caused-chemical-im balance-brain-new-study; also see Moncrief (2021). Also see The Critical Psychiatry Network, founded in the UK in 1999 by a group of psychiatrists in the UK to discuss changes to the proposed Mental Health Act: http://www.criticalpsychiatry.co.uk/.

## Chapter 1: Martinique, France, and Metaphysical Experiences

1 In a French police intelligence report from Blida, Algeria, dated November 8, 1956, he is named Frantz Marguerite Victor Fanon.
2 Though it is often asserted, Joby insists that Frantz was never Césaire's student (2014: 38).
3 Macey (2012: 100) notes that Ben Bella, the future leader of Algeria, was also awarded a medal by this man. The OAS was dedicated to destroying Algeria rather than negotiating any future.
4 Falling into convulsions. The reference to Creole here is important in the chapter "The Black and Language."

## Chapter 2: Fanon in France

1 His bestseller, *Introduction aux existentialismes*, was published in 1947.
2 When Manville asked for further explanation, Fanon said he had never met "so many idiots in his life as in dental school" (Geismar 1971: 44). In truth, as Cherki adds: "Fanon did not have much choice in the matter; the scholarships that had been earmarked for medical students from the Antilles were restricted to campuses in the eastern region of the country or in Lyon" (2006: 15).
3 Cherki points out that Fanon "spontaneously switched to Creole whenever he found himself in the company of Guyanese or Antillean friends" and was "outspoken about the way in which Creole had been relegated to its lowly status" (2006: 217–18).
4 Certainly a critically engaged anthropology can be seen in many of Fanon's works. See, for example, "The 'North African Syndrome'" (1967: 3–16), "Daily Life in the Douars" (2018: 373–84), and "Introduction to Sexuality Disorders among the North Africans" (2018: 385–93) as well as *L'An V*.
5 Socialisme ou barbarisme, which was founded in 1948, was probably the most radical of former Trotskyist groups that offers some connection to Fanon's politics. One of its founding members was the Lacanian analyst Jean Laplanche.
6 Cherki notes (2006: 6) that she as well as other friends and colleagues of Fanon's from his time in Algeria and Tunisia knew nothing of Mireille's existence until a number of years after his death.
7 Djebar remembered Josie's words in October 1988 as youth revolted across Algiers and "reached fevered pitch under Josie's balcony." The police opened fire killing 500 and injuring 1,000 people; "Once more, O Frantz, 'les damnés de la terre'" (Djebar 2000: 92).

8 This is a quote from "On Liberty," titled "La liberté existentielle," in Dufrenne and Ricoeur (1947: 144). The quote is marked up in Fanon's copy (2018: 731).

9 Burns was a British colonial governor who, much like Mannoni, was a liberal critic of racism and an advocate of a slow reform under British supervision. Fanon responds to these liberal colonists (we could also include J.C. Carothers) in *Les Damnés de la terre*: "So they say the colonized want to move too fast. Let us never forget that it wasn't such a long time ago the colonized were accused of being too slow, lazy, and fatalistic" (2004: 35).

10 Fanon attributes the quote to *Thus Spoke Zarathustra*, but it is in fact from *Ecce Homo* (see Khalfa in Fanon 2018: 179n.29).

11 Antoine Porot had also trained at the University of Lyon. He founded the Algiers school of neuropsychology; see Chapter 4.

12 The map of the departments of France included on Wikipedia (https://en.wikipedia.org/wiki/Departments_of_France) is spatially instructive with the Islands of Martinique, French Guiana, Guadeloupe, Réunion, and now Mayotte located to the East and West of the mainland.

13 Marcel Manville suggests that Fanon would have returned if there had been a job available (see Cherki 2006: 22).

14 Tosquelles's idea is quite different from the social science idea of "sociotherapy" that has developed in the anglophone world.

15 Politically conservative with a social Darwinist worldview that drew him toward National Socialist ideology, Hermann Simon (1867–1947) had an innovative approach to mental health, which drew on his practical experience. He developed the concept of a "more active therapy," perceiving patients in a holistic way, regarding them not so much as sick people but as fellow human beings, which allowed for the patient's individual views (see Walter 2002).

16 In 1938, Tosquelles and Mira y López were both named Chief of Psychiatric Services of the Republican Army (see http://www.miray lopez.com/). Tosquelles held the post until April 1939.

17 Fanon would carry this idea to Blida-Joinville Psychiatric Hospital, and developed it politically in *Les Damnés de la terre*, where the administration of things – "development" from on high – is considered a *deus ex machina* and contrasted to the messy building of a community out of day-to-day praxis (1968: 200–1).

18 Quoted in https://fr.wikipedia.org/wiki/Centre_hospitalier_Fran%C3%A7ois-Tosquelles.

19 See, for example, Merleau-Ponty's "Marxism and Philosophy," in his *Sens et non-sens* (1948).

20 To Katie Kilroy-Marac's speculation about why Senghor didn't respond (2019: 106–7), I would add that Fanon might not have stayed long in Senegal given Senghor's defense of neocolonialism.

## Chapter 3: Black Skin, White Masks

1 Fanon repeats a central question of Freudian psychoanalysis, addressed by Marie Bonaparte: "What does a woman want?" (see Jones 1955: 421).

2 One original goal of psychoanalysis for Freud was to alleviate suffering, "transforming hysterical misery into common unhappiness"; see Breuer and Freud, *Studies in Hysteria* (1895), repr. in Freud, *Selected Edition*, vol. II, pp. 304–5. On Fanon's "pedagogy of failure," see Burman (2021: 179.)

3 It was released in France as *Requins d'acier*, translated into English in *Black Skin* as "Steel Sharks."

4 The French term *petit nègre* is defined in Larousse as "elementary French used by Blacks in the colonies," a meaning that was intolerable for Fanon. The disparagement implicit in the term, especially the sarcasm in *petit*, is much stronger than is conveyed by the term "pidgin."

5 Fanon's sensitivity to language is not always caught by the English translators. The original expression *petit nègre* is not used. In its place is "gobbledygook" (a word coined by a Texas congressman in the 1940s apparently to represent the sounds of chicken pecking). Richard Philcox's translation continues, "for it means he is a gook," itself a derogatory racist term originally used by the US military in the Philippine–American war (1899–1902), and continued to be used during the Korean and Vietnam wars. The literal translation of Fanon's sentence – "Parler petit-nègre à un nègre, c'est le vexer, car il est celui-qui-parle-petit-nègre" (Fanon 2011: 82) – is, "To speak petit-nègre to a nègre is to upset him, because he is the one-who-speaks-petit-nègre."

6 Hachures are the shading on a contour map denoting elevation gradients. Markmann suggestively translates this in the 1967 translation as "across the zebra striping of my mind" (Fanon 1967: 45).

7 Established in 1946, Mayotte Capécia would become the fourth Antillean and the first Black woman to be awarded the Grand Prix Littéraire des Antilles.

8 First published in 1954, parts of novel appeared in the first and second issues of *Présence Africaine* (November–December 1947, pp. 89–110; January 1948, pp. 276–98).

9 The cohabitation between European traders and Wolof and Lebou

women traders in the seventeenth and eighteenth centuries produced a bourgeois offspring who formed an important merchant community in Saint-Louis, fully involved in the economic, social, cultural, political, and public life of the city. Saint-Louis continued to play a dominant role as the capital of French colonial Senegal until 1902. It was only in 2020 that the statue of the French general, colonist, and governor of Senegal, Louis Faidherbe, was removed from the city. Schools, streets, and squares bore his name. Léopold Cédar Senghor, Senegal's first president, called him a friend of Senegal. See https://www.nytimes.com/2022/05/05/world/africa/senegal-faidherbe-statue.html?searchResultPosition=1.

10 Another French term for the n-word.

11 This is far from an a priori criticism of all Black women. See, for example, Musser's (2014: 92–3) and Sharpley-Whiting's (1998: 37–40) responses to critics.

12 Mannoni's work was published in the journals *Psyché*, *Revue de psychologie des peuples*, *Chemins du monde*, and *Esprit*. His essay "La plainte du noir" was included in a special issue of *Esprit*, which also included Fanon's essay "L'expérience vécue du noir."

13 Mannoni's point of view has a connection with Oscar Lewis's "culture of poverty" argument developed in the postwar period, that indigenous cultures were degraded and could not adapt or "develop."

14 After 1956, the estimate was raised to 100,000.

15 "The fact of Blackness" catches the facticity of Blackness in an anti-Black world. The literal translation also highlights the connection with Merleau-Ponty's phenomenology, and the idea of body in space with which Fanon engages. Merleau-Ponty translated the German word *Erlebnis* as "lived experience," indicating another connection, namely Freud's reference to *Erlebnis* highlighting the connections Fanon is making between psychoanalysis, lived experience, and trauma. Aware of how trauma is expressed somatically, Fanon brought this sensitivity into his book, marking a new psycho-affective development.

16 At the end of the chapter he again reminds us of the little White boy on the train: "'Say thank you to the gentleman,' the mother tells her son, but we know that the son often dreams of shouting some other word, something that would make a scandal" (2008: 195).

17 In his preface to Sartre's collection, *Colonialism and Neocolonialism*, Robert Young argues that Sartre's premise was "taken from Richard Wright's observation that 'There is no Negro problem in the United States, there is only a [W]hite problem'" (Sartre 2001: xi). Later, Fanon quotes Marie Bonaparte on the connection between the anti-Semite's projection onto the Jew and the anti-Black projection onto the Black: "The anti-Semite projects onto the Jew, attributes to the

Jew all his own more or less unconscious bad instincts . . . Thus, by
shifting them onto the shoulders of the Jew, he has purged himself
of them in his own eyes and sees himself in shining purity. The Jew
thus lends himself magnificently as a projection of the Devil . . . The
Black in the United States also assumes the same function of fixa-
tion" (2008: 161n.47).

18 Of course we should note that their relationship continued and developed with Sartre's support of the Algerian revolution. Fanon read
Sartre's *Critique of Dialectical Reason* (published in 1960) and the influence of his work on *Les Damnés de la terre* is discussed by Bernasconi
(2010), Batchelor (2015), and Etherington (2016). Importantly, Sartre
was in his turn influenced by Fanon; he agreed to write a preface to
*Les Damnés*, which is considered to be him at his most radical.

19 There is an interesting connection to Merleau-Ponty's discussion in
*Phenomenology of Perception* (1945) including a reference to Lhermitte
(whom Fanon references in this chapter), that the phantom limb
lends itself neither to a purely physiological explanation, nor to a
purely psychological one. One can imagine an analogy to Fanon's
body schema (2008: 90–1) in Merleau-Ponty's discussion of the
phantom limb: "If I am sitting at my table and I want to reach the
telephone, the movement of my hand towards it, the straightening
of the upper part of the body, the tautening of the leg muscles are
enveloped in each other" (2005: 172).

20 For Freud the ego is "primarily a body ego," a psychic figure and a
"projection of a surface." In *The Ego and the Id*, Freud notes that "the
way in which we gain new knowledge of our organs during painful
illnesses is perhaps a prototype of the way by which, in general, we
arrive at the idea of our own body."

21 Bird-Pollan (2014: 135) points out that Fanon was well aware that
Freud moved away from his earlier theory, but uses it to gain insight
into the "trauma" of the Black in the White world. In *Black Skin*,
Fanon immediately turns to a determined experience at the origin of
every neurosis and states his position vis-à-vis Freud quite simply: for
Freud this is repressed in the unconscious, for the Black the drama
is played out in the open every day and is a product of "collective
catharsis" (Fanon 2008: 124).

22 Which, we should note, puts him at odds with Lacan.

23 Transgenerational trauma is often seen as mainly intrapsychic, passed
on from one generation to another. One main source, in a Fanonian
sociogenic sense, is through social institutions. Kirkland Vaughans
(2021) notes that the educational system in the US looks upon the
Black child as if they are of little value; the police department looks
upon Black children as criminal. These issues are carried through

the very structures of society. Though Fanon does not use the terms "intergenerational" or "transgenerational" trauma (terms that were not popular at the time), his analysis leads in the same direction. The lack of "a real traumatism" (2008: 124) leads Fanon to consider a "collective catharsis" and his insistence on sociogeny and social psychotherapy indicates a consistent appreciation of what would now be considered intergenerational trauma.

24 While this approach, made famous by the Frankfurt School and feminist theorists, is certainly part of the intellectual discussions of Fanon's time in postwar France, it was very marginal if not nonexistent in psychoanalytic practice (except in the area of what came to be known as institutional or sociopsychotherapy).

25 We should note that Fanon was not alone in his critique of Freud. Around the same time the British psychoanalyst and pediatrician Donald Winnicott was similarly arguing that Freud didn't have a space for cultural things in his topography of the mind, as he developed some of his key concepts during the war years addressing child trauma, separation, and class, which might have interested Fanon. Winnicott insisted on involving all staff social workers, doctors, parents, and foster parents on an equal basis.

26 Fanon did not know of Richard Wright's important role in the development of the Lafargue Mental Hygiene Clinic in Harlem. Opening in 1946, it gave the Black community access, for the first time, to psychoanalysis and psychiatry to address the emotional and psychological effects of racism. Nor was Fanon aware of the two leading Black American psychologists, Kenneth and Mamie Clark, who founded The Northside Testing and Consultation Center in Harlem the same year. The Clarks had conducted what came to be known as the "doll study" on identification among Black children, which continues to be particularly relevant for understanding the impact of internalized racism. Their study became part of the research which influenced the historic 1954 Supreme Court Case, *Brown v. Board of Education of Topeka*. *Black Skin, White Masks* can very much be considered part of these debates reflected in the discussion of how the Antillean child identifies as French and White.

27 Fanon notes (2008: 144), in a word association test, that, alongside the words sex, strong, athletic, powerful, associated with the word "nègre," some added "Nazism" and "SS." However repressive the realities they usher in, there is also an association with sadomasochism.

28 Primary processes are unconscious mental activity which, dominated by the pleasure principle, provide hallucinatory fulfillment of wishes. See https://dictionary.apa.org/primary-process.

29 One could certainly add that, based on the materiality of racism and its cultural reproduction, the fantasy has a reality, but that is not Fanon's point. He is, rather, separating the woman's fantasy of the Black man's power over her from the reality of rape.

30 There is a connection between Freud's argument and Fanon's inter-pretation of the White woman who wants to hurt herself mediated by the fantasy of the Black man. If the father figure is the symbolic White imperial father, the Black man is simply a tool in the woman's oedipal wish in the classical sense.

31 "The core fantasy," argues Mary Ann Doane (1991: 221), is not "Un nègre is raping me" but 'I am raping myself.'" Behind the fantasy of a sado-masochistic act with a Black man is that of being the Black man's puppet master, who fulfills the desire to hurt herself.

32 Later when discussing the need to embrace negritude, Fanon expresses a universalism, asking: "What about the others? Those 'who have no mouth,' those 'who have no voice.' I need to lose myself in my negritude and see the ashes, the segregation, the repression, the rapes, the discrimination, and the boycotts. We need to touch with our finger all the wounds that score our Black livery" (2008: 162–3). Earlier, he disagreed with Mannoni that relations between the French military and young Malagasy women were anything but violent, making it clear that what was occurring was the systematic rape of Black women by White men.

33 Cournot was awarded the Prix Fénéon in 1949 for his book *Martinique*. Fanon quotes from René Étiemble's critical review of the book in *Les Temps modernes* (1950): "Racial jealousy is an incite-ment to crimes of racism: for many [W]hite men, the [B]lack man is precisely that magic sword which, once it has transfixed their wives, leaves them forever transfigured ... Monsieur Cournot applies his talent to reviving the fable in which the [W]hite man will always find a specious argument: shameful, dubious, and therefore doubly effec-tive" (quoted in Fanon 2008: 149).

34 Nausea, we should remember in the frame of Sartre's "Nausea," i.e. as a concept and trope of existential phenomenology and existential psychology.

35 Unaware of Fanon's preliminary investigations into "sexual disor-ders among North Africans" (see Fanon 2018: 38–9), which were not published (in Italian) until 2012, Fuss importantly wonders: "Is it really possible to speak of 'homosexuality,' or for that matter 'het-erosexuality' or 'bisexuality,' as universal, global formations? Can one generalize from the particular forms sexuality takes under Western capitalism to sexuality as such?" (1999: 315).

36 We have already seen how ideas of color hierarchy in Martinique and

Saint-Louis are articulated by Capécia and Sadji. In the Americas, these ideas were systematized. One example is W.B. Stevenson's chart of castes in his three-volume *Twenty Years of Residence in South America*, published in 1825. At the top is the White man and then a hierarchy of 32 differentiations of color through the male line and the creation of new terms representing proportions of Whiteness. We can also consider how that powerful category of race is reproduced in the US where the one drop of "Black blood" rule was enough to be considered Black.

37  Attended by Lacan and Merleau-Ponty, but not Sartre.

38  Fanon clearly read Hegel's *Phenomenology* and while Kojèvean perspectives influenced Fanon's reading, we have no evidence that he read Kojève's book. On Fanon and Hegel, see Gibson (2003), Turner (1996), and Kistner and Van Haute (2022).

39  It should be remembered that Martinique was a British colony during the French and the Haitian (Saint-Domingue) revolution. Slavery was not abolished in Martinique as it was in Saint-Domingue and Guadeloupe during this period. When Martinique again became a French colony in 1802, slavery was restored by Napoleon, and Guadeloupe and Martinique became the most important sugar-producing colonies in the Caribbean.

40  He adds a medical analogy: "Just as a patient suffers a relapse after being told that their condition has improved and that they will shortly be leaving the asylum, so the news of emancipation for the slaves caused *psychoses and sudden death*" (2008: 194–5; my emphasis).

41  We can see this principle repeated politically in *Les Damnés de la terre* with Fanon's criticism of the nationalist elites' quick acceptance of the colonizing powers' negotiated withdrawal.

42  Fanon would later comment about the constant complaints from colonizers about the laziness and indolence of the colonized, viewing the colonized resistance as "a remarkable system of self-preservation" (2004: 220).

43  The history of the Antilles is also the history of revolt highlighted by the Haitian revolution. We should note, however, that Fanon's notion of the Antilles here is conceptually specific. That is to say, he conceives it, particularly Martinique, as postcolonial, reflected by *ressentiment* and *comparaison* (for example, see Fanon 2008: 185–7).

44  This also connects with Césaire's disgust at his own complicity and "cowardice" (Fanon 2008: 170). On a tram, he sees two young women giggling at a poor and broken Black man: "He was COMICAL AND UGLY. COMICAL AND UGLY, for sure," Césaire writes, "I exhibited a wide smile of connivance ... My cowardice recovered"

(1995: 109). Fanon critically adds: "But none of his writings indicate the mechanism of this cowardice." This was an essential critical point for Fanon, who then tells us that: "What needed to be done was . . . [to] attempt to apprehend . . . the fact . . . that there was nothing in common between this real [B]lack man and himself" (2008: 170).

45 Susan Buck-Morss (2009) has argued for the importance of the Haitian revolution as a profound, if unspoken, impact on Hegel's *Phenomenology*. History irrupted into that text through Bonaparte and Toussaint Louverture.

## Chapter 4: Fanon in Algeria

1 Many of these attitudes are expressed in *L'An V*, including an important critique of what is now, after Said, called Orientalism (see, for example, Fanon 1965: 40–1).

2 Of the Moorish café, he writes of a visit by Doctor Gambs, who said it was "an excellent terrain for relearning gestures of the outside world." "To relearn," remarks Fanon in *Notre Journal*, "I find this expression very beautiful," connecting it with the boarder rediscovering "the meaning of freedom, which is the first milestone on the way to responsibility" (2018: 332–3).

3 By June 1954, the first contribution by a Muslim patient appeared in *Notre Journal*; in July, the Moorish café opened, and by August the newsletter's heading was in French and Arabic (2018: 313).

4 Fanon was drawn to Ferenczi's work on war neuroses and body movement; Ferenczi's idea of mutual therapy might also have appealed to him as well as his "active interference" technique (see Gibson and Beneduce 2017: 211–15, 222nn21–3). One of Ferenczi's most famous papers is "Confusion of the Tongues Between Adults and the Child: The Language of Tenderness and of Passion": https://www.sas.upenn.edu/~cavitch/pdf-library/Ferenczi_Confusion.pdf.

5 Joby insists that Fanon was already secretly attending Algerian nationalist meetings before November 1, 1954.

6 See "The First International Congress of African/Black Writers and Artists and the Crisis of Cultures – September 19–22, 1956": http://peace-int.org/en/2021/06/05/first-international-congress-of-african-black-writers-and-artists/#. That there were no women among the presenters was highlighted by Wright in *Présence Africaine* (1956: 347–60). See Merve Fejzula, "Women and the 1956 Congress of Black Writers and Artists in Paris": https://arcade.stanford.edu/content/women-and-1956-congress-black-writers-and-artists-paris.

7 François Maspero, *Le Monde*, September 21, 2000.

8 Benkhedda and Abane were close; Benkhedda considered "the anti-

imperialist revolution [as] only the first step towards victory in the social revolution." He was a revolutionary intellectual "for whom cerebral conclusions and concrete actions could not remain separate. This explains the paradoxical image of the bookish [B]enKhedda directing a bomb-throwing network" (Mathews 1962).

9 M'hidi was particularly important at the Soummam conference. His revolutionary intellect is displayed in a conversation with Ali LaPointe in Pontecorvo's *The Battle of Algiers*: "BEN M'HIDI: 'Wars aren't won with terrorism, neither wars nor revolutions. Terrorism is a beginning but afterward, all the people must act . . . This is the reason for the strike, and its necessity: to mobilize all Algerians, count them and measure their strength.' And then suggesting the necessity of what Fanon calls the 'second phase of liberation,' he adds: 'Do you know something Ali? Starting a revolution is hard, and it's even harder to continue it. Winning is hardest of all. But only afterward, when we have won, will the real hardships begin'" (Solinas 1973: 101).

10 Jeanson writes about the question of friendship and his relationship with Fanon in his 1965 afterword, "Reconnaissance de Fanon": http://bouhamidimohamed.over-blog.com/2018/11/francis-jeanson .reconnaissance-de-fanon-postface-peau-noire.masques-blancs.html.

## Chapter 5: The Algerian Revolution and Beyond: Fanon in Tunis

1 Cherki notes that everyone knew him as Fanon, and Dr. Farès may only have been used for administrative purposes (2006:102).

2 Published in *La Tunisie médicale* in 1959.

3 Fanon wrote 14 articles in 1957 (his first in August), 22 in 1958, 3 in 1959, 3 in 1960, and 1 in 1961. *Résistance algérienne*, the FLN's publication intended for international consumption, was edited in Morocco, Tunis, and Paris from October 1955 until July 1957, when it was replaced by *El Moudjahid*.

4 The outstanding articles are collected by Jean Khalfa and Robert Young in *Alienation and Freedom* (Fanon: 2018).

5 Her first novel, *La Soif* (*The Mischief*), was published in 1957.

6 Just two years older than Fanon, he had joined the nationalist Parti du peuple algérien (PPA) in 1942 before moving to study in Paris. He was imprisoned in 1948 and expelled from the PPA's successor organization, the Movement for the Triumph of Democratic Liberties (MTLD), before joining the FLN and becoming its representative in New York City.

7 These borders were named, respectively, the Morice and Challe lines after the French airforce general Maurice Challe, who led the

counterinsurgency against the ALN in 1959. Challe was one of the four generals who took part in the Algiers putsch in 1961.

8 In *Les Damnés de la terre* Fanon notes: "In the unpublished introduction of the first two editions of *L'An V de la révolution algérienne*, we already indicated that an entire generation of Algerians, steeped in collective, gratuitous homicide with all the psychosomatic consequences this entails, would be France's human legacy in Algeria. The French who condemn torture in Algeria constantly adopt a strictly French point of view. This is not a reproach, merely an affirmation: they want to safeguard the conscience of present and potential torturers and try and protect French youth from moral degradation" (2004: 183n.22).

9 Made from drawings and stories of children collected by Jacques Charby and Frantz Fanon, the film was released in 1961. The new Algerian government credited it as being "prepared by Frantz Fanon and R. Vautier."

10 Edited by Jacques Charby and Giovanni Pirelli, *Racconti di bambini d'Algerie: testimonianze e disegni di bambini profughi in Tunisia, Libia e Marocco* (Stories of children from Algeria: testimonies and drawings of refugee children in Tunisia, Libya and Morocco) was published anonymously in 1962.

11 Fanon's biographers Cherki, Geismar, and Macey, all have different analyses of the attacks. Implying that Fanon was not an important target, Macey wonders whether he warranted the attention of *La Main rouge* (a terrorist organization operated by the French intelligence agency). Almost reluctantly, Macey concedes that Fanon was involved in high-level FLN meetings in 1959 as a "specialist," drawing up a political program and proposals for the FLN's statutes to be approved by the CNRA (National Council of the Algerian Revolution). Fanon had declared that "the goal of the war was 'the liberation of the national territory' and 'the social and economic revolutions form a whole . . . and do not constitute two distinct stages'" (Macey 2012: 392).

12 See "His Holiness Replies," *Présence Africaine* XXIV–XXV/1 (1959): 469–70.

13 Her husband, Gilbert, was working as an engineer in Tunisia doing social service instead of military service (see Aubenas 2017).

14 Abbas had joined the FLN in 1956 and would later became the prime minister of Algeria. Fanon had wanted him to write the introduction to *L'An V de la révolution algérienne*. Like Fanon, Abbas emphasized the importance of women in the liberation struggle (see Vince 2015: 75).

15 Manuellan's description of the meeting about the book with Fanon

in a plaster cast seems contrary to Cherki, who writes that the book was almost finished when he was involved in the "car accident" (2006: 129).

16 Fanon was not pleased when Maspero changed the title to *Sociologie d'une révolution* once it was no longer the fifth year of the revolution.

17 Maspero thought it added nothing and was "essentially a statement of principles, a violent statement . . . lacking nuance." Apparently, he had also shown the book to Césaire who was enthusiastic about it but agreed with Maspero about the introduction (see Fanon 2018: 679–80).

18 In February 1956, the socialist Robert Lacoste became resident minister and governor general of Algeria.

19 "The doctor," of course, referred to Fanon. Presumably for security reasons, Géronimi is listed as a "former intern at the Saint Anne Psychiatric Hospital in Paris," not at Blida-Joinville (1965: 163n.15).

20 Note that the English translation has his name as Bresson Yvon. He was also named Yves in Mohamed Maougal's book *The Algerian Destiny of Albert Camus 1940–1962*.

21 This was especially true after he was put in charge of a police station. He was arrested in November 1956.

## Chapter 6: Writing from Inside the Algerian Revolution: *L'An V de la révolution algérienne*

1 Juminer's first novel, *Les Bâtards*, was published in 1961 and focused on the racism experienced by newly qualified doctors returning to French Guiana. His later novels were concerned with the psychological complexities of decolonization.

2 On the contemporality of Fanon, see Horton (2018).

3 See Alloula (1986), which includes popular images of Algerian women on French postcards in the period 1900–30.

4 Fanon spoke at the World Assembly of Youth conference in Accra in 1960 alongside the Congolese minister of youth, Maurice Mpolo, who was later murdered with Lumumba.

5 Thinking of the horrible tortures that many of the women endured after capture by the French police or army (Djamila Boupacha was raped with a broken wine bottle; Louisette Ighilahriz, who joined the FLN after her father was seized by colonial authorities, was imprisoned and tortured in Algiers' notorious Barbarossa prison in 1957), Fanon writes that "the Algerian woman rises directly to the level of tragedy" (1965: 50).

6 Torture is normal under colonialism, argues Fanon. The French denied its existence, as did the Americans in the 2000s.

7 Known as the Mokrani Revolt after one of its leaders, Sheikh Mohamed El-Mokrani.

8 As soon as the Paris Commune was crushed, troops were sent to Algeria to destroy the uprising. Survivors of the massacres in Paris and Algeria were sent to New Caledonia. One of those deported, Louise Michel, would write about the Algerian Commune in her memoirs and, on her release, would campaign for an amnesty for the Algerian deportees.

9 See, for example, the "debate" included in my collection *Rethinking Fanon*: Helie-Lucas (1999); McClintock (1999); Fuss (1999); and Sharpley-Whiting (1999). Also see the oral interviews with the women participants in Vince (2015).

10 Moradian (2022: 207–9, 229) argues that "Fanon's analysis of the relationship between women's agency and revolutionary activity" became re-envisioned in Iran in the 1970s, and became expressed in resistance poetry: "Now I have joined the endless waves I exist in struggle." There were echoes of this in 2022, as well as when women took to the streets and questioned the promise of the 1979 revolution that year, shouting: "At the dawn of freedom, we have no freedom."

11 I date this to reflect this moment of radical possibility when the daily resistance and demonstration in Iran has not stopped, despite repression.

12 We should note the importance of the Iranian Kurds (a minority in Fanon's terms) in this movement, who have had a long radical history and are once again playing an important role, resonating with Fanon's "minorities question," and making new connections, what we might call the intersectionalities of a new generation of revolutionaries demanding freedom.

13 Shariati states that Fanon composed it in "the last days of his life" (2018: 668).

## Chapter 7: Fanon, a Revolutionary Pan-Africanist Ambassador and His Last Days

1 Cherki reports that Fanon was "taken aback by the unfriendliness of the Algerians" toward the Africans (2006: 124).

2 Reports of Fanon's speech can be found in Young (2005). *The Times* report, "Tactics of the African Nationalists," and Fanon's speech, under a subtitle "Outwitting Imperialists," can be found at https://www.thetimes.co.uk/archive/page/1958-12-10/8.html?region=global.

3 Grant was the managing editor of a Caribbean-focused newsmaga-

zine *Our Sphere* published in London. He left London to report on and take part in the struggle for African independence in 1957.

4  This was in December 1958 before the creation of the Pan-Africanist Congress in South Africa (April 6, 1959), which occurred before the Sharpeville massacre (March 21, 1960). The ANC and PAC were banned on April 8, 1960. It was at the same time that Fanon gave his address to the Accra Positive Action Conference (April 1960). Both the ANC and the PAC created official armed wings in 1961.

5  He was likely referring to the 1958 conference. The confusion comes from his statement, "In 1960, I attended the All-African Peoples Congress in Accra, Ghana." That conference was in 1958. The 1960 conference was called the "Positive Action Conference for Peace and Security in Africa." Fanon spoke on violence on both occasions.

6  Nkrumah showed no animosity to Fanon for his intervention and said in 1967 that *The Wretched of the Earth* was a "powerful book" and Fanon was "ideologically sound" (Nkrumah: 1991: 174).

7  Nkrumah's commitment to Pan-Africanism can also be traced to the year he spent in the US during the war. He played an important role in the 1944 Pan-African Congress and was a principal organizer of the fifth Pan-African Congress in Manchester, England, in 1945.

8  The history of the Sahel (coast) is one of movement and people across the Saharan desert indicating that there was never a division between North Africa and "sub-Saharan Africa" but a constant movement – *great navigation channels* – across the desert as if it were a sea with ports on all sides.

9  Harbi is a former FLN activist and now historian of the FLN, who met Fanon in Tunis.

10  He had expressed himself in similar terms in an answer to Francis Jeanson about a sentence in *Black Skin, White Masks*: "I cannot explain this sentence. When I write things like that, I am trying to touch my reader affectively, or in other words irrationally, almost sensually. For me, words have a charge."

11  "Cool thinking" reminds us of his introduction to *Black Skin, White Masks* where he speaks about writing the book while feeling wary of zealousness. This is in stark contrast to the oft-repeated notion from the 1960s and 1970s, especially in the US, that Fanon was a man of rage.

12  Cherki reports that Fanon was critical of the Soviet psychiatrists he met while in Moscow and was far from impressed by the psychiatric unit he was allowed to visit (2006: 156).

13  Cherki says he left for Moscow in mid-January and stayed for just a couple of weeks (2006: 156). Macey suggests it was in the Spring of 1961, and that he was back by early April (2012: 441).

14 Since Fanon's comrade Moumié was poisoned, it is not unreasonable to speculate whether Fanon's leukemia was also a result of poisoning.

15 Lanzmann, who visited Ghardimaou on Fanon's insistence in 1961, notes that the combatants he spoke with heard Fanon give one seminar on Sartre's *Critique of Dialectical Reason*.

16 Macey argues: "Between April and the beginning of July, Fanon worked fast against the clock . . . Little or no research was done . . . Fanon's hopes and fears for the future are expressed with powerful emotion, but he rarely justifies them with hard facts" (2012: 451). Macey's critique is disingenuous, especially given the perspicacity of Fanon's analysis.

17 Along with reading Marx's *Eighteenth Brumaire of Louis Bonaparte*, Fanon was involved in these discussions in Lyon.

18 Marx's conception of the revolution in permanence, which should not be confused with Trotsky's, was not limited to a critique of alliances with bourgeoisie. Clearly it related to revolution itself as an ongoing process, as he argues in the 1844 manuscripts: "Communism is not the goal of human development" but, rather, the form in which "*positive* Humanism, beginning from itself" can emerge.

19 The FBI file on Fanon has, however, been released (see Browne 2015: 2).

20 Indicating the importance of keeping up relations between the FLN and the US after Fanon's death, Iselin was invited to Fanon's funeral at Ghardimaou and also accompanied the coffin into Algeria.

21 Josie committed suicide in January 1989. Returning to Algeria after liberation, she worked as a journalist for the Algerian press and the Paris-based *Demain l'Afrique*. Djebar writes that, in the summer before her death, she visited Fanon's grave and all the places they had lived in Tunis.

## Chapter 8: *Les Damnés de la terre*: The Handbook of Revolution

1 In the 1968 Farrington translation, "l'affirmation échevelée d'une originalité posée comme absolue" is rendered as "the untidy affirmation of an original idea propounded as an absolute"; in 2004, Richard Philcox translated this as "the impassioned claim by the colonized that their world is fundamentally different" (2004: 6). On the two translations, see Gibson (2007) and Gibson (2020a).

2 The 2004 Philcox translation is cited first; where I prefer the Farrington translation (1968), that comes first.

3 For discussion of the importance for Fanon of Marx's *The Eighteenth Brumaire*, see Martin (1999) and Gibson (2020b).

4 Decades later, political science developed this into a theory of elite

transition – that is, the transition from authoritarian rule to democratic rule does not address structural inequalities. The result in South Africa, for example, is that, since the formal end of apartheid, the unequal society has become even more unequal as the inequalities between rich and poor have widened.

5 To an audience that included South African revolutionaries, Fanon argued that "there is unanimity that only armed struggle will bring about the defeat of the occupation."

6 Sekyi-Otu translates this is as "'Each one shits for himself', that godless form of salvation," and points out that "le démerdage" is no longer an object of opprobrium in neoliberal Africa where the ethics of primitive accumulation aid "the unrestrained accumulation of wealth by a new class of hustlers" (2023: 105–6; see also 2019: 162).

7 Part of the Napoleonic Wars fought in 1807–14 in the Iberian Peninsula between the French and the English, who were aided by Spanish and Portuguese allies.

8 Fanon hoped for the end of the American empire, seeing a global rejoicing with end of the almighty dollar whose security "is only guaranteed by the slaves of this world, toiling in the oil wells of the Middle East, the mines of Peru and the Congo, and the United Fruit or Firestone plantations" (2004: 54n.9).

9 The neocolony often becomes a kind of rentier state (for extractive industries) as the national bourgeoisie plays a role in opening up the country as "resorts and playgrounds" for "the Western bourgeoisies who happen to be tourists enamored of exoticism, hunting and casinos" (2004: 101).

10 This is exactly what happened in South Africa. After waiting patiently, the poor in Durban created the shack-dwellers' movement, Abahlali baseMjondolo, which has frequently been violently attacked and its leaders killed. In 2008, S'bu Zikode, president of the organization, said: "We are finished with being ladders for politicians to climb up over the people . . . Our politics starts by recognizing the humanity of every human being . . . We are the people that are not meant to think. We are the people that are not meant to participate in planning and to debate on issues that affect us . . . The poor are strongly opposed to these dehumanizing human characteristics of the top-down system that has terrorized our communities and our lives" (see Gibson 2011).

11 This is Lenin's argument in *What is To Be Done?* written in 1902. Well known for the idea that the workers could only attain a trade union consciousness, and that socialism had to be brought to the workers from outside by intellectuals in the party (an idea that Lenin reversed after the 1905 revolution, when he argued that workers

were spontaneously revolutionary), he also argues that the intellectuals needed to be disciplined by the workers at local meetings.

12 The WHO sponsored Carothers's *The African Mind* (1954), because he was, in their opinion, "the most internationally renowned ethnopsychiatrist with clinical experience" (Heaton 2013: 44).

## Conclusion

1 An earlier version of this conclusion can be found in Gibson 2020c.

2 In the US, even as free Blacks were given the vote after independence, they systematically became disenfranchised.

# References

Abane, Beläid. (2011). "Frantz Fanon and Abane Ramdane: Brief Encounter in the Algerian Revolution," in Nigel C. Gibson (ed.), *Living Fanon: Global Perspectives*. New York: Palgrave, pp. 27–43.

Adler-Bolton, Beatrice, and Artie Vierkant (2022) *Health Communism*. London: Verso.

Ahlman, Jeffrey (2010) "The Algerian Question in Nkrumah's Ghana, 1958–1960: Debating 'Violence' and 'Nonviolence' in African Decolonization," *Africa Today* 57/2: 67–84.

Alexander, Robert J. (1991) *International Trotskyism 1929–1985: A Documented Analysis of the Movement*. Durham, NC: Duke University Press.

Alloula, Malouda (1986) *The Colonial Harem*. Minneapolis: University of Minnesota Press.

Arnall, Gavin (2020) *Subterranean Fanon: An Underground Theory of Radical Change*. New York: Columbia University Press.

Aubenas, Florence (2017) "In the Shadow of Frantz Fanon." https://www.versobooks.com/blogs/3491–in–the–shadow–of–frantz–fanon.

Babu, A. M. (1989) "New Introduction," in Frantz Fanon, *Studies in a Dying Colonialism*, trans. Haakon Chevalier. London: Earthscan Publications.

Batchelor, Kathryn (2015) "Fanon's *Les Damnés de la terre*: Translation, De-Philosophization and the Intensification of Violence," *Nottingham French Studies* 54/1: 7–22.

Beauvoir, Simone de (1989 [1949]) *The Second Sex*. New York: Vintage books.

Beauvoir, Simone de (1992 [1964]) *Hard Times: Force of Circumstance* (The Autobiography of Simone de Beauvoir, vol. 2). New York: Paragon House.

Bernasconi, Robert (2010) "Fanon's *The Wretched of the Earth* as the Fulfilment of Sartre's Critique of Dialectical Reason," *Sartre Studies International* 16/2: 36–47.

Bernasconi, Robert (2022) "Introduction: Fanon's French Hegel," in

Ulrike Kistner and Philippe Van Haute (eds.), *Violence, Slavery and Freedom between Hegel and Fanon*. Johannesburg: Wits University Press, pp. xiii–xxiii.

Bhopal, Kalwant, and John Preston (eds.) (2011) *Intersectionality and "Race" in Education*. New York: Routledge

Biko, Steve (1979) *I Write What I Like*. London: Heinemann.

Bird-Pollan, Stefan (2014) *Hegel, Freud, and Fanon: The Dialectic of Emancipation*. Lanham, MD: Rowman & Littlefield.

Bouvier, Pierre (1971) *Fanon*. Paris: Éditions universitaires.

Briefel, Aviva (2015) *The Racial Hand in the Victorian Imagination*. Cambridge: Cambridge University Press.

Browne, Simone (2015) *Dark Matters: On the Surveillance of Blackness*. Durham, NC: Duke University Press.

Buck Morss, Susan (2009) *Hegel, Haiti, and Universal History*. Pittsburgh, PA: University of Pittsburgh Press.

Bulhan, Hussein. A. (1985) *Frantz Fanon and the Psychology of Oppression*. New York: Plenum Press.

Burman, Erica (2019) *Fanon, Education, Action: Child as Method*. London: Routledge.

Burman, Erica (2021) "Frantz Fanon and Revolutionary Group Praxis," *Group Analysis* 54/2: 169–188.

Burns, Alan (1948) *Colour Prejudice*. London: Allen & Unwin.

Capécia, Mayotte (1997) *I Am a Martinican Woman & The White Negress*, trans. Beatrice Stith Clark. Pueblo, CO: Passeggiata Press.

Caute, David (1970) *Frantz Fanon*. London: Penguin.

Césaire, Aimé (1995 [1939]) *Notebook of a Return to the Native Land*, trans. Mireille Rosello and Annie Pritchard. Hexham: Bloodaxe Books.

Césaire, Aimé (2000) *Discourse on Colonialism*. New York: Monthly Review.

Cherki, Alice (2006) *Frantz Fanon: A Portrait*. Ithaca, NY: Cornell University Press.

Cherki, Alice (2016) Interview with Gaele Sobott. https://gaelesobott .wordpress.com/2016/11/.

Ciccariello-Maher, George (2012) "The Dialectics of Standing One's Ground," *Theory & Event* 15/3.

de Lauretis, Teresa (2002) "Difference Embodied: Reflections on *Black Skin, White Masks*," *Parallax* 8/2: 54–68.

Djebar, Assia (2000) *Algerian White*. New York: Seven Stories Press.

Djemai, Cheikh (dir. 2001) *Frantz Fanon: His Life, His Struggle, His Work*. Documentary. https://vimeo.com/ondemand/frantzfanon.

Doane, Mary Ann (1991) *Femmes Fatales: Feminism, Film Theory, Psychoanalysis*. New York: Routledge.

Dosse, François (2011) *Gilles Deleuze and Félix Guattari: Intersecting Lives*. New York: Columbia University Press.

Du Bois, W.E.B. (2009) *The Souls of Black Folk*. New York: Oxford University Press.

Dufrenne, Mikel, and Paul Ricoeur (1947) *Karl Jaspers et la philosophie de l'existence*. Paris: Seuil.

Ehlen, Patrick (2001) *Frantz Fanon: A Spiritual Biography*. Spring Valley, NY: The Crossroad Publishing Company.

Ellison, Ralph (1964) *Shadow and Act*. New York: Vintage.

Etherington, Ben (2016) "An Answer to the Question: What is Decolonization? Frantz Fanon's *The Wretched of the Earth* and Jean-Paul Sartre's *Critique of Dialectical Reason*," *Modern Intellectual History* 13/1: 151–178.

Fanon, Frantz (1965 [1959]) *A Dying Colonialism*, trans. Haakon Chevalier. New York: Grove Press.

Fanon, Frantz (1967 [1952]) *Black Skin, White Masks*, trans. Charles Lam Markmann. New York: Grove Press.

Fanon, Frantz (1967 [1964]) *Toward the African Revolution: Political Essays*, trans. Haakon Chevalier. New York: Monthly Review Press.

Fanon, Frantz (1968 [1961]) *The Wretched of the Earth*, trans. Constance Farrington. New York: Grove Press.

Fanon, Frantz (2004 [1961]) *The Wretched of the Earth*, trans. Richard Philcox. New York: Grove Press.

Fanon, Frantz (2008 [1952]) *Black Skin, White Masks*, trans. Richard Philcox. New York: Grove Press.

Fanon, Frantz (2011) *Oeuvres*. Paris: Découverte.

Fanon, Frantz (2018) *Alienation and Freedom*, trans. Steven Corcoran; ed. Jean Khalfa and Robert J.C. Young. London: Bloomsbury.

Fanon, Joby (2014) *Frantz Fanon, My Brother: Doctor, Playwright, Revolutionary*, trans. Daniel Nethery. Lanham, MD: Lexington Books.

Filostrat, Christian (1978) Interview with Frantz Fanon's Widow, Josie Fanon. https://frantzfanonspeaks.wordpress.com/2011/04/26/frantz-fanons-widow-speaks/.

Fuss, Diana (1999) "Interior Colonies: Frantz Fanon and the Politics of Identification," in Nigel C. Gibson (ed.), *Rethinking Fanon: The Continuing Legacy*. Amherst, NY: Humanity Books, pp. 294–328.

Garcia, Jay (2006) "*Home of the Brave*, Frantz Fanon and Cultural Pluralism," *Comparative American Studies: An International Journal* 4/1: 49–65.

Geismar, Peter (1971) *Fanon*. New York: Dial.

Gendzier, Irene (1973) *Frantz Fanon: A Critical Study*. New York: Grove Press.

Gibson, Nigel C. (ed.) (1999) *Rethinking Fanon: The Continuing Dialogue*. Amherst, NY: Humanity Books.

Gibson, Nigel C. (2003) *Fanon: The Postcolonial Imagination*. Cambridge: Polity.

Gibson, Nigel C. (2007) "Relative Opacity: A New Translation of Fanon's *Wretched of the Earth* – Mission Betrayed or Fulfilled?" *Social Identities* 13/1: 69–95.

Gibson, Nigel C. (2011) *Fanonian Practices in South Africa*. New York: Palgrave Macmillan.

Gibson, Nigel C. (2020a) "Connecting with Fanon: Postcolonial Problematics, Irish Connections, and the Shack Dwellers Rising in South Africa," in Dustin J. Byrd and Seyed Javad Miri (eds.), *Frantz Fanon and Emancipatory Social Theory: A View from the Wretched*. Leiden: Brill, pp. 111–138.

Gibson, Nigel C. (2020b) "Fanon and Marx Revisited," *Journal of the British Society for Phenomenology* 51/4: 320–336.

Gibson, Nigel C. (2020c) *Fanon and the "Rationality of Revolt."* Quebec: Daraja Press.

Gibson, Nigel C. (ed.) (2021) *Fanon Today: Reason and Revolt of the Wretched of the Earth*. Quebec: Daraja Press.

Gibson, Nigel C., and Roberto Beneduce (2017) *Frantz Fanon, Psychiatry and Politics*. Lanham, MD: Rowman & Littlefield.

Gilroy, Paul, Tony Sandset, Sindre Bangstad, and Gard Ringen Høibjerg (2019) "A Diagnosis of Contemporary Forms of Racism, Race and Nationalism: A Conversation with Professor Paul Gilroy," *Cultural Studies* 33/2: 173–197.

Gordon, Lewis R. (2000) *Existentia Africana: Understanding Africana Existential Thought*. New York: Routledge.

Gordon, Lewis R. (2015) *What Fanon Really Said*. New York: Fordham.

Grant, Stan (1973) *The Call of Mother Africa*. Kingston, Jamaica: Courier Press.

Guex, Germaine (2015 [1950]) *The Abandonment Neurosis*, trans. Peter D. Douglas. New York: Routledge.

Hansen, Emmanuel (1974) "Frantz Fanon: Portrait of a Revolutionary Intellectual," *Transition* 46: 25–36.

Hansen, Emmanuel (1977) *Frantz Fanon*. Columbus: Ohio State University Press.

Healy, David (1997) *The Antidepressant Era*. Cambridge, MA: Harvard University Press.

Healy, David (2004) *The Creation of Psychopharmacology*. Cambridge, MA: Harvard University Press.

Heaton, Matthew (2013) *Black Skin, White Coats: Nigerian Psychiatrists, Decolonization, and the Globalization of Psychiatry*. Columbus: Ohio University Press.

Hegel, G.W.F. (1931) *The Phenomenology of Mind*, trans. J.B. Baillie. London: George Allen and Unwin.

Helie-Lucas, Marie-Aimee (1999) "Women, Nationalism, and Religion in the Algerian Liberation Struggle," in Nigel C. Gibson (ed.), *Rethinking Fanon: The Continuing Legacy*. Amherst, NY: Humanity Books.

Henry, Paget (2000) *Caliban's Reason: Introducing Afro-Caribbean Philosophy*. New York: Routledge.

Horne, Alistair (1978) *A Savage War of Peace: Algeria 1954–1962*. New York: Viking Books.

Horton, Richard (2018) "Frantz Fanon and the Origins of Global Health." https://www.thelancet.com/journals/lancet/article/PIIS014 0-6736(18)32041-5/fulltext.

Jones, Ernest (1955) *The Life and Work of Sigmund Freud*, vol. 2. New York: Basic Books.

Judt, Tony (2011) *Past Imperfect: French Intellectuals 1944–1956*. New York: New York University Press.

Keller, Richard C. (2007) *Colonial Madness: Psychiatry in French North Africa*. Chicago, IL: University of Chicago Press.

Kestleloot, Lilyan (1974) *Black Writers in French: A Literary History of Negritude*. Philadelphia, PA: Temple University Press.

Khalfa, Jean (2018) "Fanon, Revolutionary Psychiatrist," in Frantz Fanon, *Alienation and Freedom*, trans. Steven Corcoran; ed. Jean Khalfa and Robert J.C. Young. London: Bloomsbury.

Kipfer, Stefan (2022) *Urban Revolutions: Urbanisation and (Neo-) Colonialism in Transatlantic Context*. Chicago: Haymarket Books.

Kilroy-Marac, Katie (2019) *An Impossible Inheritance: Postcolonial Psychiatry and the Work of Memory in a West African Clinic*. Oakland: University of California Press.

Kistner, Ulrike, and Philippe Van Haute (eds.) (2022) *Violence, Slavery and Freedom between Hegel and Fanon*. Braamfontein: Wits University Press.

Kojève, Alexandre (1947) *Introduction to the Reading of Hegel: Lectures on the Phenomenology of Spirit*. Paris: Gallimard.

Kunene, Mazisi (1969) "Introduction," in Aimé Césaire, *Return to My Native Land*, trans. John Berger and Anna Bostock. Baltimore, MD: Penguin Books.

Kwarteng, Kwasi (2011) *Ghosts of Empire: Britain's Legacies in the Modern World*. London: Bloomsbury.

L (2022) "Women Reflected in Their Own History," September: https://www.e-flux.com/notes/497512/women-reflected-in-their-own-history; also available as "Figuring a Women's Revolution: Bodies Interacting with their Images": https://www.jadaliyya.com/Details/44479/Figuring-a-Women%E2%80%99s-Revolution-Bodies-Interacting-with-their-Images.

Laing, R.D. (1965) *The Divided Self: An Existential Study in Sanity and Madness*. Harmondsworth: Pelican Books.

Lanzmann, Claude (2012) *The Patagonian Hare: A Memoir*. New York: Farrar, Straus and Giroux.

Lazreg, Marnia (1993) *The Eloquence of Silence: Algerian Women in Question*. New York: Routledge.

Leval, Gaston (1975) *Collectives in the Spanish Revolution*. London: Freedom Press.

Lingiardi, Vittorio, and Nancy McWilliams (2017) *Psychodynamic Diagnostic Manual* (PDM-2). New York: Guilford Press.

Lumumba, Patrice (1972) *Lumumba Speaks: The Speeches and Writings of Patrice Lumumba, 1958–1961*. Boston, MA: Little, Brown.

Macey, David (2012) *Frantz Fanon: A Biography*. London: Verso.

Mannoni, Octave (1990 [1950]). *Prospero and Caliban: The Psychology of Colonization*. Ann Arbor: University of Michigan Press.

Manuellan, Marie-Jeanne (2017) *Sous la Dictée de Fanon*. Coaraze: L'Amourier.

Manville, Marcel (1992) *Les Antilles sans fard*. Paris: Éditions L'Harmattan.

Martin, Tony (1999) "Rescuing Fanon from the Critics", in Nigel C. Gibson (ed.), *Rethinking Fanon: The Continuing Dialogue*, 2nd edn. Lanham, MD: Rowman & Littlefield, pp. 83–102.

Marx, Karl (1852) *The Eighteenth Brumaire of Louis Bonaparte*. https://www.marxists.org/archive/marx/works/1852/18th-brumaire/.

Marx, Karl (1975) *Capital*, vol. 1. London: Penguin.

Marx, Karl and Friedrich Engels (1848) *The Communist Manifesto*. https://www.marxists.org/archive/marx/works/1848/communist-manifesto/index.htm.

Mathews, Richard (1962) Letter to Richard Nolte, Institute of Current World Affairs, February 22. http://www.icwa.org/wp-content/uploads/2015/10/RKM-2.pdf.

Mbembe, Achille (2017) *Critique of Black Reason*. Durham, NC: Duke University Press.

Mbom, Clément (2004) "Frantz Fanon," in Alba della Fazia Amoia and Bettina L. Knapp (eds.), *Multicultural Writers Since 1945*. Westport, CT: Greenwood Press, pp. 211–215.

McClintock, Anne (1999) "Fanon and Gender Agency," in Nigel C.

Gibson (ed.), *Rethinking Fanon: The Continuing Legacy*. Amherst, NY: Humanity Books.

McDonnell Nieto del Rio, Guilia (2021) "Darnella Frazier, the Teenager who Recorded George Floyd's Murder, Speaks Out." https://www.nytimes.com/2021/05/25/us/darnella-frazier.html.

Meany, Thomas (2019) "History Unclassified: Frantz Fanon and the CIA Man," *The American Historical Review* 124/3: 983–995.

Merleau-Ponty, Maurice (1964) *The Primacy of Perception: And Other Essays on Phenomenological Psychology, the Philosophy of Art, History and Politics*. Evanston, IL: Northwestern University Press.

Merleau-Ponty, Maurice (2005 [1945]) *Phenomenology of Perception*. London: Routledge.

Metzl, Jonathan M. (2010) *The Protest Psychosis: How Schizophrenia Became a Black Disease*. Boston, MA: Beacon Press.

Metzl, Jonathan M. (2012) "Mainstream Anxieties about Race in Antipsychotic Drug Ads," *Virtual Mentor* 14/6: 494–502.

Meyers, Todd (2014) "Jean Oury and Clinique de La Borde: A Conversation with Camille Robcis." https://somatosphere.net/2014/jean–oury–and–clinique–de–la–borde–a–conversation–with–camille–robcis.html/.

Mezine, Hassane (dir. 2018) *Fanon, Yesterday, Today*. https://vimeo.com/ondemand/fanonhieraujourdhui.

Mirzoeff, Nicholas (2011) *The Right to Look: A Counterhistory of Visuality*. Durham, NC: Duke University Press.

Mirzoeff, Nicholas (2012) "'We Are All Children of Algeria': Visuality and Countervisuality 1954–2011." http://scalar.usc.edu/nehvectors/mirzoeff/jai–huit–ans–analysis?path=main–route.

Moncrief, Joanna (2021) *A Straight Talking Introduction to Psychiatric Drugs: The Truth About How They Work and How to Come Off Them*. Monmouth: PCCS Books.

Moradian, Manijeh (2022) *This Flame Within: Iranian Revolutionaries in the United States*. Durham, NC: Duke University Press.

Musser, Amber Jamilla (2014) *Sensational Flesh: Race, Power and Masochism*. New York: New York University Press.

Ngugi wa Th'iongo (1993) *Moving the Centre*. London: Heinemann.

Oberst, Timothy (1988) "Transport Workers, Strikes and the 'Imperial Response': Africa and the Post World War II Conjuncture," *African Studies Review* 31/1: 117–133.

Panaf Editors (1975) *Fanon*. London: Panaf Books.

Pieterse, Jan Nederveen (1995) *White on Black: Images of Africa and Blacks in Western Popular Culture*. New Haven, CT: Yale University Press.

Platts–Mills, Ben (2021) "Asylum." https://aeon.co/essays/patients–and –psychiatrists–fought–against–fascism–together–at–saint–alban.

Ray, David, and Robert M. Farnsworth (1973) *Richard Wright: Impressions and Perspectives*. Ann Arbor: University of Michigan Press.

Razanajao, Claudine, and Jacques Postel (2007) "La Vie et l'œuvre psychiatrique de Frantz Fanon," *Sud/Nord* 22: 147–174.

Robcis, Camille (2016) "François Tosquelles and the Psychiatric Revolution in Postwar France," *Constellations* 23/2: 212–222.

Robcis, Camille (2021) *Disalienation: Politics, Philosophy, and Radical Psychiatry in Postwar France*. Chicago, IL: University of Chicago Press.

Roberts, Neil (2015) *Freedom as Marronage*, Chicago, IL: University of Chicago Press.

Robinson, William I. (2023) "The Unbearable Manicheanism of the 'Anti-Imperialist' Left." https://thephilosophicalsalon.com/the-unbea rable-manicheanism-of-the-anti-imperialist-left/.

Ruedy, John (1992) *Modern Algeria: The Origins and Development of a Nation*. Bloomington: Indiana University Press.

Sartre, Jean-Paul (1965 [1948]) *Black Orpheus*, trans. S.W. Allen. Paris: Présence Africaine.

Sartre, Jean-Paul (2001) *Colonialism and Neocolonialism*, preface by Robert J.C. Young, introduction by Azzedine Haddour. London: Routledge.

Sayles, James Yaki (2010) *Meditations on Frantz Fanon's Wretched of the Earth*. Montreal: Kersplebedeb Publishing.

Sekyi-Otu, Ato (1996) *Fanon's Dialectic of Experience*. Cambridge, MA: Harvard University Press.

Sekyi-Otu, Ato (2019) *Left Universalism, Africacentric Essays*. New York: Routledge.

Sekyi-Otu, Ato (2023) *Homestead Homeland Home: Critical Reflections*. Quebec: Daraja Press.

Sharpley-Whiting, T. Denean (1998) *Frantz Fanon: Conflicts and Feminisms*. Lanham, MD: Rowman & Littlefield.

Sharpley-Whiting, T. Denean (1999) "Fanon's Feminist Consciousness and Algerian Women's Liberation: Colonialism, Nationalism, and Fundamentalism," in Nigel C. Gibson (ed.), *Rethinking Fanon: The Continuing Legacy*. Amherst, NY: Humanity Books.

Shatz, Adam, and Alice Cherki (2002) "An Interview with Alice Cherki, *Historical Reflections/Réflexions Historiques* 28/2: 293–300.

Shatz, Adam, and Mohammed Harbi (2002) "An Interview with Mohammed Harbi," *Historical Reflections/Réflexions Historiques* 28/2: 301–309.

Solinas, Piernico (1973) *Gillo Pontecorvo's The Battle of Algiers*. New York: Scribner's.

Stawarska, Beata (2022) "Struggle and Violence: Entering the Dialectic with Frantz Fanon and Simone de Beauvoir," in Ulrike Kistner and Philippe Van Haute (eds.), *Violence, Slavery and Freedom between Hegel and Fanon*. Braamfontein: Wits University Press.

Swartz, Sally (2018) *Ruthless Winnicott: The Role of Ruthlessness in Psychoanalysis and Political Protest*. New York: Routledge.

Taylor, Keeanga-Yamahtta (2021) *From #BlackLivesMatter to Black Liberation*. Chicago, IL: Haymarket.

Thomas, Greg (2007) *The Sexual Demon of Colonial Empire: Pan-African Embodiment and Erotic Schemes of Empire*. Bloomington: Indiana University Press.

Trimbur, Lucia (2021) "The NFL's Reversal on 'Race Norming' Reveals How Pervasive Medical Racism Remains," NBC News, June 8. https://www.nbcnews.com/think/opinion/nfl–s–reversal–race–nor ming–reveals–how–pervasive–medical–racism–ncna1269992.

Turner, Lou (1996) "On the Difference between the Hegelian and Fanonian Dialectic of Lordship and Bondage," in Lewis R. Gordon, T. Denean Sharpley-Whiting, and Renee T. White (eds.), *Fanon: A Critical Reader*. Oxford: Blackwell.

Turner, Lou (2011) "Fanon and the Biopolitics of Torture: Contextualizing Psychological Practices as Tools of War," in N. C. Gibson (ed.), *Living Fanon: Global Perspectives*. New York: Palgrave.

Turner, Lou, and Helen Neville (eds.) (2020) *Frantz Fanon's Psychotherapeutic Approaches to Clinical Work: Practicing Internationally with Marginalized Communities*. New York: Routledge.

Turner, Lou, and Kurtis J.B Kelley (2021) "When Black Liberation Mattered: Frantz Fanon in the Theory and Practice of Pan-Africanism in the Black Power Era, 1965–1975," in Nigel C. Gibson (ed.), *Fanon Today: Reason and Revolt of the Wretched of the Earth*. Quebec: Daraja Press.

Vaughans, Kirkland (2021) "Object Relations Theory." Part of the Freud Museum, Psychoanalytical Schools of Thought after Freud, January 29. https://www.youtube.com/watch?v=vO0GhlBijss&ab_channel=sig mundfreudmuseum.

Vince, Natalya (2015) *Our Fighting Sisters: Nation, Memory and Gender in Algeria, 1954–1962*. Manchester: Manchester University Press.

Walter, Bernd (2002) "Hermann Simon: Psychiatriereformer, Sozialdarwinist, Nationalsozialist?" *Der Nervenarzt* 73/11: 1047–1054.

Woodis, Jack (1972) *New Theories of Revolution: A Commentary on the Views of Frantz Fanon, Régis Debray and Herbert Marcuse*. London: Lawrence and Wishart.

Wright, Richard (1948) "Such Is Our Challenge." http://europe-solidai
re.org/spip.php?article51779.

Wright, Richard (1956) "Tradition and Industrialization: The Plight of
the Tragic Elite in Africa," *Présence Africaine* 8/10: 347–360.

Young, Robert J.C. (2005) "Fanon and the Turn to Armed Struggle in
Africa," *Wasafiri* 20/44: 33–41.

Young, Robert J.C. (2018) " Fanon, revolutionary playwright," in Frantz
Fanon, *Alienation and Freedom*, trans. Steven Corcoran; ed. Jean Khalfa
and Robert J.C. Young. London: Bloomsbury, pp. 11–79.

Zahar, Renate (1974) *Frantz Fanon: Colonialism and Alienation.* New
York: Monthly Review.

Zeilig, Leo (2016) *Frantz Fanon: The Militant Philosopher of Third World
Revolution.* New York: I.B. Tauris and Co.

Zikode, S'bu (2008) "Land and Housing." https://libcom.org/article/lan
d–and–housing–sbu–zikode.

# Index

Malagasy 104, 105, 106, 107–8,
    110
  Senegalese soldiers, role
    108–9
Malek, Redha 178, 179, 180, 183,
    262
Malraux, André 254
Manicheanism 2, 84, 97, 101, 141,
    144, 197, 205, 210, 268
Mannoni, Octave 102
  dependency of the colonized
    104–6
  dream analysis 107–8
  Fanon and 102
  inferiority complex 104
  *Psychologie de la colonisation* 102
  racial inferiority 110
Manuellan, Gilbert 13
Manuellan, Marie-Jeanne 11, 13,
    188–92
Manville, Marcel 15–16, 39, 48,
    51, 165, 171, 175
Maran, René, *Un Homme pareil
    aux autres* 97–8, 101, 102
Martin, Trayvon 81, 131
Martinique 24, 34, 36, 37,
    309n39
  dialectic of recognition 132,
    133
  racism in the context of Vichy
    37–8
  slavery 132
Marx, Karl 75, 78, 138, 250, 257
masochism, unconscious 122–3
Maspero, François 54, 163, 179,
    192, 194, 195, 234, 244,
    247–8, 249
masses, the 136, 187, 204, 259,
    264, 270–1, 274, 275, 277–8,
    279, 280
Mau Mau revolt 109, 260, 264,
    289
McAree, Françoise 206, 207

medicine
  and colonialism 218
  "modern" 216
  "traditional" 216
Ménil, Reni 27
mental health
  chemicalization 18, 20
  racism and imperialism 19
  and social self 154
  and social world 83
mental illness
  Maghrebi Muslim attitudes
    151–2
  in warfare 287–8
  among women refugees 185
  *see also* trauma, of war
mental liberation 290
Merleau-Ponty, Maurice 46, 48,
    49, 55, 83, 149
Merzouk, Nahle 292–3
M'Hidi, Larbi Ben 167, 168, 181,
    311n9
Mohammed V, King (Morocco)
    171
Mosole, Pierre 16, 48
Moumié, Félix 239
  murder 238–9
Mounier, Emmanuel 47
Mugniery, Leon 63–4
mulatto 98, 99
Muslim
  women, psychological testing
    152–3
  *see also* Blida-Joinville
    Psychiatric Hospital

name changes at independence
    260
Nardal, Jane 28
Nardal, Paulette 28
national bourgeoisie *see*
    bourgeoisie, national
national consciousness 211, 220,

224, 246, 260, 263, 278, 280, 281
*see also* humanism, new
National Council of the Algerian Revolution 169
National Liberation Army (ALN) 166
National Liberation Front of Algeria *see* FLN
nationalism, African 224, 229, 250
nationalist parties 261, 269–70
  elitism 273
  function 274, 275
  ideology 270, 277
  organizational form 270, 273
  voluntarist short cut, limitations of 276–7
nationalist urban groups 264
nationalization 272, 280
negotiation 228, 254, 259, 298
negritude 22, 27, 28, 30, 31, 32, 33, 114–15, 116, 284, 285
negrophobia 123–4
nepotism 259
neuropsychology Algiers school 70
neurosis, psychoanalysis of 83, 129
Nkrumah, Kwame 226, 230, 273, 315n6, 315n7
North African brain 288–9
"North African syndrome" 19, 67, 70–2
"The 'North African Syndrome'" (Fanon) 64, 67, 70, 72, 109, 142, 144, 173
Northside Testing and Consultation Center 307n26
*Notebook of a Return to My Native Land* (Cesaire) 27, 29–33, 61

objectification 8, 19, 57, 63, 71–2, 82, 86, 110, 113

Oedipus complex 122, 126, 127
"L'Oeil se noie" *see* "The Drowning Eye"
*Organisation spéciale* 264
Oury, Jean 18
Oussedik, Omar 13, 159

Pan-Africanism 30, 230–2, 236, 315n6, 315n7
"Parallel Hands" (play; Fanon) 57, 59, 60, 61, 62
party, role of in new society 275
PCF (Communist Party of France) 47, 50
peasantry 263, 265, 280, 281, 282–3
Péju, Marcel 245
perception 54–5
"petit nègre" 93, 95, 304n4, n5
phobia 83, 124, 126, 127, 128
  bourgeois 266
Pirelli, Giovanni 186
plays and playwriting 54, 58, 60
  *see also* names of individual plays
political meeting, local 282
politics
  of hatred 268
  of impoverished masses in new society 279–80
Porot, Antoine 70, 71, 110, 143, 151, 288
Positive Action Conference for Peace and Security in Africa 232–3
poverty, culture of 305n13
praxis 140, 259, 268, 269, 270, 278, 281, 298
*Présence Africaine* 65,195
primitive accumulation 317n6
production committees 283
production for export 272